THE POLITICAL ARMY

THOMAS CROSBIE

THE POLITICAL ARMY

How the U.S. Military Learned to Manage
the Media and Public Opinion

COLUMBIA UNIVERSITY PRESS

NEW YORK

Columbia University Press
Publishers Since 1893
New York   Chichester, West Sussex

Copyright © 2025 Thomas Alexander Crosbie
All rights reserved

Library of Congress Cataloging-in-Publication Data
Names: Crosbie, Thomas (Writer on military affairs), author.
Title: The political army : how the U.S. military learned to manage the media and public opinion / Thomas Crosbie.
Other titles: How the U.S. military learned to manage the media and public opinion
Description: New York : Columbia University Press, [2025] | Includes bibliographical references and index.
Identifiers: LCCN 2024036411 (print) | LCCN 2024036412 (ebook) | ISBN 9780231219778 (hardback) | ISBN 9780231219785 (trade paperback) | ISBN 9780231562898 (ebook)
Subjects: LCSH: United States. Army—Public relations—History—20th century. | United States. Army—Press coverage—History—20th century. | United States. Army—Political activity—History—20th century. | United States. Army—Public opinion—History—20th century. | Armed Forces and mass media—United States. | Politics and war—United States. | Civil-military relations—United States. | Press and politics—United States. | United States—Politics and government—20th century. | Public opinion—United States.
Classification: LCC UH703 .C76 2025 (print) | LCC UH703 (ebook) | DDC 355.3/420973—dc23/eng/20241024

Cover design: Milenda Nan Ok Lee
Cover photo: Photo of Horst Faas: AP Photo/Courtesy AP Corporate Archives

*all the newsboys had their war faces on
so turtle eggs under the trestle went
unreported, but it was still a miracle.*

—Darrell Epp, "My Doombot Is Late"

CONTENTS

Acknowledgments ix
List of Abbreviations xiii

INTRODUCTION: THE DEMOCRACY OF WAR 1

PART I. THE BIRTH OF THE POLITICAL ARMY

1. THE ARMY ASCENDANT: MARSHALL'S MEDIA MANAGEMENT, 1939–1945 27

2. ARMY OVERREACH: DOMESTIC POLITICS AND COMMAND CULTURE, 1945–1963 52

PART II. THE FALL OF THE POLITICAL ARMY

3. OUTPACED: THE PRESS AND PUBLIC AFFAIRS IN VIETNAM, 1963–1968 77

4. THE TET PARADOX: MEDIA-MANAGEMENT REGIMES IN VIETNAM, 1968–1975   96

5. TET SUPPRESSED: ARMY DOCTRINAL INNOVATIONS, 1976–1982   120

PART III. THE RISE OF THE POLITICAL ARMY

6. RECOVERY: SMALL WARS AND ORGANIZATIONAL RENEWAL, 1983–1989   141

7. THE TEST: MEDIA-MANAGEMENT REGIMES IN THE GULF WAR, 1990–1991   160

8. LESSONS LEARNED AND NOT LEARNED, 1991–2000   189

CONCLUSION. THE BIRTH, FALL, AND RISE OF THE POLITICAL ARMY   212

Notes   217
Index   255

ACKNOWLEDGMENTS

A **BOOK OF** this sort, written in fugitive stages over a period of fifteen years, will inevitably give rise to so many debts from so many sources that a number of words equal to the text itself could be profitably spent in acknowledging them. This acknowledgment is thus—and regrettably—merely notional, capturing in spirit a fraction of the generosity and support I have received as I have struggled to untangle a knot worth untangling. The knot, the puzzle at the center of this book, is how to use social science to support the democratic role played by militaries, and so it is fitting that so many people supported this effort—as, indeed, the lesson of the book is that we all are responsible for the democracies of war. Any failings of this book are, of course, mine alone.

The story told in these pages primarily concerns the professional lives of U.S. Army officers (in particular senior leaders and public-affairs officers) and journalists (bureau chiefs, war correspondents, and combat photographers). It is, in a sense, a tale of two professions, officers and journalists. Because of the nature of these professions, the journalists inevitably come into sharper focus, for it is they who through their collective efforts drove the officers to work toward (or, as might be the case, resist) organizational reform. The cover image shows one such journalist: the much-celebrated combat photographer

Horst Faas, who won Pulitzer Prizes for his work covering the Vietnam War in 1965 and again covering the Bangladesh War of Independence in 1972. The image, which shows Faas in camo, a faint smile on his lips, pointing his camera to the left (backward, from the reader's perspective), captures something essential about the role of the *individuals*, rather than the social groups, who so often dominate this narrative. As the reader will discover, only by looking at the microlevel of individual behavior can we make sense of the mesolevel, how the media and the military transformed over the decades covered in this research, and ultimately the macrolevel of broader sociopolitical change. From a research perspective, my greatest debt is therefore likewise to those individuals who provided access to these worlds: the librarians at the archives I visited, the friends who brought me into military circles, and especially the individuals who spoke with me on and off the record about their firsthand experiences.

The research for this book began under the supervision of Julia Adams, with critical support from Miguel Centeno, Philip Smith, and Jonathan Wyrtzen. Later, Meredith Kleykamp provided guidance and encouragement during my time at the University of Maryland. Colonel Thomas Funch Pedersen, Major Jacob Vik Hansen, as well as the team of officers and researchers at the Institute for Military Operations, Royal Danish Defence College, have my deepest thanks for providing the environment in which I could complete this long-gestating project.

When I started my research into the political agency of military organizations, there was no field of study to receive it, so we had to make one. The "we" encompasses the large group of scholars who have worked collectively to establish the military politics perspective, an alternative to the long-dominant tradition of civil–military relations. This group includes the many participants in the Military Politics conference and PhD course in Copenhagen in 2020, cosponsored by the University of Southern Denmark and the Royal Danish Defence College, as well as the contributors to the subsequent book series, with special thanks to Tom Bonnington and the rest of the team at Berghahn Books.

Friends and colleagues who provided additional critical support at various stages of this project (wittingly and unwittingly) include

Stefan Beljean, Ian Bowers, General James D. Campbell, Shai Dromi, Vincent Keating, Anthony King, Joseph Klett, Tamir Libel, Holger Lindhardtsen, Leslie A. Lopez, Edward R. Lucas, Jeff Lucas, Katrine Lund-Hansen, Jon Rahbek-Clemmensen, Jeffrey M. Reilly, Samuel Rivera-Paez, Jonathan Roberge, Carsten F. Roennfeldt, Jensen Sass, Simon J. Smith, Samuel Stabler, Andrew Stewart, Ori Swed, Luke Wagner, Brad West, Craig Whiteside, and the late (and much missed) Xiaohong Xu.

One of the great pleasures in working on this project has been connecting with Columbia University Press. I especially thank Sharon K. Weiner for guiding me to the press and Stephen Wesley for his incredible support. Special thanks to Julie Quistgaard for her help with the manuscript.

Parts of this book appeared previously and in different form as articles in *Parameters* and *War in History*. I wish to acknowledge and thank the editors of those journals for their generosity in allowing me to present the work in an updated format in the pages that follow.

Thanks to Darrell Epp, one of the great poets of our unsettled times, for the epigraph.

Finally, and most of all, I thank my wife, Jill, for the support and encouragement she has provided without fail for more than twenty years and our children, Rae and Calvin, for their particular ways.

ABBREVIATIONS

AP	Associated Press
ARVN	Army of the Republic of Vietnam
BPR	Bureau of Public Relations
CENTCOM	U.S. Central Command
CMH	Center of Military History
CONARC	Continental Army Command
DOD	U.S. Department of Defense
DTIC	Defense Technical Information Center
GDP	gross domestic product
JIB	Joint Information Bureau
MAAG	Military Assistance Advisory Group
MAAG-V	Military Assistance Advisory Group, Vietnam
MACOI	Military Assistance Command Office of Information
MACV	Military Assistance Command, Vietnam
NATO	North Atlantic Treaty Organization
OCI	Office of the Chief of Information
OCPA	Office of the Chief of Public Affairs
OWI	Office of War Information
PAO	public-affairs officer
ROTC	Reserve Officer Training Corps

SASC	Senate Armed Services Committee
SGAC	Senate Governmental Affairs Committee
TRADOC	Training and Doctrine Command
UMT	Universal Military Training
UPI	United Press International
USAMHI	U.S. Army Institute for Military History
USIA	United States Information Agency
USIS	United States Information Service

INTRODUCTION

The Democracy of War

Among the calamities of war may be justly numbered the diminution of the love of truth, by the falsehoods which interest dictate and credulity encourages.

—Samuel Johnson, *Idler*, no. 30 (November 11, 1758)

THE DEMOCRATIC state, the most successful political configuration of our time, is marked by a peculiar tension in the way power and information inform its sovereignty. The democratic impulse toward inclusion and representativeness hinges on open debate, the rule of law, and the capacity of elected officials to oversee actions done in the name of the state. But the state is a thing of exclusion. It is an exclusion of space: inside is the state; outside, the world. It invites the exclusion of time, a community imaging a story of itself as it moves through the decades and centuries. Both trigger further exclusions—of race, class, sex, and language (among others)—between the powerful and the powerless.[1] The peculiar alchemy of the democratic state depends in great part on information—its flow, its perception of flow, and ultimately its control. A more credulous age dreamed of states built on self-evident truths, but even that age's people were skeptical of the state's honesty and worked hard to create systems of checks and balances that would allow a society to concentrate its collective force in the structures of the state while retaining as much of individual rights and liberties as possible.

This book concerns itself with democracies of war—that is, with war as a network of democratic processes. For too long, war has been treated by social scientists as a state of exception, something foreign to the state that must be resolved for the real life of the state to continue. From that perspective, the politics of war begins and ends at the battlefield. Meanwhile, the battlefield itself is ignored, viewed as the exclusive domain of military professionals (dubbed the "managers of violence" by Samuel P. Huntington in 1957).[2] From this traditionalist perspective, the "why" of war (why we go to war, why some wars are short and some are long, why some alliances fail to deter conflicts and others don't, and so on) is all that matters, while the "how" of war (how we fight, how we organize war, and how we decide who ends up on the front line) is more or less ignored.

I belong to a generation of scholars awakened to political life with the terrorist attacks of September 11, 2001, witnesses to a "forever war" that despite its astounding costs was normalized and sectored into the normal functioning of the democratic state—and, ultimately, lost. From our perspective, the "how" of war is very much a political question. We do not assume that the way wars are fought is a pure expression of military expertise. Instead, we have grown accustomed to the possibility that military expertise has been distorted (rightly or wrongly) by the gravitational effects of democratic politics. For us, war is democratic in a deep sense, a grand compromise between how military experts want to fight and how they believe their political masters and their global publics will allow them to fight. This book is a first attempt at accounting for one democracy of war—namely, the entwining of media management and military thought over six decades from 1939 to 2000.

How does this story compare with the way we normally understand the relationship between war and democracy? For many scholars, Max Weber's vision of the state is the inevitable starting point in making sense of these tensions. Weber famously described the state as "a human community that (successfully) claims the *monopoly of the legitimate use of physical force* within a given territory."[3] He presented this perspective on the state shortly after his involvement with writing the Weimar Republic's new constitution in 1919, a failed effort to draw a democratic state from the embers of war.[4] One hundred and thirty years earlier, the framers of the U.S. Constitution were engaged in a similar, if more successful, enterprise. Perhaps tellingly, in the first State of the Union address George Washington set as the most immediate order of concern the question of military power, noting that "to be prepared for war is one of the most effectual means of preserving peace." To this end, he hoped, "the proper establishment of the troops which may be deemed indispensable, will be entitled to mature consideration." Washington's concern was with "hostile tribes of Indians," and a small standing army was duly organized.[5] Today, the U.S. Department of Defense (DOD) houses the greatest concentration of force on the planet, with yearly expenditures accounting for nearly 40 percent of the world's defense spending.[6]

The sovereignty of the democratic state, in particular the U.S. state, is in this sense a sort of conjoined twin to its own violent capacities. Democracies have much to fear from their militaries, after all. Coups d'états and pronunciamentos pose existential threats, but military power can also corrupt the democratic process in a variety of other ways.[7] Legal, cultural, and economic checks help balance the state's power by holding its actions accountable to the public, but all these checks require the free flow of information, at least among elected officials and their agents. The key theorists of civil–military relations established the scholarly understanding that this sort of formal control, which I term *civilian oversight*, is a necessary precondition for democratic states with powerful militaries to remain democratic.[8] However, the recent emergence of new recording technologies and distribution platforms has created new scenarios where very broad publics share in that oversight, a situation that I describe in this work as the emergence of *democratic oversight* alongside civilian oversight. Democratic oversight is reliant in particular upon the work of professional journalists, whose interests awkwardly intersect with military preferences for autonomy.

What is military autonomy? The question does not yield a simple answer. Steffen Böhm, Ana Dinerstein, and André Spicer argue that the concept of autonomy is "infested with meanings" and note three common uses: autonomy from capital, autonomy from the state, and autonomy from colonial domination or dependency.[9] The military's autonomy from capital has been addressed in work on the military-industrial complex.[10] Its autonomy from the state has been analyzed by many civil–military relations scholars.[11] Its autonomy from colonial logics of domination has been addressed by historical sociologists and area studies specialists.[12] Yet while the empirical reality of military self-rule in contemporary democratic states certainly rests on each of these three forms of autonomy, there is another site of control that military organizations seek to escape: autonomy from oversight by people outside the organization who have the power or are perceived as having the power to affect its fortunes.

My focus on *autonomy from oversight* is an original formulation that aims to establish a new perspective on the term *autonomy*. American sociologists have tended to focus more on the autonomy from capital, especially in the long tradition of Marxian scholarship that analyzes the coercive and extractive capacities of the state. Peter Evans, Dietrich Rueschemeyer, and Theda Skocpol's edited volume *Bringing the State Back In* (1985) cemented the autonomy-from-capital perspective as arguably the dominant one in the discipline and certainly the dominant one in the subfield of historical sociology.[13] Charles Tilly offered a grand historical narrative in his vision of war triggering extractive and administrative capacities that in turn enable more and more effective warring.[14] Although many still follow this emphasis on analyzing the state's autonomy from capital alongside its capacity to extract or coerce, subsequent generations of scholars have found various faults with this perspective.[15]

Regardless of the specific critiques, each of these perspectives on autonomy reflects and contextualizes the other uses of the concept and points to its multidimensional character. For example, military leaders may believe that they act autonomously from capital or other state structures when in fact they tailor their decisions to better obtain procurements or to avoid antagonizing their civilian commanders. This sort of subjective account easily slides into the realm of false consciousness. By focusing on oversight, we gain more leverage on the concept, although the focus does not entirely detach our analysis from the other theories of autonomy because in the background of concerns with oversight are the familiar shadows of capital, state, and sovereignty. The possibility I raise throughout this book is that powerful state organizations, in particular militaries, are increasingly concerned with how democratic oversight restricts their ability to pursue their ends as they see fit, possibly overriding their attempts to obtain autonomy from other perceived sources of control.

The military's autonomy from democratic oversight hinges in large part on the ways its actions are mediated by journalists and the control it can exert over their output. This mediation may be a mere annoyance when the state is at peace, but during times of war the information necessary for civilian and democratic oversight is transformed, and its significance is heightened. Information is inevitably a military concern, both a liability and a potential asset. In times of peace, information about military affairs is often less guarded but also less valuable and less interesting. In times of war, such information gains economic value even as it gains strategic value, although the two are rarely commensurable. Disinformation, deceit, emotional manipulation, mass persuasion, misdirection, and silence are all tools of statecraft, no more so than during times of war. Journalists use these tools as well, sometimes out of ignorance, sometimes out of principle (e.g., the case of Robert Sherrod described in chapter 1), and sometimes out of corporate interest (e.g., William Randolph Hearst's role in the Spanish-American War).[16] For centuries, commenters have noted the threat to truth and honesty during times of war.[17] War's effect on journalism and on the capacity for both civilian and democratic oversight is in this sense a particular danger to the life of a democracy.

While the changing relationship between democratic polities and the work of journalists has been a topic of considerable interest to political sociologists, the active role played by militaries in shaping democratic oversight has largely been ignored, although some exceptions are noted later.[18] The chapters in this book offer historical vantage points on how democratic oversight has increasingly intruded upon the autonomy of one immensely powerful state structure, the United States Army.[19] Although intended as a critical intervention, this book ultimately affirms the value of Weber's view of the state. His definition has elsewhere been accused of portraying the state as overly monolithic and homogenous, ignoring that many contemporary states exist as a collection of multiple and often competing state structures.[20] I argue here that the legitimacy of individual state structures to use violence, although central to the continuing shared project of statehood, is more contingent and negotiated than social scientists tend to think. The future of the state is therefore likely to include a far more complex relationship between the monopoly on violence and the autonomy of the state to enact that violence than we have seen over the past 500 years.

Why should we think that the future of the democratic state should look any different from its past? The alchemy that once allowed open democratic processes to combine happily with closed state structures must now be adapted to account for the emergence of democratic rather than civilian oversight. In the United States, as many have noted, media technology and the culture of news coverage have changed enormously since the beginning of World War II.[21] This change has in turn increased the tempo of negotiation between state structures and their societies, prompting organizations to become more responsive to public debate.

In the case of the U.S. Army, this responsiveness can be assessed across various dimensions. From the outside looking in, regulatory and legislative processes have restricted the use of many types of weapons, have canceled various weapons systems requested by the service, and have ended the Army's most powerful social tool, the conscription of civilians, in addition to forcing other changes. At the same time, internal "learning processes" have resulted in reformulated doctrine and cultural attitudes intended in part to bring about better relations with the public.[22] More overtly, Army leaders are also equipped with a variety of organizational tools that can be used to shape the political and social contexts within which they operate. Although some of these tools are designed and intended for use in foreign publics, leaders also have many resources that exist solely to interfere in politics at home, and together these resources encompass what I term the Army's *domestic political strategy*. Simply put, this book examines the Army's domestic political strategy in times of war and peace with respect to its management of the press.

THE OROGENY OF THE STATE

An important feature of Weber's definition of the state is the link it creates between the materiality of the physical world and the immateriality of the social world. From his perspective, the state gains substance both through physical acts of accumulating certain instruments of violence and removing them from the reach of ordinary citizens as well as through the cultural act of investing those instruments and their sanctioned use with legitimacy, marking all other violent acts as illegitimate. I pursue a course throughout these chapters that aims to demonstrate the enduring heuristic value of the classical definition in analyzing the flow of power between state and society, especially for understanding the United States in the second half of the twentieth century and beyond. However, I focus on only one dimension of the state's monopoly on legitimate violence—namely, the violence it projects beyond its borders or that it marshals defensively. Michael Mann and others call this dimension "military power," but an important initial consideration is that the military and the modern state are complexly intertwined.[23] Indeed, one problematic inheritance from Weber, especially for students of military organization, is the conflation of his theory of the state with his theory of bureaucracy.

Weber's large corpus includes many productive tensions, of course. While Weberian perspectives on the state often focus on bureaucracies, Weber was equally concerned with the life of status groups (such as the military) that enjoy distinctive if partial autonomy from the state. He recognized the honor system of the Prussian military as an important element of internal solidarity and external separation, a recognition that has been repeatedly reaffirmed in military organizations ever since. The distinctive cultural cohesion that sets military life apart from other lifeworlds in a given state has also been critiqued constructively by several generations of scholars, including Anthony King in his recent discussion of the modern combat soldier.[24]

Although Weber was aware of the existence of richly diverse status groups within the state, including some occupying functional roles as organs of the state, as in the case of the military, his later definition of the state would efface that awareness and set his interpreters down a path of analysis that has sometimes conflated the state with its bureaucratic structures, downgrading the status group from a primary analytical role. This conflation is not limited to military sociology, although it is a distinctive feature of that tradition. As elsewhere, its inheritance has created problems felt across the many subfields that address the state's coercive capacities.

The problem at hand is a conceptual binding that occurs when the state's monopoly on violence is viewed through the lens of multiple autonomous organizations expressing that monopoly over distinct submonopolies. For Weber, this binding made a great deal of sense, especially when thinking in terms of the Prussian military, with which he was personally familiar. Weber stressed the importance of discipline in the various developmental tendencies of modernity. He unequivocally dated these tendencies back to a specific configuration of military discipline: "military discipline gives birth to all discipline."[25] Military discipline has taken many forms, paradigmatically among the Spartans, the medieval chivalric class, the Swiss infantry, and finally the Prussian military, which rationalized war through the development of a meritocratic and protobureaucratic officer corps.[26] For Weber, statehood emerged through warring, but the modern state was born with the creation of a closed military bureaucracy and the bureaucratic logic that would be isomorphically adopted across state structures.

Weber was much impressed with bureaucracies and thought "the power position of a fully developed bureaucracy is always overtowering."[27] He was not much impressed with the power of the polity and had little sense of an empowered and independent public sphere. In a discussion intended to link bureaucracy and democracy, he reveals a very skeptical view of the latter: "The *demos* itself, in the sense of an inarticulate mass, never 'governs' larger associations; rather, it is governed, and its existence only changes the way in which the executive leaders are selected and the measure of influence which the *demos*, or better, which social circles from its midst are able to exert upon the content and direction of administrative activities by supplementing what is called 'public opinion.'"[28] If democratic governance is simply the selection of executives by empowered social groups, the power of an entrenched bureaucracy with its specialist language and other trappings of expertise is understandably expected to outmaneuver the political "dilettantes" who formally command them.[29]

What sort of America would conform to this Weberian vision? Imagine an archipelago of closed bureaucracies governing discrete areas of the social world, separated from one another by deep regulatory and cultural waters. In the domestic sphere, police departments monopolize the legitimate violence used to enforce laws, and correctional institutions monopolize the violence used to punish those found guilty of breaking laws. Violence directed beyond the territory of the state is divided among the U.S. Navy, which monopolizes sea power; the U.S. Marine Corps, which monopolizes the projection of power from sea to land; the U.S. Air Force, which monopolizes airpower; and the U.S. Army, which monopolizes conventional land power.

However, scholars have repeatedly pointed to the erosion of the boundaries between each of these islands of monopolized violence. Much research points to the blurring of corrections, detention, and welfare-state structures.[30] The regulatory and cultural waters separating the islands have receded, leaving peaks of organizational concentrations with large fields of overlapping activity. Moving beyond the archipelago metaphor is yet another step along the path of freeing sociology from its midcentury assumptions.

For students of military affairs, this shift is especially significant because it reveals the increasing role played by the state's coercive institutions in shaping their social and political environments. Much of the preceding argument points to the problem of conflating the state with its bureaucracies, which risks losing sight of the productive tensions between the state and the multiple lifeworlds of status groups, including military organizations. This conflation makes even less sense today, when the mass of the state is rising above the waters of cultural and regulatory separation to reveal far stronger linkages between state structures than has traditionally been the case.

We might think of this configuration metaphorically as the state's *orogeny*, a term borrowed from geology to suggest the rising of a continental landmass. The orogeny of the state calls for a reappraisal of Weber's two styles of state power, the concentration of means of violence in legitimate organizations and the blocking of access to means of violence by nonlegitimate competitors. The blurring of the boundaries between the state's violent bureaucracies suggests that something is triggering a reconfiguration of both the concentration of force within those bureaucracies and the perception of who exactly threatens its monopoly. My focus on democratic oversight is intended to allow for the analytical possibility that leaders of state agencies have an increasing sensitivity to democratic oversight as the challenge to state sovereignty that is of the most immediate concern, supplanting both foreign challenges and rival organizations as the threat that must be met. This is not to say that state bureaucracies will or do deploy their full reservoirs of violence against civil society, which is manifestly not the case. Rather, the possibility raised in this book is that solving the problem of oversight may come before solutions to problems of geopolitical order or problems of scarce resources in state funding.

Accordingly, this book focuses on the historical emergence of one of the most important sites of domestic political strategy for the U.S. Army, the field of media management—a topic that social scientists have almost entirely neglected, with the exception of pioneering work by a handful of British sociologists.[31] These scholars remind us that military organization (or police organization or corrections organization and so forth) must not be conflated with state power: any given state bureaucracy can lose its submonopoly if it fails in its domestic political maneuverings. The United States Army, for example, "lost" its control over air combat through the creation of the Air Force in 1947, but skillful bureaucratic maneuvering allowed it to regain its own air-power component and thereby challenge its sister service for appropriations, mission control, and symbolic capital.[32]

States do monopolize violence, and they do overwhelmingly house their means of violence in closed military bureaucracies. However, democratic oversight places increasing tension on that arrangement. Citizens now have access to far more of the battlefield than ever before. This greater access creates pressures to hide state violence in new state structures, as, for example, in U.S. Special Operations Command, a military command created in 1987 outside normal regimes, or simply to outsource state violence to the private contractors or "corporate warriors" who now make up a large percentage of any military operation.[33]

All these topics should reasonably interest political and cultural sociologists, but the issues remain firmly outside the mainstream of the discipline. The neglect of the topic is unmistakable. For example, leading American sociological journals have barely registered the past two decades of U.S. war.[34] In the two most widely cited journals in the discipline, the *American Journal of Sociology* (*AJS*) and the *American Sociological Review* (*ASR*), only thirteen articles have featured the word *war* or *military* in their title since the terrorist attacks of September 11, 2001—with only a single such article appearing in *AJS* (see table 0.1). Of the total thirteen, seven have nothing to do with U.S. military affairs.[35] Of the remaining six, three include notes indicating that the authors perceived their work to be outside the mainstream of the political and cultural sociology.

The lack of mainstream sociological interest in the U.S. military is troubling for the absence it implies in the broader debates. I have already noted that U.S. military procurements account for nearly 40 percent of the world's defense spending and that the DOD currently boasts the most powerful concentration of force in the world. Within the American national context, the enormous scale of the DOD is no less overwhelming. The DOD has experienced extraordinary relative growth for decades, matched by only two other departments of the federal government: the Department of Health and Human Services and the Department of the Treasury (now the department with the

TABLE 0.1 *American Journal of Sociology* and *American Sociological Review* Articles with *War* or *Military* in the Title, 2002–2024

Year	Source	Authors	Topic
2002	ASR	McAdam and Su	Vietnam War
2003	ASR	Kiser and Cai	Qin China
2004	ASR	Zuckerman	Turf wars
2004	AJS	Dechter and Elder	World War II
2006	ASR	Wimmer and Min	Explaining wars, 1816–2001
2008	ASR	Lundquist	U.S. military
2008	ASR	Rivera	Croatian tourism
2008	ASR	Gartner	U.S. war casualties
2008	ASR	Hillmann	English Civil War
2009	ASR	Marks, Mbaye, and Kim	socialist parties before World War I
2010	ASR	Hooks and McQueen	U.S. military-industrial complex
2011	ASR	Büyükokutan	U.S. poetry
2021	ASR	Broćić and Miles	culture wars

largest share of the budget). Although the remaining departments have comparable budgets and have experienced similar growth, the Departments of Health and Human Services, Defense, and Treasury are far larger, making up 71 percent of the federal budget for fiscal year 2024.[36] "Bringing the state back in" surely means bringing in its departments as well, after all. These entities are formidable by any standard. The DOD can compete with sovereign states in its economic pull: its $1.6 trillion budget for fiscal year 2024 would rank it sixteenth in the list of nations by gross domestic product (GDP), between Spain and Indonesia.[37] A mesolevel American sociology cannot afford to ignore the direct effects, opportunity costs, and cultural significance of these massive agencies.

Although all the major departments of the U.S. government demand sociological investigation, the military has additional claims on our interest. "Pax Americana" is backed by U.S. military power, but much of the world has recognized this military power, at least since the spectacular reversals of the Vietnam War, as bound up in domestic public opinion. Conversely, the democratic voice of foreign publics has been repeatedly silenced in favor of short-term geopolitical advantages. Our current global configuration has been profoundly marked by decades of American adventurism, ill-considered support for dictators, and the exchange of foreign collateral damage for fewer dead American soldiers.

Accordingly, the U.S. military has been a central conduit in the global flow of opportunity and constraint for the past eight decades. The wealth and debt, freedom and tyranny, understanding and ignorance of billions of people have been shaped by the course of U.S. military force through direct action, the threat of action, and restraint in the face of provocation. For virtually all this period, the military has continuously increased its efficacy and capacity, while the burden of executing this immense power has been placed on fewer shoulders. Today's DOD is by almost any measure the most powerful coercive force that *ever* existed, and there are no longer any realistic physical checks on its power. Indeed, both of the most important traditional checks—the balance of a large conscript force against a small professional force and the balance of competition between the armed forces—have been brushed aside in the name of combating militarism through the end of conscription and improving efficiency in the name of "jointness."[38] Yet I will not recount the story of one fragment of the state eclipsing and dominating the social world but rather a story of compromise between the state and society in ways that have proven to be very stable. The role played by the U.S. Army in helping to maintain this stability is the subject of this book.

SHAPING DOMESTIC POLITICS

A state organization's monopoly over a given subfield of violence is tied (in Weber's view) to the perception of its right to do so, its legitimacy. As noted earlier, the concentration of means of violence is generally matched by efforts to prevent challengers from concentrating means of their own. The theoretical intervention being made here is to rethink what it means to compete for the state's monopoly on violence. By focusing on the autonomy of the state's bureaucracies from various forms of oversight (not, as previous generations of scholars have argued, from capital, as already noted), we gain leverage on two new categories of "challengers" in the quest to monopolize legitimate violence. Both civilian leaders and the mass public periodically challenge the military's monopoly over violence by demanding changes in policy driven by sociopolitical rather than operational concerns.

This is not a new idea. Any attempt to view military affairs through the lens of politics owes much to the insights of Carl von Clausewitz, who described military strategy as inextricably rooted in policy.[39] For our purposes, however, Clausewitz is still too constrained in his thinking to be of much use in making sense of how contemporary militaries have changed in their relations with other state structures and the public. What is missing is the reflexive character of how politics shapes military strategy, which in turn shapes politics, producing recursive loops that may constrain, propel, or lead militaries to evolve in entirely new directions. Scholars have recognized this reflexive vision of military-political exchange but have yet to find a shared theoretical vocabulary for it.[40]

A starting point for attempting to move beyond Clausewitz and begin to account for such reflexive, intentional statecraft by military organizations can be found in the influential work of the historian Michael Howard. In a widely cited *Foreign Affairs* article published in 1979, Howard outlined what he considered the "forgotten dimensions of strategy," adding to operational strategy the overlooked fields of logistic strategy and what he called "social strategy."[41] He worried that, given the millions of people then subject to direct Soviet propaganda and censorship, social strategy (directed at shoring up the domestic public) might well rise above operational or logistic strategies and decide the Cold War on a playing field that the West had largely ignored.

Howard's notion of social strategy did not emerge as a major theoretical tool in either U.S. national strategic studies or international security studies.[42] However, a cognate concept has developed in organizational studies that offers more leverage in making sense of how the U.S. Army shapes its political environment. From an organizational studies perspective, the sort of social strategy Howard described might better be labeled "political strategy." In the field of management studies, Barry Baysinger describes this strategy as actions intended to shape the public-policy environment more favorably.[43] For a military, the policy environment is indeed shaped by both politicians and the public, but the significant shift brought about by adopting this language is to think of military leaders as concerned primarily with "the firm" (in this case the Army) and not the work of the firm (in this case fighting wars).

How do organizations shape their political environment? In one example, Douglas Schuler, Kathleen Rehbein, and Roxy Cramer, following Amy Hillman and Gerald Keim, use a logic of supply and demand to clarify the goals of the organization.[44] A limited supply of public policy (from legislators) is demanded by interest groups eager to shape the regulatory environment. The authors model a variety of tactics used by major corporations to gain political advantage, including funding political action committees; maintaining offices in Washington, DC; and hiring lobbyists. Baysinger adds public relations, involvement in trade associations, and agency hearings to the list of corporate political tactics, and Ivar Berg and Mayer Zald add educational programs and advertising.[45]

Clearly, corporate tactics of this sort cannot be directly applied to state structures, which swim in very different regulatory and cultural waters. Since the U.S. Information and Educational Exchange Act (Smith-Mundt Act) of 1948, the Army has been restricted in precisely these overt forms of overt lobbying and electioneering.[46] Nevertheless, by aggregating up from tactics to corporate political strategy, we can find several more general lessons on where to look for military political strategy. The tactics listed earlier fall within organized strategic units: marketing departments, public-relations departments, internal lobbying departments, and external lobbyists. In addition, a strand of management scholarship notes the importance of domain maintenance and buffering, or efforts to resist external forces and avoid undesirable public oversight.[47]

Organizational studies literature provides three insights that will prove to be valuable. First, it encourages us to think of military leaders as concerned with the life of their organizations in addition to the winning of wars. Second, it prompts reflection on the link between the multiplicity of an institution's specialized organizations concerned with shaping the political environment (the strategic level) and their specific forms of action (the tactical level). In the private sector, these organizations and actions can be multiple and contradictory.[48] Third, it encourages us to think in terms of resistance to being shaped as a core strategic concern among military leaders. We should perhaps follow Howard in noting that great military leadership can also be found among those who excel in managing logistics and interfacing with the public. Few names spring to mind when considering the Army's most distinguished logistic or political strategists, but perhaps they should.[49]

MONOPOLY, AUTONOMY, AND THE U.S. ARMY

The U.S. Army boasts remarkably sophisticated organizational structures dedicated to precisely the sorts of public-sector political strategy described here. Important work has been done in investigating the statecraft of military organizations in the early U.S. state and in contemporary foreign states, but we lack a corresponding account of the contemporary U.S. case.[50] To begin to develop such an account, we might first recall that the regulatory environment for military political strategy is shaped profoundly by the Smith-Mundt Act of 1948, which ended the military's right to propagandize the American public.[51] The act essentially expanded the restrictions on the use of military violence within the United States enshrined in the Posse Comitatus Act of 1878. Just as the Posse Comitatus Act is far less restrictive than is commonly thought, so, too, the Smith-Mundt Act falls far short of an absolute embargo on domestic military political strategy.[52] Indeed, at least five separate doctrine streams grant the Army direct organizational capacities to shape its political environment in ways that resemble the political strategy of the public sector.

The most obvious site of Army political strategy is the work of *legislative liaising*. Split between the Army's Office of the Chief of Legislative Liaison and an assistant secretary of defense for legislative affairs, legislative liaising is described by Mordecai Lee as "simply a fancy word for agency lobbying."[53] Stephen Scroggs advances a more nuanced argument that both regulatory restrictions and informal norms effectively restrict DOD agency liaisons from lobbying as overtly as do private lobbyists. Nevertheless, agency liaisons act in much the way outsiders might imagine lobbyists acting, and the restrictions actually restrain only "overly crude styles of agency liaising; attempts to limit or control congressional ties back to the agencies; and a clear extra-legal prohibition against liaising its appropriators."[54]

Army legislative liaising is conducted in Washington, DC. It is supplemented at local levels (mainly around Army installations) by a second category, *community relations*, which is housed in the broader field of public affairs and concerns liaising with local political elites in addition to liaising with local publics.[55] Overlooked entirely by scholars, this field should not be dismissed as an important site of Army statecraft. Indeed, in an interview a former Army chief of public affairs, Major General Anthony Cucolo, stressed to me the importance of public affairs as an organized field in the Army and as a resource called upon by commanders in bases around the country.[56]

A third category is the field of *command information* (formerly called *troop information*), the Army's internal-communication program, which, like community relations, is housed in public affairs. By regulation, the Army is allowed to inform its troops but can no longer indoctrinate them directly.[57] However, command information can be considered a site of political strategy to the degree that the Army directs efforts to influence soldiers' habits and to use soldiers to effectively proselytize Army interests to their friends and family.

The fourth category of political strategy is the one that concerns us here. *Public information* is the field of Army work dedicated to shaping the work of civilian journalists. Also housed in public affairs, it can be viewed as the Army's home of media management.[58]

Finally, a fifth category is *marketing and public relations*, although much of this work is contracted out of the Army.[59] This category, of course, extensively concerns recruitment but has applications in wartime as well.[60] For example, the public-relations firm Hill & Knowlton was hired by a group of Kuwaiti nationals. In her history of that firm, Karen Miller notes, "Its mission was clear: to build public support for President George Bush's plan for American military intervention in the crisis in Kuwait."[61] The back-channeling implicit in the Kuwaiti group's plan can serve as a reminder of the enormous complexity and opacity of this category in particular.

It is an irony of the literature that scholars have ignored these organized sites of overt and sophisticated military statecraft in favor of far more transient sites. Risa Brooks offers a rich take on this issue and outlines a spectrum of observed forms of military politicking, including public appeals, grandstanding, alliance building, and shoulder tapping.[62] Although these insights are valuable, we can gain far more leverage by considering the larger category of routine activities intended to change the military's domestic political environment. By not looking in the right places for military political activity, we risk missing it altogether.[63] As I have argued elsewhere, traditional civil–military relations approaches have failed time and again to acknowledge the political agency of military organizations.[64] A military politics perspective, which understands militaries to be political actors (even as they remain professional and nonpartisan), is essential to moving the field forward.

Much of the story of U.S. war is inevitably a story of external factors acting upon the military. This may include foreign aggressors setting the stage of conflict, domestic civilian leaders directing military affairs, or allies aiding or undermining military efforts. However, the military does have powerful capacities to shape its environment. The story told in each chapter of this book is how the single state capacity of media management is deployed in an effort to achieve military ends in whatever level of autonomy Army leaders happen to encounter.

THE DATA

Chapter 1 explores a time when the Army's command structure was not yet subject to jointness and it still enjoyed a very positive relationship with the nation. I focus on the Army's top soldier, General George C. Marshall, as a key conduit through which media-management principles were expressed and work was accomplished. Coincidentally, Marshall's tenure as Army chief of staff began on the day war began in Europe in 1939, and he remained in this role for the duration, making him an ideal candidate for study. Marshall was also unique in his bureaucratic diligence and strict routines, and he left probably the best personal archive of any American military leader. I was able to analyze his personal involvement in media management by tracking down several hundred references to the press in three sources: the published volumes of his collected papers, Forrest C. Pogue's four-volume biography, and the original copies of Marshall's papers held by the George C. Marshall Foundation in Lexington, Virginia.

Research for the subsequent chapters was less straightforward. The full history of Army public information remains unwritten, although one remarkable document, Jack E. Pulwers's "A Quest for Excellence: The History of US Army Public Affairs, 1763–1981," has been preserved in hard copy at the U.S. Army Institute for Military History (USAMHI) at Carlisle Barracks in Pennsylvania. Over the course of thousands of pages paginated separately in dozens of sections, Jack E. Pulwer's monumental, unpublished manuscript tells the story of Army public affairs, building largely on his interviews with many of the former Army chiefs of information.

There are two excellent sources of historical data on the day-to-day work of Army information officers. The first is the *Army Information Digest*, compiled by the Army Information School for the purpose of keeping commanding officers and their staff informed about information affairs. Its issues have been digitally archived by Hathi Trust and cover the years 1947 to 1966. The second is the Annual Historical Reports of the chief of information, held at the Center of Military History (CMH) at Fort McNair in Washington, DC. These reports exist only for the years 1966 through 1991 and so continue the story, albeit in rather different terms, told in the *Digest*. I supplemented and cross-tabulated these reports with the Annual Historical Reports of the U.S. Army writ large, hard copies of which I was given by exceptionally generous CMH librarians.

Unfortunately, the agencies in charge of media management from World War II to the Vietnam War did not leave many other direct traces. One important exception is a 250-page document I found filed among the Army staff records at the National Archives. This document provides an at times phantasmagoric vision of an expansive Army public-relations plan that would encompass much of American civil society. More significantly, one key public-affairs officer, Brigadier General Winant Sidle, left rich archival records to the United States Army Heritage and Education Center at Carlisle Barracks.

The Vietnam chapters draw upon my research on both the Army side and the civilian side of the relationship. Thanks to LexisNexis's digital archives, I was able to access an enormous volume of war correspondence and combat photography. In addition, I gained the trust of several war correspondents, who invited me to join the Vietnam Old Hacks Google discussion group. This lively community is an invaluable resource in assessing the accuracy of the enormous volume of secondary literature (memoirs, works of art, and scholarly monographs) that is still being produced on the subject. From that community, I made contact with several Vietnam-era war correspondents who discussed their experiences in long interviews (varying from one hour to an hour and forty-five minutes), which were recorded and transcribed. A snowball-sampling technique led to various other interviews, including with two general officers and a former public-information officer who had served in Vietnam, among others.

Although these resources were very rich, the archival resources on Vietnam are much less so, and I remain heavily reliant on the work of one military historian, William M. Hammond, throughout the chapters. Hammond's two-volume history of public affairs in Vietnam not only is a major scholarly accomplishment but is also based on records that were subsequently lost (Hammond's personal copies of these records were deposited at a military archive, but they subsequently disappeared).[65]

Chapters 3 through 6 hinge upon our ability to reconstruct what was happening behind closed doors within the Army's highest levels of leadership. The annual reports I found at Fort McNair provided me with the records of the Pentagon's Information Office. I then supplemented them with the records of the chiefs of staff of the Army, held by the United States Army Military History Institute in Carlisle Barracks. Each chief of staff has managed the office differently, and there is no pattern in what was preserved. In managing this material, I have privileged speeches to Army audiences and especially internal memoranda over material that might have a more obvious performative character.

As we move closer to the present, the historical record dries up considerably, and much of the most important information remains classified and inaccessible to researchers. The Desert Storm chapter would have been impossible to write except for two small collections of records. The first, held at CMH, includes a collection of telex messages regarding public affairs collected by the Public Information Office. The second, held at USAMHI, includes a number of oral histories and other documents of interest. I discovered many other valuable documents online in military databases, in particular the Defense Technical Information Center (DTIC). The U.S. Air Force's 350-page *Public Affairs After Action Report* provides an exceptionally rich reference source. The *Congressional Record* figures largely in several chapters and is an invaluable resource for understanding those events in this book that rose to the level of broad political debate.

OVERVIEW OF CHAPTERS

The book is divided into three parts, each aiming to answer an overarching question over the course of two or three chapters. In part 1, I ask how the Army managed the press during the "golden age" of military media management: World War II and its immediate aftermath. The Army before World War II was in almost every important sense a completely different institution than during and after the war: a small, low-status force managed by a tiny collection of poorly paid officers and enlisted men and periodically supplemented with an influx of conscripts during periods of conflict. The pre–World War II Army jostled alongside the state militias and National Guard and competed (at times bitterly) with the U.S. Navy. The total mobilization of World War II created the modern Army (thereby "birthing" the political army), but it was also the high-water mark of the Army's authority over information.

In chapter 1, I look at the press work conducted by the man at the top of the Army's hierarchy, Chief of Staff General George C. Marshall, to gain a detailed sense of what media management entailed at this moment of unprecedented and unrepeated Army ascendancy. In chapter 2, I describe the ways in which Marshall and his fellow senior officers exited the war with a totally skewed conception of how the Army fit into the broader American political landscape. I describe the Army overreach in this period as a reflection of "utopian" thinking, a belief among this circle of officers that a better world was possible through the application of Army know-how throughout social and political life.

Part 2 asks why the Army lost its control over the press during the Vietnam War. Chapter 3 provides the first piece of the explanation: by looking closely at how Army commanders and journalists separately sourced information about the conflict and how they shared and fought over information, we see that unrealistic expectations of Army authority and competence led to disastrous media-management policies. In chapter 4, the tension in the unhappy media–military relationship comes to a head with the paradox of the Tet Offensive, where the enemy failed operationally but managed nevertheless to succeed strategically. In chapter 5, I explore how the Tet paradox for the United States (operational success but political failure) was recognized but suppressed in the rich period of doctrinal innovation that followed the Vietnam War.

Part 3 asks why and how the Army finally took media management seriously as a command concern. What I argue in chapter 6 is that despite initial indicators of success in the Army's new, antipolitical approach to war, some of its leaders came to recognize that information concerns are in fact central to how wars are fought. This realization led to the creation of the Sidle Panel Report, which argued for a variety of doctrinal and organizational changes that would institute core lessons from Vietnam. In chapter 7, I explore how aspects of the report were tested, including through (mismanaged) press pools in operations in Panama (Just Cause) and the Persian Gulf (Desert Shield and Desert Storm). Chapter 8 concludes the story of Army public affairs by highlighting the lessons learned and suppressed from the Gulf War, which culminated in the development of a new Army and joint doctrine that placed information close to the center of command concerns.

The three parts highlight the Army's agency in affecting its political and social environment. Each also stresses the recursive character of military strategy in mediated democracies, making them effective glimpses of reiterated problem solving in Jeffrey Haydu's sense (and indeed of learning processes in Gregory Daddis's sense).[66] Military strategy is recursive in the sense that repeated iterations of the military–media interface, particularly as enacted by military public-affairs officers and war correspondents, have given rise to learning processes within the military, reflected in its doctrine and practice. By borrowing the perspective of key Army leaders at critical moments in the organization's relationship with the state, we see clearly the contingency of the current configuration of violent means overseen not only by elected and appointed officials but also by millions of people, Americans and others, who contribute to the civil-military conversation.

The impact of the public sphere on the state's most powerful, most closed, and most autonomous structures has been underestimated. For Army leaders, at least, managing the press and, through it, the public has slowly come into focus over the period covered here as one of the highest-level concerns of their organization. In this sense, the democracy of war not only manifests in the decision to go to war or not but also inheres equally in how wars are fought, how they are resourced, whether they will be outsourced, and how long they last. But too rarely do we ask the following questions: Who should die in the name of democracy? What are we willing to pay? How are we to fight the wars we choose to fight? These questions demand answers that can be provided only by an informed public in dialogue with but not dominated by its professional military.

PART I
The Birth of the Political Army

1

THE ARMY ASCENDANT

Marshall's Media Management, 1939–1945

THE EVOLVING relationship between military commanders and the mass media has long been the subject of interest for scholars and soldiers alike, but much remains unknown.[1] It has often been assumed that in the American context World War II marked the most stable period in this relationship, a golden age of unquestioning press obedience to military command and unflagging public interest in (if not always support for) military affairs. However, few scholars have examined the degree to which press matters occupied the time and attention of the highest levels of military command—if they did at all.

By carefully examining the daily work of Army chief of staff General George C. Marshall, we can glean a rather more complex portrait of this golden age of media–military affairs. Marshall has been called "the principal military architect of the Western democracies' ultimate victories over the Axis powers."[2] As chief of staff, Marshall occupied a pivotal position connecting the most powerful uniformed service to its civilian leadership, and his unique personality made him particularly effective in the role. His unglamorous but unstinting bureaucratic labors have also left us with a remarkably detailed record of his contribution to the war. His vast archives reveal that he was consistently occupied by a number of characteristic press concerns, sometimes casting the press as an ally in the war, other times positioning it as an opponent in a struggle to shape public opinion.

I argue that Marshall's leadership of the U.S. Army included persistent engagement with press concerns. This contact gave rise to three strategic preferences: a preference for anticipating the needs and expected output of journalists; a preference to persuade journalists to voluntarily align their interests with those of the Army and thereby to act as a conduit for Army propaganda; and, finally, a less pronounced preference to misdirect the press and the public when it would benefit the war effort. If this era was indeed a golden age from the army's perspective, this happy state of affairs was the result of constant effort by both public-affairs agencies and at least one top army commander.

A GOLDEN AGE

In what sense are we justified in describing World War II as the U.S. military's golden age of press relations? That this war marked an ideal alignment of media and military interests is repeatedly affirmed by scholars of war correspondence and military media management. The alignment was the culmination of an oft-repeated story of incremental improvement (from a military perspective) in relations with journalists. The Crimean War (1853–1856), waged shortly after the invention of the telegraph, is commonly taken as the starting point of this story.[3] William Howard Russell, often called the first war correspondent, galvanized the British public with his highly critical news reports from the field of combat.[4] This impact came as a surprise to the military, which had essentially ignored Russell's presence on the battlefield.[5] Russell and the other telegraphic front-line correspondents of the Crimean War enjoyed a high degree of access to potential news but at the cost that they could not or would not comment on military action and were to report instead on logistics, living conditions, and the like. Hence, this first generation sacrificed control over the message in exchange for the access and support they needed to obtain information.[6]

Russell and many of his colleagues next turned their attention to the U.S. Civil War (1861–1865). Despite the large number of war correspondents and extensive network of war reporting, the Civil War was characterized by more censorship than was the Crimean War.[7] The Russell tradition of criticizing logistics and management did find some proponents but failed to gain the public's interest, and Russell's own work was poorly received by military command.[8] The military's autonomy over both the fighting of war and the content of the journalists' message was now generally accepted by correspondents, leaving only the questions of access and support.

During World War I, the next major test of media–military relations, the issues of access and support would also swing to privilege the interests of the military. Some journalists, including notably Arthur Moore in his "Amiens Dispatch," challenged censorship, but war correspondence had generally narrowed from Russell's day to become a form of nationalist cheerleading.[9] Perhaps the most remarkable evidence of this can be found in the American coverage of trench warfare. Although war correspondents gave their lives to report from those very trenches, they did not succeed in revealing the truth of the Western Front during the war, presenting only the most antiseptic insights.[10]

Scholars argue that war correspondents grew even more aligned with military interests during World War II, an alignment that gave rise to an era that I term the "golden age" of American media–military relations. This term is appropriate for three reasons: first, the alignment of interests was generally found agreeable to journalists and military agents alike; second, there was extensive censorship of journalists, but there was also considerable self-censorship among journalists; and, finally, journalists actively executed the military's propaganda goals (sometimes knowingly, sometimes not). With these three elements in place, military leaders could feel confident that operational security would be maintained, public opinion would be cultivated, and congressional interference would be minimized, while any mistakes or unpleasant necessities would be overlooked—certainly a desirable information environment for the military of any democracy.

The willing obedience of the press to toe the line during World War II is frequently noted. Clarence Wyatt argues that "the reporters believed in the cause for which the nation was fighting."[11] Philip Knightley explains, "War correspondents went along with the official scheme for reporting the war because they were convinced that it was in the national interest to do so. They saw no sharp line of demarcation between the role of the press in war-time and that of the government."[12] William Hammond describes the press as cooperative, and Mary Mander is even more emphatic: "This rhetoric of service to one's country was never really questioned in World War II[,] where it was as familiar as old wallpaper."[13] In a lavish catalog for the National Portrait Gallery's exhibition on World War II's correspondence, Alan Fern argues that "the press was by no means a homogenous cheering section," but he tellingly goes on to clarify, "This is another subject, to be dealt with in another context."[14]

The attitude of obedience extended to acceptance of fairly stringent censorship guidelines, so much so that one scholar notes that journalists "took it upon themselves to police their ranks."[15] In a study of the reporting of atrocity, Kendrick Oliver stresses the particular self-censoring surrounding stories of American soldiers committing acts of violence or cruelty: "Neither U.S. media outlets themselves nor their readers and listeners seemed particularly receptive to stories that disturbed, however faintly, the discursive nexus between war-making and national virtue." This was true, too, of atrocities committed against American soldiers by enemy forces.[16] Correspondents became so accustomed to censorship that Knightley quotes one at the end of the war asking where he should go now to clear his stories. Dale Minor also stresses this habit of mind, attributing the timidity of American journalists in the face of Senator Joseph McCarthy's witch-hunts "in large part to a hangover from the experience of [the press's] war-time relationship with government and men in power." Frederick Voss notes, "Generally speaking, journalists and the news-consuming public alike were sympathetic ... to regulations and mechanisms designed to limit and to a large extent channel the war's news coverage."[17]

Historians of propaganda have stressed the importance of war correspondents' collaboration with the U.S. military to disseminate immense quantities of "white" propaganda in what has been called "the greatest propaganda battle in the history of warfare." Another historian notes, "It was systematic mobilisation of propaganda and manipulation of public opinion. Although journalists soon realized this, few if any confronted the system." And Charles Lynch, recalling his experiences as a World War II correspondent, affirms this view: "It's humiliating to look back at what we wrote during the war. It was crap—and I don't exclude the Ernie Pyles or the Alan Mooreheads. We were a propaganda arm of our governments. At the start the censors enforced that, but by the end we were our own censors. We were cheerleaders."[18] From the perspective of critical readers of the news and of repentant correspondents like Lynch, the state of the American public sphere during World War II was perhaps more an Orwellian nightmare than a golden age. Yet the term *golden age* has value as a heuristic device for clarifying just how ideal the situation was from the military's perspective and just how remote that era is from our post-Vietnam perspective.

In my analysis in subsequent sections, I accept the scholarly consensus that American war correspondents did by and large willingly follow the U.S. government's information policies. By turning to examine in depth the press work of the Army's top soldier, General George C. Marshall, we will discover the degree and character of the military effort undergirding this arrangement. As it turns out, this golden age required considerable command attention.

PRESS WORK BEFORE WORLD WAR II

The term *press work*, borrowed from Glora Goodman, is used here to refer to a class of organized, intentional activity that broadly overlaps with what is now termed the "public-information" element of military public affairs.[19] U.S. military public affairs has traditionally been divided between three fields, as described in the introduction: *public information*, which involves military agents liaising with, managing, and observing the work of the civilian press; *command information* (formerly *troop information*), which concerns the internal audience of soldiers and officers; and *community relations*, which concerns liaising with the local domestic governments and civil society actors that surround military bases.[20] In this section, I isolate work undertaken personally by Marshall that falls under the organizational category of public information.

Why choose this narrow definition? I have done so primarily to maintain a focus on efforts directed at the press itself rather than at the diffuse political processes that involve the press. A broad definition of *press work* might encompass any act done by officers or soldiers where there is some purposeful intent to interfere with the processes of reporting on military affairs, which includes news gathering, reporting, and then transmitting, editing, publishing, and promoting such reports. That broader use would cut across multiple organizational divisions within the military, including, for example, the work of liaising with top U.S. government officials (called *legislative liaising* and, later, *legislative affairs*); managing the actual governance of foreign publics (called *civil affairs*, a major concern in the North African theater); as well as public relations, marketing, and advertising. It would also include special-branch activities, such as Samuel A. Stouffer's research efforts and Frank Capra's films. Although Marshall was involved in all these activities, including all of them in the analysis here would distract us from the goal of understanding how the press factored as a point of specific command concern.

Our focus, then, is on Marshall's press work in the narrow sense of his public-information work—that is to say, his efforts to manage the civilian American press. I exclude Marshall's involvement with *Stars and Stripes* and *Yank* magazines, for example, because they concerned the primary audience of American soldiers and so are classified as command-information activities. Similarly, I exclude instances such as Marshall's memorandum for General Thomas T. Handy where he recommends expeditiously informing family members of soldiers' injuries through the Adjutant General's Office—a policy he describes as "good propaganda" but not one involving the civilian press.[21] Incidentally, this narrower approach aligns with both William M. Hammond's pioneering work on public affairs and Sarah Maltby's recent work on military media management.[22]

As the war progressed, the U.S. government's capacities to manage information expanded dramatically. All such activity can be broadly classified as having propagandistic or censoring functions, with the public-information activities (or press work) done by American soldiers partaking of both. In this work, uniformed press workers were joined by three major civilian staffs. First, the Office of War Information (OWI) executed "white propaganda," efforts to persuade Americans that were clearly marked as such. Second, the Office of Strategic Services executed "black propaganda," attempts to persuade that were not clearly marked as propaganda—in other words, deceptive propaganda and psychological warfare.[23] These two offices had little to do with one another.[24] Third, the Office of Censorship executed standard forms of security-oriented censoring, with no publicity function at all. Indeed, the office did not even have a press agent.[25]

Within this field of propaganda and censorship activities, top military leaders soon recognized the need to engage in their own full-scale propaganda and censorship activities. When Marshall was appointed Army chief of staff in September 1939, Army public-information activities were under the Information Division, or G-2, as they had been since World War I. This meant in practice that each unit conducted its own independent form of public relations with little centralization.[26] In July 1940, the Press Relations Bureau, now free from the limiting purview of Army intelligence, was set up under Major Ward Maris, who was directly responsible to the deputy chief of staff for operations. Marshall's biographer notes, "This bureau controlled information for the War Department; information on units outside Washington still came under G-2. . . . [Secretary of War Henry L.] Stimson and General Marshall became convinced of the need for supplying more information on Army activities to the nation's newspapers. Secretary Stimson concluded that he must have a War Department Bureau of Public Relations directly under his control."[27]

On February 11, 1941, Stimson formed the Bureau of Public Relations (BPR) to succeed the Public Relations Branch. He directed Major General Robert C. Richardson, the head of the old branch, to shift over and head the new bureau. This bureau "was created to implement those things which General Richardson felt were necessary to keep Army PR apace with the expanding forces. . . . He remained the director of the Bureau for only six months, however, being given a command assignment."[28] The preference for a command assignment would continue to strip the BPR of talent for the rest of the war.

Major General Alexander Surles replaced Richardson on August 8, 1941, and would become Marshall's primary correspondent and aide in press matters for the rest of the war. Surles enjoyed a good reputation, and though, like Richardson, he would have preferred to leave the office for a command assignment, he was willing to remain in place. As one historian notes, "In the words of one Washington editor '[Surles] came through with laurels and the affectionate respect of the newspapermen with whom he had to deal.'"[29] Under Surles, the BPR worked with both the OWI and the Office of Censorship (but not the Office of Strategic Services). The BPR's Review Board (in charge of censorship) had a tense relationship with the OWI because the OWI "argued for the release of 'everything known to the enemy or that would not give him aid,'" but "in general, relations were quite harmonious with [Elmer] Davis [as OWI chief], and especially so, as one might well expect, with Bryon Price and the Office of Censorship."[30]

In Surles, Marshall had a thoughtful and dedicated press chief heading a vast press office that worked closely with both the primary propaganda and primary censorship departments of the U.S. government. And, notably, Marshall himself was not oblivious to the role of the press in war. During World War I, when he was General John J. Pershing's aide, and they were campaigning through France, Marshall gave one rare intimation of this understanding. According to one historian, immediately before a battle at Cantigny, France, and "foreshadowing a technique made famous in World War II, [Lieutenant Colonel] Marshall then briefed the assembled news correspondents on the plan, in part to commit them to its security."[31] This ethic would come to define Marshall's relations with the press during the next world war.

TOP SOLDIER AND PRESS CHIEF

Marshall's tenure as chief of staff began on September 1, 1939, coincidentally the day that Hitler's forces crossed into Poland. He left the post in November 1945, three months and nine days after the bombing of Nagasaki. Although there are important distinctions between his work as chief of staff before the United States joined the fray on December 7, 1941, and his work in that position after the United States joined the war, I focus here on both parts. Doing so not only gives us a more complete picture of his press work but also reflects the simple fact that Marshall's time as chief of staff before the official entry into the war was spent with the full expectation that the country would join the war.

The nomination process reveals something of Marshall's initial view of the press. At the time of his appointment, he was the fifth officer in line who met all eligibility criteria. The more senior General Hugh A. Drum was publicly campaigning for the position and could boast considerable political support. Certainly, Marshall, too, benefited from a roster of highly influential supporters, including his former commander, Pershing (perhaps the most respected military figure in the country at that time). More importantly, Marshall was an astute political strategist and carefully guided his supporters in moderating their support until the last minute for fear of showing his hand as the clear favorite. He viewed the press at this time as an obstacle to avoid rather than as a resource to exploit and considered his reputation for not seeking promotion as a major asset. In turn, the announcement of his appointment met with little enthusiasm among reporters, who, in his biographer's words, "knew Marshall only slightly by reputation, if at all."[32]

Marshall's reluctance to deal directly with journalists would pass, and he soon entered routines of engaging the press and his public-affairs staff. But precisely what sorts of press work occupied Marshall's attention during his term as Army chief of staff? To answer this question, I have drawn from several hundred references to the press in three sources: the published volumes of his collected papers; Forrest C. Pogue's four-volume biography; and the original copies of his papers held by the George C. Marshall Foundation in Lexington, Virginia.[33] From that large collection, I have narrowed down a list of 119 items for which we have confirmation that Marshall was directly involved and for which we have a specific date and action (table 1.1). Marshall's personal press work emerges from this body of material as constituting four primary types of action: dictating to his secretary

TABLE 1.1 Types of Press Activity Personally Conducted by George C. Marshall, by Year

	Memoranda	Letters	Briefings	Speeches	Misc.	Press Releases	Total
1939	0	0	0	1	0	0	1
1940	4	6	1	0	2	2	13
1941	10	8	0	2	2	1	22
1942	8	4	7	0	1	1	20
1943	17	3	4	2	1	0	27
1944	11	7	1	5	1	1	25
1945	1	5	0	0	0	0	6
Total	51	33	13	10	7	5	119

(and, on occasion, handwriting) letters and memoranda; meeting with journalists in off-the-record briefings; giving speeches; and editing press releases.

Table 1.1 offers us a broad portrait of Marshall personally working on press-related matters about twice a month during the most intense phases of the war. In terms of the data, it is important to acknowledge that individual letters or memos written by Marshall may have been lost or that additional briefings and speeches pertaining to the press were not recorded. However, it seems unlikely that the missing material would dramatically alter our understanding. Marshall, after all, was a creature of well-recorded habits who spent much of every day in this period behind a desk dealing with paperwork (duly archived) or attending high-level public or political events that were assiduously recorded. Throughout the war, Marshall adhered to a strict routine to "keep his health and sanity." In addition to the recorded items, the routine included a "quick look" at various newspapers in the morning (his biographer singles out the *New York Times*, the *Washington Post*, and the *Christian Science Monitor*) and at magazines or books in the evening: "Of the many magazines to which they subscribed, he preferred the *Saturday Evening Post* and *Readers' Digest*."[34] Also not included in my accounting is Marshall's involvement in drafting discussion points for Secretary of War Stimson's Thursday press conferences, although we do know that Marshall was regularly involved in that task.[35]

We also have no record of what generally crossed Marshall's desk from his press-relations officers. On this point, perhaps the best we can do is to extrapolate from a memorandum from late in the war sent by Colonel Luther L. Hill to Marshall. In this memorandum, Hill describes the routine press services provided by the BPR to the top combatant commanders, Dwight D. Eisenhower, Douglas MacArthur, Joseph T. McNarney, and Albert Coady Wedermeyer. Up to May 5, 1945, these generals were given a weekly "book cable," which was then switched at Eisenhower's request to a daily update with immediate dispatches for urgent matters.[36]

The most extensive category of press work Marshall did (84 of the 119 items) unsurprisingly comprises the memoranda and letters that he dictated because they were systematically collected for the historical record. The preponderance of this material is appropriate given the large portion of his day that such work generally occupied. In contrast, the "briefings" category is almost certainly incomplete: Wyatt describes them as "regular," and Larry Bland (editor of Marshall's collected papers) as "occasional," but we have dated reference for only thirteen items in this category.[37] The "press release" category refers only to official Army public-relations releases that Marshall dictated or edited by hand, but it is possible that more of these passed his desk and occupied his attention than were retained in the relevant archival folder. As a final point to consider, a miscellaneous category of seven items encompasses meetings, discarded drafts, and a dinner event that defied easy classification; one suspects many other exceptional events were glossed over in the recordkeeping process.

In sum, then, we know that Marshall was personally involved in at least 119 instances of press work during his time as Army chief of staff. We can add to this number an unknown number of other off-the-record briefings; a steady stream of material from his press-relations bureaus that would have crossed his desk at least weekly; his involvement with Stimson's Thursday press conferences; and his personal daily perusal of several magazines and newspapers. And so although the total class of 119 actions may seem trivial in the context of Marshall's unceasing labors during these long six years, they in fact reflect a fairly consistent effort on his part both to act upon press matters that came to his direct attention and to oversee and intervene in press work done by his staff.

Marshall experienced several periods of heightened activity in his press work. To understand Marshall's media management at its most intense, this chapter explores the two most defined peaks: the first in October 1941 and the second in January 1943. I collected the press work done in the five-month periods centered on those two dates. By targeting these loose dates, we are able to focus on a narrower subset of reports in greater detail. The risk is that we exaggerate the amount of Marshall's press work, but this risk is outweighed by the benefit of better understanding what sorts of actions he would take when press work was occupying his attention.

CASE 1: AUGUST–DECEMBER 1941

Between August and December 1941, Marshall was personally involved in thirteen press matters (see table 1.2). Categorized by type of media, they included four letters, four memoranda, two meetings, two speeches, and one press release. Categorized as propaganda or censorship or mixed, they included five cases that were strictly propagandistic, four that were strictly concerned with censorship, three that involved both, and one for which we have too little information to determine. The column of most interest, however, is the one listing the directives that Marshall issued in this press work. These directives reveal what role commanders such as Marshall actually played in managing public information during the war.

In his letter to General Wade Haislip on August 18, 1941, Marshall is quite straightforward: "I think it is important that a press release be made tomorrow morning on the question of extension of service. . . . We must not appear to be taking action because of unfavorable reactions."[38] Marshall's letter gave Haislip the authority to issue a press release but also guided Haislip in what the release was intended to accomplish—namely, to convey the false impression that the Army was not concerned with recent reports of discontent among soldiers. This release was, in other words, propaganda delivery via the press.

TABLE 1.2 Marshall's Press Work, August 18, 1941–December 13, 1941

Date	Type	Addressee	Category	Directive
8.18.41	memo	Gen. Wade H. Haislip	P	Write a press release
8.19.41	letter	Bernard M. Baruch	P/C	Build morale and counteract reports
9.6.41	memo	President F. D. Roosevelt	P/C	Delegate work
9.29.41	memo	BPR	P	Distribute photo
10.13.41	memo	Gen. Alexander Surles	P	Distribute photo
10.21.41	letter	Commanders	C	Prepare for bad publicity
10.25.41	letter	Gen. Ben Lear	C	Stop potboiling
11.11.41	speech	Citizens' Defense Corps	P	Be on guard against enemy propaganda
11.13.41	press release	American press	C	End rumor
11.15.41	meeting	Six correspondents	P/C	Spread propaganda, censor rumor
12.7.41	speech	Eds. of African American newspapers	Unknown	Unknown
12.13.41	letter	F. Warren Pershing	P	Enlist in Public Relations Section
12.21.41	meeting	Robert Sherrod	C	Background

Note: P = propaganda, C = censorship.

Indeed, Marshall was very concerned with the issue of troop morale. At the heart of the problem was the Selective Training and Service Act of 1940, which had drafted large numbers of American men without clear indication of what they were to do because the country had yet to join the war. A movement had developed around the acronym OHIO, which stood for "Over the Hill in October"—"over the hill" referring here to desertion. This issue also occupied Marshall's attention in his letter on August 19 to Bernard M. Baruch, a famed Washington insider described by Pogue as "a pipeline to centers of influence."[39] In this cordial letter, Marshall simply thanks Baruch for his support, shares his own feelings on the OHIO movement, and writes that he hopes they get to eat lunch together soon. In one revealing comment, he notes, "There is no more delicate problem than troop morale, and with such a slender margin of public approval behind us, it is no easy matter to build up the highly trained and seasoned fighting force that we must have available as quickly as possible."[40] But the letter is also an indication of a more systematic effort on Marshall's part that he would later relate to his biographer. Behind the scenes and leaving no traces other than these letters, Marshall "strengthened the Army's Press Relations organization and set it to work telling the positive side of the Army's training program. The Morale Branch was enlarged and more camp shows were organized to entertain men at the various posts."[41]

On September 9, 1941, Marshall would address his concerns in this matter directly to the president. He notes, "The present morale situation in the troops of the Army, resulting from the debates in Congress, as well as press and radio activities, presents a very difficult problem. . . . Within the War Department organization we are doing our best to counteract this weakness on the home-front, but as it relates to the civil population, I recommend that this phase of the matter be taken in hand by the Civilian Defense organization. . . . In my opinion, Mr. President, prompt action is necessary."[42] Here, then, Marshall's directive is to encourage the president to "prompt action" in delegating more authority to the Civilian Defense organization in raising troop morale.

Twenty days later, Marshall's attention was taken up by a more mundane matter. Marshall had come across a picture of himself taken by Maurice Constant and requested that the BPR gain the rights to the picture so he could make it his official portrait. Coincidentally, the next month Marshall had another photograph that he wanted the BPR to distribute—a photo of "the first German prisoner captured" by American forces. Marshall sent the photo to BPR for simple propaganda but reveals in the note what might today be considered a major scandal at the heart of the picture, although this scandal appears to have little moral or strategic concern: "Confidentially, there were few heroics in the procedure, as he wandered into our lines to deliver food, having taken the wrong trench. There the poor fellow, who had been injured in the head, I think, was questioned until he died, because after our G-2, the officer in this picture, was finished with him, all the observers in the rear echelons of an impatient AEF [Allied Expeditionary Force] started to work on him."[43]

In October, Marshall wrote to a number of generals who he had heard were to be subject to criticism in the press. His directive was simply to prepare for the bad news. He later wrote again to one of those generals, Ben Lear, to discuss the matter in more detail: "Our problem here is to avoid having columnists, radio men and the press generally involve us, with deliberate intention, in denials or assertions regarding leading, and frequently baseless statements. It is news to them to keep the pot boiling." This awareness led Marshall to reveal that "General Surles and I have discussed at length the proper procedure, and as a result he is endeavoring to arrange at the White House to have the President use this incident as an example of destructive press practices."[44]

On November 11, Marshall used NBC Radio to broadcast a message directed to the Citizens' Defense Corps. It was simply a warning to be on guard against enemy propaganda. Two days later, he personally edited a press release denying the rumor that "we are preparing troops for a possible expedition to Africa or other critical area outside this hemisphere." This was another nod to the OHIO movement and broad morale problems. Then two days after that, he held a secret conference with six correspondents (Robert Sherrod of *Time*; Edward E. Bomar of the Associated Press [AP]; Charles W. B. Hurd of the *New York Times*; Bert Andrews of the *New York Herald Tribune*; and Ernest K. Lindley of *Newsweek*). Sherrod recorded, "There were some things that he had to tell to key press correspondents in order that their interpretations of current and forthcoming events did not upset key military strategy of the United States."[45] Marshall revealed to these correspondents that the country was on the brink of war with Japan and that the U.S. government had a secret source on all Japanese information about the United States—a major strategic asset. He had hatched a complicated scheme and was seeking support from the press. The key issue was that the Japanese believed the United States was preparing only to fortify the Philippines rather than for offensive war. Marshall wanted the press to help in keeping U.S. power in the region secret so that the "Army fanatics" in Japan did not force the Japanese state into attacking the United States to save face. Instead, Marshall wanted to leak the U.S. force information directly to the Japanese ambassador to the United States, Saburo Kurusu, so that he could warn his government against antagonizing the United States. Marshall also cautioned that the danger period was the first ten days in December.

Of this remarkable conspiracy, Marshall's biographer notes, "The Chief of Staff had learned that the best way to keep a secret out of the newspapers was to reveal it to the responsible newsmen and then explain why it could not be printed." He goes on, "The briefing was successful in gaining secrecy if not in reporting accurately all of his plans."[46] This is reflected in the fact that on the day of the Pearl Harbor attacks, Marshall was busy meeting with the editors of African American newspapers to help build targeted support in African American communities. But perhaps the most remarkable expression of this close relationship is seen in a one-on-one meeting between Marshall and correspondent Robert Sherrod two weeks after the attack. The earlier secret meeting acknowledged the vulnerability of General Douglas MacArthur's Philippine air force, and, in the event, MacArthur spectacularly failed to protect against the bombing attack on December 7. Marshall told Sherrod, "I just don't know how MacArthur happened to let his planes get caught on the ground."[47] This is clear indication of the confidence Marshall had in Sherrod, who would wait to tell the story in a postwar collection.[48] But surely on the date of the attack much could have been made in the press over MacArthur's blunder and over division at the very highest levels of Army leadership. The relationship between Marshall and Sherrod was such that this story was not reported.

Only a week after Pearl Harbor, Marshall would find himself corresponding directly with General John J. Pershing's son, a stockbroker in New York, who wanted desperately to join the war effort. Marshall's nuanced public-relations sensibility is revealed in his response. Marshall felt that commissioning the younger Pershing directly would cause resentment, so instead he advises him to join the Public Relations Section in a civilian capacity, after which he would be given a commission. He alternately suggests Pershing enlist: "I am certain that the public reaction would be immediate and extremely favorable to such an action on your part."[49]

This five-month period involved Marshall in an array of both propagandistic and censoring activities. He worked to end rumors (that were true) then circulating in the press. He managed his own media profile. He gave advice to top generals to guard against anticipated criticism and warned the public to guard against German propaganda. And, most remarkably, he took a group of leading war correspondents into his confidence in an effort to guide them toward censoring certain information and promoting other information.

CASE 2: NOVEMBER 1942–MARCH 1943

Moving forward to the next major peak in Marshall's press work, between November 1942 and March 1943, we see his time was taken up by no fewer than twenty-one events (see table 1.3). By type of media,

TABLE 1.3 Marshall's Press Work, November 7, 1942–March 20, 1943

Date	Type	Addressee	Category	Directive
11.7.42	draft	President Roosevelt	C	Warn the president
11.15.42	briefing	Reporters	Unknown	Unknown
11.20.42	letter	Gen. Dwight D. Eisenhower	P	Publicize a general
11.23.42	press release	Gen. Alexander Surles	P	Write a press release
11.25.42	memo	Gen. Alexander Surles	P	Convince press
12.1.42	memo	Gen. Alexander Surles	P	Distribute propaganda
12.7.42	memo	Gen. Alexander Surles	P	Convince press
12.13.42	letter	Gen. Dwight D. Eisenhower	P	Convince press
12.15.42	memo	Gen. Alexander Surles	C	Discourage press reports
1.4.43	briefing	Reporters	Unknown	Unknown
1.7.43	letter	Walter Lippmann	C	Discourage press reports
1.30.43	briefing	Reporters	Unknown	Unknown
2.7.43	memo	Gen. Alexander Surles	P	Misdirection
2.13.43	speech	American Society of Newspaper Editors	C	Court press
2.21.43	memo	Gen. Alexander Surles	P	Promote a story
2.22.43	memo	Gen. Alexander Surles	C	Discourage press reports
2.22.43	memo	Gen. Alexander Surles	P	Promote a unit
2.24.43	draft	Gen. Alexander Surles	P/C	Promote a story
3.1.43	letter	Gen. Alexander Surles	P	Court press
3.15.43	memo	Col. McCarthy	P	Distribute propaganda
3.20.43	memo	Gen. Alexander Surles	C	Protect a general from criticism

Note: P = propaganda, C = censorship.

this period included ten memoranda, four letters, three briefings, two drafts, one press release, and one speech. Eleven cases were strictly propagandistic; five were strictly concerned with censorship; one involved both; and for four we have too little information to determine their purpose.

Unlike the earlier period, this five-month interval was marked above all by Marshall's frequent messages to General Alexander Surles, which make up twelve of the twenty-one events. Accordingly, it reveals important information about what Surles's BPR actually did. Marshall's first memorandum to Surles in this period is a directive to write a press release providing Army and Navy casualty figures from the North African theater. On November 25, 1942, two days after writing this memo, Marshall has cause to mention press "attacks" on the War Department prompted by what the correspondents considered to be too little information coming to them about Eisenhower's campaign in North Africa. This was in fact the result of Eisenhower having major radio communications problems, a serious strategic risk: "We cannot advertize [sic] to the world that he is having communication difficulties but you could tell these press men that when the commander is in trouble over communications they certainly cannot expect voluminous press releases. As a matter of fact they know practically as much as we know and we regret that it is not organized as a New York newspaper office."[50]

Two more memoranda to Surles would follow in the next few weeks, the first directing Surles to send a propaganda film to England and France, where it will "stimulate morale and . . . produce a healthy effect." In the second, Marshall complains to Surles that too much of the press coverage of the North African campaign comes from British sources, which has caused the *New York Times* to complain in print about the British stranglehold on information: "Whatever the trouble is see if you can't straighten it out because it is unfortunate to be building up anti-British prejudices."[51]

In a memo in mid-December 1942, Marshall provides Surles with quotations for use in deflecting criticisms that the Army is too large. On February 7, 1943, Marshall strategizes with Surles to distract the press: "Find out if Navy has any objections to the release of the following [information about Guadalcanal]. . . . This release at this time might take some of the heat off the pressure of the question about what is happening in the Solomons."[52] On February 21, he sends Surles information that he thinks may have "possible news value." The next day he writes to Surles twice. First, he writes of his frustration with the still-growing anti-British sentiment spreading in the American press. Second, he also sends Surles statistics on the continued expansion of the various Army departments. Two days later, he sends Surles several rambling paragraphs musing on the need to intervene in debates over manpower by correcting the tendency to overlook the cost and time associated with training troops properly. Surles notes that he will use the pieces "in different places, where he could."[53] In the last two messages to Surles during this period, on March 15 and 20, Marshall first writes to ask him to help finalize details about a meeting with leading newspaper publishers and later in March writes to ask Surles for his thoughts on adverse comments being made about General Lloyd Fredendall. Although a deeply problematic commander, Fredendall still had Marshall's faith at this point, and Marshall typically was working hard to shore up the general's reputation.

Throughout this period, then, Marshall kept in steady contact with Surles about a wide range of press matters, involving both strategies to guide press interests and more mundane instances of pushing propaganda or censoring reports. At the beginning of this period, Marshall had considered writing the president about "the obvious campaign in a large number of newspapers directed against the increase of the Army" but decided to send Roosevelt a milder warning instead.[54] Given this circumspect concern, it is likely that Marshall's three press briefings during this period (off the record, as usual), would have been more covertly intended to court the press back to supporting the Army's interests.

The North Africa campaign had become a bit of a press paradox in part because of growing tensions with the British in the press. Marshall wanted more positive coverage of the American forces but was wary of strategic risks associated with too much information being revealed. He admitted as much in an eyes-only, urgent message to

Eisenhower on November 20, 1942: "I am doing my utmost to support you by meetings with the press, with members of Congress, with State Department and with the President."[55] During the invasion of Northwest Africa, according to Pogue, "Marshall was strongly bent on making the public aware of American contributions to victory." To this end, Marshall informed Eisenhower that "a wonderful press kept at its same tone by filling in gaps in communiqué business with details regarding personal items." As it happens, there was a bit too much fluff for Marshall's liking, and he would complain to Eisenhower two weeks later that "there was more about the loss of [General Mark Clark's] pants . . . than there was of the serious phase of the war."[56]

Eisenhower, for his part, blamed this type of coverage on his lack of an experienced public-relations officer.[57] In a letter to Elmer Davis, who was the chief of OWI and as such the country's top propagandist, Marshall requested as much support as possible for Eisenhower in managing the press. And, indeed, Marshall himself jumped into the fray, writing to the famed columnist Walter Lippmann personally in early January 1943 to tell him, "We must pause for the moment in our impatient desire to accomplish miracles of readjustments and reforms and put some faith in the judgment and intelligence of Eisenhower [and his staff] . . . who are on the ground and who are responsible for the success or failure of our effort in Africa."[58]

In mid-February, some of the frustration Marshall must have been feeling with these press concerns came to the fore in an informal talk to the American Society of Newspaper Editors. His reflections on that occasion are worth quoting at length:

> In my past dealings with members of the press and the radio I have scrupulously avoided what might be called propaganda proposals and have endeavored, through a frank presentation of the situation, so far as permissible, merely to give them the facts, leaving the conclusions to their own judgment. The War Department will always be embarrassed by the insatiable demand of our people for "hot" news, and with related perils involved in releasing certain information. The situation is inevitable and the safeguard I turn to is to build up a general understanding of the problems by you gentlemen who present carefully considered views in your editorial columns.[59]

Of course, as we have seen, there was much more to Marshall's press-management strategy than "a frank presentation." Throughout this second period, we see instances of Marshall working to shape the reputation of his top generals and to direct the press toward or away from certain stories. In his mid-March letter to a Colonel McCarthy, Marshall reveals his enthusiasm for propaganda as a militarily valuable resource, directing further distribution of *Desert Victory*, a British propaganda film that the president thought was "the best thing that has been done about the war on either side."[60]

MAKING SENSE OF MARSHALL'S PRESS WORK

The thirty-four events discussed in the two cases make up about 29 percent of the total number of events. The reports are chosen from two five-month periods, or about 14 percent of Marshall's total tenure as the Army's chief of staff. This is a robust sample of Marshall's total recorded press work from which we can glean a number of insights into the way the office of chief of staff (and, indeed, other top military leadership roles) may reach out to shape the work of journalists. Several broad categories of strategic effort can be identified in these cases to help focus future work on this complex topic.

ANTICIPATE

Perhaps the most consistent theme in Marshall's press work is the importance of anticipating rather than reacting to the press. This approach involves both the anticipation of bad news, as we see in his warning to the generals on October 21, 1941, as well as the anticipation of what the press will need to produce, stories that the Army wants disseminated, as, for example, in his tendency to send along to Surles whatever newsworthy material crossed his desk.

Looking outside our cases, we can see many examples of Marshall's emphasis on anticipation. In a worried letter to Roosevelt's aide Lowell Mallett, Marshall requests "an immediately available background of publicity" for the Selective Service Act, something that no one else appears to have considered worth doing.[61] Marshall took particular care with the reputation of his generals and worked hard both to anticipate negative coverage, as in the case of Fredendall, and to anticipate good public-relations opportunities and newsworthy material that would show his generals in their best light. These points converged in an eyes-only memo to Surles on April 4, 1943, concerning General Orlando Ward:

> Ward is being relieved from command because he suffered a slight wound and a considerable shock under the pressure of the German attacks[;] . . . it seems to me that it would be a good thing to get into one of your press releases, as quickly as possible, the fact that General Ward had been wounded in action, without any comment as to his relief of command. That would develop later, and the previous announcement would serve to protect him against the usual newspaper—columnists—dissertations. What do you think about it? Destroy this memorandum.[62]

In any event, the memorandum was preserved, and we can see in this directive that Marshall was playing a long game with the press regarding his generals' reputations. A more mundane example of this is a memorandum for BPR handwritten by Marshall that complains about a "wretched photo" of General Charles Corlett and supplies a better one.[63] Verging on micromanagement, this careful pruning reflects the high value Marshall assigned positive coverage of American generals and the importance of anticipating press needs to cultivate such coverage.

ALIGN

A corollary to the strategy of anticipation is the strategy of alignment that Marshall practiced assiduously throughout the war. Our first indication of this strategic preference dates back to his work meeting with war correspondents outside Cantigny in World War I. And, as we have seen in the two five-month periods covered here, Marshall worked to win over the press quite overtly, as in his plea to the American Society of Newspaper Editors for support on February 13, 1943. Looking beyond our cases, Marshall deployed this strategy in perhaps the most famous instance of Army–press tensions during the war: General George Patton's slapping incident. Writing "in the *utmost* confidence" to the editor of the *Kansas City Star* in early April 1943, Marshall pleads for editorial intervention: "I feel I must depend on you and your most influential associates to protect us from his business of throwing pop bottles at the umpire in the hope of influencing his decision, when the thrower of the bottle has not even played sand-lot baseball."[64]

To persuade journalists to align their interests with those of the Army, Marshall was conscious that his broad censorship powers needed to be handled judiciously. On April 13, 1943, he wrote to Eisenhower about a minor flap over British criticism of an American unit (the Thirty-Fourth Division), which had been traced back to Eisenhower's command. Marshall makes clear that he thinks negative reports of this kind are "to our national disadvantage" but that "the problem of censorship is a delicate one and frankness has its eventual reward."[65] But if pushed, this strategy of alignment went only so far. As late as November 22, 1944, Marshall considered withdrawing his confidante Robert Sherrod's credentials after Sherrod published a piece that criticized Army soldiers in comparison with U.S. marines.[66]

MISDIRECT

That being said, while Marshall's press management sometimes bears the traces of the Carnegie method of persuasion, there are also glimmers of Machiavellian subtlety in certain instances of misdirecting the press. We have seen misdirection in his memo to Surles on February 7, 1943, when information about fighting at Guadalcanal was intended to distract reporters from discussing setbacks in the Solomon Islands.[67] This was perhaps a more important principle before the United States entered the war because Marshall was tasked with building up a military force without the support of the public. On May 15, 1940, he warned a staff member that "we must be prepared in the next few days—and immediately in conversations with the press, to off-set the clamor that will be raised by the opponents of the Administration."[68]

Misdirection in that case referred to reorienting press coverage from one subject to another. This principle was more commonly a second-order strategy, based first on having aligned the press to Army interests and then on persuading key journalists to act as a conduit to misdirect public opinion, with the ultimate goal being to allow continued secrecy of operations. Marshall's meeting with various reporters shortly before the Pearl Harbor attacks is the most significant instance of that form of misdirection. This two-stage strategy (court the press, then use journalists as conduits for propaganda) was difficult to pull off, and at times these attempts fell flat. On September 9, 1944, for example, Marshall was forced to admit to the independently minded General MacArthur that he was unable to persuade *Time* to increase its coverage of the Pacific theater—Marshall blamed this shortcoming on MacArthur's unwillingness to work with his local war correspondents.[69]

LESSONS FROM WORLD WAR II

As chief of staff of the Army for the entirety of World War II, George C. Marshall occupies an important and unique role in the history of the U.S. Army's relations with the American people. Marshall relied on a press-management staff that was very competently headed by General Alexander Surles, but as we have seen, Marshall himself was very engaged with managing the complex processes linking the Army to the public through the work of journalists. At the very least, he conducted 119 separate acts of press work during his tenure as chief of staff. More likely there were many more because we should add to that number both Stimson's weekly press conferences as well as dozens more unrecorded off-the-record press briefings. This would bring the total to a conservative estimate somewhere closer to 400 acts of press work. And in that active total we must also consider Marshall's passive encounters with the press, including both whatever documents he read from the BPR (which were, at minimum, sent in weekly books) as well as his daily rituals, which involved reading the news every morning and every evening. These actions and encounters surely informed his conduct of the war.

However, the goal of this chapter has not been to establish a definite claim about what proportion of Marshall's work as chief of staff was dedicated to the management of the press. Such a claim would need to be suspended within a much richer analysis of the War Department's overarching information management. Instead, this chapter builds a foundation for the logics of media control that emerged among top Army leaders during World War II. What we have found is a rich diversity of press work resulting in an equally rich diversity of directives. Marshall was ecumenical in his efforts, dedicating time equally to propagandistic actions (such as building up generals' reputations, encouraging coverage of infantrymen, and covering the Pacific theater) and to censoring activities (such as writing Walter Lippmann to discourage certain reports).

From this diversity, we can identify three strategic principles that Marshall often invoked in his press work. Most importantly, he worked to *anticipate* the opportunity for positive coverage and the inevitability of negative coverage. Also of clear importance, he worked to *align* the press voluntarily with Army interests. Only rarely did these principles spill over into a third posture, *intentional misdirection*, but Marshall did not hesitate to engage in the latter as the situation required. Notably, this body of material includes no instances of Marshall lying outright to journalists. Before the United States entered the war, Marshall met with the Committee on Military Affairs in the House of Representatives, and there had occasion to state his preferred posture: "I want to go right straight down the road, to do what is best, and to do it frankly and without evasion."[70] It is tempting to view such assertions as declaratory statecraft, and, certainly, Marshall's vision of the proper place of the press and the public admitted wide latitude to domestic propaganda and censorship. Yet for Marshall the principle of honest dealings with the press seems to have been genuine, and from that principle sprang enormous strategic benefits.

But what do we gain from this analysis of Marshall's press work? First, we are forced to recognize that even when the military of a democracy may appear to enjoy the most beneficial arrangements imaginable with its citizenry, the power of a relatively free press to shape the fighting of wars is immense. Marshall and other top American officials had at their disposal vast propaganda and censorship capacities that have since been outlawed. Yet even with those resources, press work was an important component of the top soldier's workload.

2

ARMY OVERREACH

Domestic Politics and Command Culture, 1945–1963

THE U.S. ARMY'S domestic political strategy—how it relates to Americans—inevitably bears the imprint of the underlying attitudes and assumed meanings that form the Army's unique culture. To understand why the Army lost control over the press during the Vietnam War (the topic of part 2), we must first understand how the Army's command culture fell out of synch with the media following World War II.

This chapter details a peculiar cultural structure or set of institutionalized patterns that arose during the post–World War II drawdown period and that directly relate to how the Army's warfighting approach going into the Vietnam War conceptualized the role of the media. I call this cultural structure "Army utopianism," a vision of the Army as a central structure of governance that was expected to meaningfully connect a large proportion of citizens to the state and to the world. This cultural structure is ultimately a manifestation of a deeper well of civic republican thought in the American political tradition, reflecting in part what Samuel P. Huntington would later praise as the "military ideal."[1] However, Army utopianism can and, I will argue, should be analytically separated from those concepts to pinpoint one specific way that Army leaders tended to envision civil-military relations at a transitional moment. The existence of this set of assumptions led leaders to make poor decisions that ultimately contributed to the profound alienation of millions of Americans from the Army.

Army utopianism emerged as a consequence of the massive mobilization of the country during World War II and was cultivated by some Army leaders over the next three decades. It was initially reflected in a major debate within the newly formed Department of Defense over the role of a conventional ground force and, specifically, President Dwight D. Eisenhower's New Look policies. Subsequently, when President John F. Kennedy pivoted from New Look to an emphasis on irregular warfare in the early days of U.S. involvement in Vietnam, Army utopianism emerged again when the Army was challenged to justify its continued monopoly over a conventional ground force. Together, these pressures, piped through the utopianism of a cadre of Army leaders, led the institution to favor a form of involvement in Vietnam that would prove politically disastrous.

UTOPIANISM AS A U.S. ARMY CULTURAL STRUCTURE

In chapter 1, Marshall's press work was used to understand how the Army learned about media management during World War II. Marshall's influence, however, was deeper than that. The Army of the Cold War was in many ways Marshall's Army, an organization whose internal policies and leadership culture had been profoundly shaped by his tenure as its chief of staff during World War II. Organizational culture can be notoriously hard to quantify, but a sense of his preferred command style can be gleaned from a commencement address he gave at Trinity College in Hartford, Connecticut, on June 15, 1941: "This Army of ours already possesses a morale based on what we allude to as the noblest aspirations of mankind—on the spiritual forces which rule the world and will continue to do so. Let me call it the morale of omnipotence. With your endorsement and support this omnipotent morale will be sustained as long as the things of the spirit are stronger than the things of earth."[2]

"Things of earth" eclipsed "things of the spirit" more quickly than Marshall may have hoped: while public support for the military remained at "unprecedented levels" throughout the war, this support quickly dried up after V-J Day.[3] At the same time as public support was declining, demobilization and drawdown were shrinking the armed services if not back to prewar levels (which has still not occurred), then still quite significantly.

It is hard to specify exactly how drawdown affected information activities because these activities were never separately accounted for. Our best indicator comes from a congressional request for information in 1942, which triggered a one-time accounting of all publicity functions within the Department of War. This report was resubmitted (and preserved for the historical record) with an updated total for fiscal year 1946, although without the full accounting from 1942. We can nevertheless sense the logic of the drawdown from the totals. In 1946, the total Department of War publicity budget, including staffing and expenses, dropped by 37 percent across the board from the preceding year. Recruiting made up about two-thirds of the publicity budget, and the cuts were taken largely out of a 46 percent reduction in information activities other than recruiting, although this reduction still left the Department of War nearly $2 million for nonrecruiting efforts (equivalent to about $32 million in 2024).[4] Marshall and other Army leaders recognized the threat of Soviet power and believed that the public needed to maintain its close attachment to the military in order to provide the groundwork for another mass mobilization, not least because even after the war had ended, the Army still needed fresh recruits to do the work of building peace.

If the problem in 1946 was maintaining public support with less money, without a war to justify that support, and with only a nebulous threat from Russia in the place of war, the solution to Marshall's mind was Universal Military Training (UMT).[5] Described as "the most revolutionary proposal[] ever made to the American Congress," UMT would encompass peacetime conscription, military training for young people, a reserve of alumni trainees, and refresher training for alumni for six years.[6]

Scholars have generally followed Alfred Vagts in understanding militarism as a sort of cultural froth around military affairs, a "vast array of customs, interests, prestige, actions and thought associated with armies and wars yet transcending true military purposes."[7] Such froth held little interest for the eminently practical Marshall, and UMT is better understood as a sort of military-inflected socialization stripped of pomp and circumstance, or what another sociologist at the time, August Hollingshead, called "militarization."[8] UMT aimed to instill a fundamental concern with military affairs in the average voter, thus militarizing the country in this specific sense. UMT would become the dissemination point for the Army utopianism of senior officers, a rethinking of public life that put the Army at the very center. Today, such a proposal would seem extremely heavy-handed, a risky attempt at overtly shaping American society that was likely to engender an antimilitary backlash. These leaders saw no particular risk to the Army, though, because they assumed that the public and the media would react favorably to such an overture.

Although UMT was an important site where Army leaders attempted to militarize American society, it was not the only one. Significantly, they also did so in part through the work of public affairs. By surveying the developments in Army public affairs in the early Cold War period, we can gain a rich sense of how Army utopianism was integrated into the Army's basic messaging to the public. Several top Army leaders championed messaging in general and public affairs in particular in this period. This reversed the trend set during World War I, which had seen the Creel Committee (the first major U.S. military effort to shape public opinion) unceremoniously disbanded after the war and its lessons quickly forgotten.[9]

Shortly after World War II, two reports were submitted to the Army's top leadership that underscored the centrality of messaging activities to military success and helped trigger the modest rise of public affairs. The Page Report of 1945, recognizing the low prestige of public affairs, called for a high-ranking officer to lead the new Army public-affairs department that would replace the World War II–era Bureau of Public Relations. The Army obliged by naming J. Lawton Collins to lead the Office of the Director of Information. Collins was a rising star and would become the Army chief of staff only four years later. His appointment was a clear vote of confidence. Working alongside Collins and his office was the Public Relations Division, headed by Major General Floyd L. Parks, another experienced and respected officer.[10]

Under Collins and Parks, the new departments commissioned the Lockhart Report in 1946, which advocated for the centrality of the Bureau of Public Relations to the Army and the importance of aligning public-relations activities with Army goals, "so as to gain maximum public benefit."[11] Park spelled out what precisely this meant to the corps of information officers in an issue of *Army Information Digest* in August 1946. Parks noted, "Every action dealing with the media of public relations, should be calculated to advance the purpose of the Army as a whole toward the larger objective."[12] He then followed this with a four-paragraph "Creed for Army Public Relations," which stressed the transparency of Army information and its "public utility function." A tension within Parks's article is evident today: How could one expect information officers to conceive of their role as both active instrument of Army command and passive public utility? At any rate, few would have mistaken Parks's own clear preference for the former over the latter. These early documents suggest strongly the belief that if the Army were to exist within the broader society, it must pursue its objectives in part by shaping that society.

An indication of what such a process of shaping might require can be found in an obscure report by two junior officers, Winant Sidle and someone identified only as "Notestein," then working for the Sixth Army at the Presidio in San Francisco.[13] Sidle and Notestein had presented the report to Major General Milton B. Halsky (who signed it) for distribution among professors of military science and tactics for the Senior and Junior Division Reserve Officer Training Corps (ROTC, Sixth Army Area)—in other words, professors at colleges that had an ROTC program and ran summer camps in the San Francisco area. The nine-page report spelled out eleven points of advice for tailoring a sequence of news releases to promote each camp. The instructors were encouraged to prepare biographical cards for each cadet; write a release for the cadet's hometown newspapers as well as school publications; take an effective headshot of each cadet; and tailor a final release to the same publications once the camp finished. More general suggestions included building relations with media in the vicinity of the camp by encouraging press tours and open houses. The authors of the report noted that they expected these stories would be based around each camper's hope that he would be offered a commission, at that time viewed as something worth boasting about. All this media work was intended to promote ROTC programs as having significant value for national security—"gag" or humorous stories were strongly discouraged.

It is difficult to imagine an era of journalism in which ROTC training might conceivably give rise to dozens if not hundreds of stories spread across local media outlets summer after summer. The plan, however, was clearly given serious consideration, as a note on the archival copy of the report indicates: "CINFO [chief of information, Parks's successor] is sending out to all CONUS [contiguous United States] Armies."[14] What accounts for this enthusiasm? The Sidle-Notestein report reflects a spirit of immense enthusiasm and confidence in the Army's capabilities in actively engaging with press in an overt quest to shape public opinion. This optimistic assessment, the authors' version of Army utopianism, suggests a near-perfect synthesis of military and public interest and a press compliant enough to allow the Army to use it as a mere conduit. Of course, it is unclear how journalists would have reacted to this attempt at shaping their work: it is possible that they would have refused to take the bait. There is also no cause to view this scheme as sinister or even disingenuous. Rather, it may well simply reflect the great optimism of the report's authors as well as of the chief of information.

In retrospect, this optimism seems to be out of step with the immediate postwar period, when both military pomp and government propaganda had definitively lost their luster. Both Elmer Davis's Office of War Information and the Office of Censorship closed in 1945, with significant congressional pressure acting on the former. The Smith-Mundt Act of 1948 outlawed domestic propaganda, a major blow to the Office of War Information's successor, the new United States Information Agency (USIA). However, it should be recalled that what might today look like moral stances taken against the corruption of the democratic process were at the time more like partisan squabbles, the concern being that domestic propaganda would be used by one party against the other. Similarly, many Army leaders still believed that George C. Marshall's vision of UMT might yet come to pass. So although militarism may have been out of season, it was being replaced by a more sophisticated form of militarization. This new form in turn was predicated on a very optimistic assessment of the press's willingness to serve as a conduit for military messaging and equally of the public's appetite for being militarized.

Army utopianism was a way of looking at the United States through an Army lens. It was expressed by senior leaders Marshall, Collins, and Parks and reflected in the public-affairs plans developed by Sidle and Notestein. The broader importance of this cultural structure, however, can best be seen in how the Army's leaders navigated two critical periods: the brief "atomic monopoly" enjoyed by the United States from August 6, 1945, to August 29, 1949, and the U.S. involvement in the Korean War from June 25, 1950, to July 27, 1953.

LAND POWER AND THE ATOMIC MONOPOLY

The Army utopians viewed their institution as the natural locus for postwar national renewal on the home front. So, too, they viewed the Army's core strengths, the employment of conventional land power, as the natural foundation for future U.S. force projection. There were dissenters, of course, most obviously among the leaders of the semi-independent U.S. Army Air Force. For these leaders, strategic airpower was the decisive operational factor in the war, far more so than tanks and artillery and infantry brigades. Whereas the enduring importance of land power seemed obvious to most Army leaders, it was not at all obvious to the Army Air Force generals or to the war-weary public and certainly not to the political elites, all of whom had seen the war brought to a close not by infantry and artillery but by two silver bullets, the atomic bombs dubbed Little Boy and Fat Man.

It is hard to imagine from our distant vantage point how seductive these horrific bombs must have been, a perfect political weapon. Through the early summer of 1945, the Army and the American public alike were preparing for a long and bloody process of invading Japan to force an end to the war. Although ultimate Allied victory was now a certainty in the minds of the leaders on both sides, what remained unknown was whether Japanese forces could resist sufficiently to achieve a negotiated peace "with honor." Millions and millions of lives still hung in the balance. Could a handful of bombs achieve what would otherwise require an invasion involving millions of service members?

Little Boy was dropped on Hiroshima on August 6, 1945. The next day President Harry Truman broadcast his message to the world introducing the atomic bomb as "harnessing the basic power of the universe." The headline of the *New York Times* was equally epochal: "FIRST ATOMIC BOMB DROPPED ON JAPAN ... NEW AGE USHERED." Dozens of stories about the incredible power of these new atomic bombs immediately followed.

Fat Man was dropped on Nagasaki on August 9, seemingly proof that the United States could destroy any place in Japan at will. That same day the Japanese Supreme Council met at the Imperial Palace to discuss immediate surrender, to which the emperor agreed.[15] On August 10, the headline of the *New York Times* read "JAPAN OFFERS TO SURRENDER." In four short days, Americans went from reading about the millions of soldiers on their way to invade Japan to reading about the shocking revelation of atomic war, Japan's unconditional surrender, and the end of the war. Nuclear power was thus introduced to the U.S. arsenal, and virtually the entire public immediately recognized its political and operational significance.

The causal link between atomic bombing and war's end was reinforced by the atomic tests held at the Bikini Atoll in 1946. These tests were widely discussed in the press and gave rise to a popular conception of nuclear weapons as the "most terrible weapon," in the words of the famed military observer Hanson W. Baldwin.[16]

If atomic bombs can end wars on their own, as many then believed, what did that mean for the way Americans structured their military? This question would come to a head in the coming year with debates over the National Security Act of 1947, but in 1946 the public was still unsure what to think about nuclear weapons. The Social Science Research Council surveyed nearly 3,000 Americans before and after the Bikini tests to gauge public perceptions of the "most terrible weapon." Although more than 99 percent of respondents knew of the atomic bomb and recognized its use as an extraordinary event, they disagreed on what this meant for the military. Most notably, survey respondents were told the figures for the size of the wartime Army (8.3 million), Army Air Force (2.3 million), and Navy (3.5 million) in 1945 and then asked what size each branch should maintain in peacetime. Although answers varied widely, the median in all three cases was considerably higher than the prewar figures for the services and in fact significantly higher than the actual numbers in 1946.[17] Americans had a newfound tolerance for large standing forces, something entirely unexpected from a country that had always resisted the concentration of force in the hands of its federal government. For decades, the Army had previously fluctuated from 130,000 to 190,000 active-duty soldiers. At the end of the war, it was bigger than ever, and though it shrunk rapidly, it was still by a large margin at its biggest-ever peacetime size (a little less than 2 million active-duty soldiers) at the close of 1946. Regardless, more than a third of the survey respondents in 1946 preferred an ever-larger force of 3.5 million or more.[18]

These survey findings can dispel the notion that most Americans viewed nuclear weapons as a straightforward replacement for conventional forces. This would have been the one moment in time when a Pax Americana backed solely by the threat of nuclear annihilation might have been enforced. Americans in 1946 had quite compelling reasons to think of nuclear weapons as their salvation from endless war, a way to maintain a very small standing force yet still enjoy the benefits of hegemony. After all, only Americans had the ultimate weapon, and they jealously guarded its secrets. But the militarization of American social and political life had progressed sufficiently that this was not in fact the survey respondents' interpretation of these weapons' significance. Mostly convinced that the secret would get out eventually, they put little faith in the atomic monopoly securing American interests. About two-thirds of respondents urged the United States to keep to itself the secret of making atomic bombs, but about the same number thought that the secret would get out anyway and that atomic bombs would likely be used against the United States.[19]

Already accustomed to a much larger military presence than before the war, Americans at the end of the 1940s accepted the need for a large and expensive Army and Navy and indeed called for the creation of a separate service, the United States Air Force, to ensure that advances in airpower (mainly in the sense of strategic bombing, including the use of atomic bombs) were safeguarded by a dedicated bureaucracy. With the passing of the National Security Act of 1947 and its revision in 1949, the Army lost its claims on airpower and lost control over the country's nuclear arsenal. More importantly in terms of the Army's command culture, the senior officers least supportive of conventional land power had by and large left the service to join the new Air Force.[20] Conventional land power was one thing that the remaining Army leaders knew that the Army did well, even as they were faced with unexpected new challenges for which they were ill-prepared and ill-disposed to address.

Certainly, victory on the battlefield had brought many unanticipated headaches. Almost immediately after V-J Day, the Army's leaders began to feel two enormous counterbalancing pressures: first, to rapidly demobilize and cut costs; second and in exact contradiction, to staff large occupying forces (with many new personnel) in Europe and Japan. Bringing the veterans home and recruiting replacements were equally difficult tasks, and both were further plagued by protests inside and outside the services.[21]

At this point, the Army utopians might have taken note of a major setback. Marshall's UMT plan was advanced with such optimism that President Truman elected not to renew the Selective Service Act when it expired, expecting rather to be flooded with high-quality trainees provided through UMT. Congress, however, rejected the plan entirely, and the military was left without the right to conscript anyone at all.[22] And then on August 29, 1949, the Soviet Union dropped its own plutonium-core bomb, RDS-1, in a successful test that effectively ended America's atomic monopoly.

In the language of the private sector, the Army of the 1940s was dramatically downsizing its experienced staff of veterans, rapidly hiring inexperienced new staff through recruitment drives, expanding into new markets as an occupying force in Europe and Japan, and grappling with the paradigm-changing new technology of atomic bombs, a technology now also being added to the product list of the Army's chief competitors. If that were not enough for the Army's leaders to juggle, they suddenly had to manage another war.

INFORMATION AND OPERATIONS IN THE FORGOTTEN WAR

The Korean Peninsula had been under Japanese control throughout World War II. When the emperor agreed to unconditional surrender after the bombing of Nagasaki, Japanese forces in Korea surrendered to Russian forces north of the 38th parallel and to Lieutenant General John R. Hodge of the U.S. Army to the south. This dual surrender created two zones, which in turn became two states. Hodge established the United States Army Military Government in the southern zone, which slowly evolved into a South Korean independent government built on an anticommunist platform. This evolution was in large part a response to developments in the northern zone, where Kim Il-sung's Soviet-backed government undertook major land reforms that triggered a mass exodus. The two governments bitterly competed for legitimacy on the world's stage, and both prepared for war even as the occupying forces withdrew. For their part, U.S. forces left South Korea in 1949, although General Douglas MacArthur's Far East Command was still relatively nearby in Tokyo.[23]

War erupted on June 25, 1950, when the North Korean army crossed the 38th parallel and invaded South Korea. MacArthur, who was responsible for the theater, heard about the attack six and a half hours later via telegram to his headquarters in Tokyo. That same day he sent a ship filled with ammunition and other supplies to aid the South Korean forces. On June 26, American dependents were ordered to evacuate and did so by air and sea the following day. Meanwhile, MacArthur had dispatched an advance command group to assess the situation. This group, headed by Major General John H. Church, quickly established a joint headquarters with the U.S. ambassador to South Korea and his team and with the South Korean army chief and his staff. By June 28, Church had seen enough to conclude that to repel the North Korean invasion, U.S. ground forces would have to be deployed.[24]

Although no American war correspondents accompanied Church's advance team, MacArthur decided to visit Korea on June 28 and brought with him the four bureau chiefs for the main wire services (AP, United Press International [UPI], International News Service, and

Reuters).²⁵ Very soon there were sufficient print reporters as well as a handful of radio correspondents and newsreel producers that MacArthur decided to issue press guidance. In a decision that appears bizarre today, MacArthur's instinct was to completely free the press to report what they thought best—a direct response to the uncivil character of the World War II censorship regime. MacArthur pointedly stated that he "did not desire to re-establish wartime censorship" and would instead allow correspondents to "establish a voluntary code that will ensure the security of operations and the safety of personnel."²⁶

MacArthur is a unique figure in U.S. military history and cannot easily be lumped together with the Army utopians. Thin-skinned, narcissistic, Douglas MacArthur in 1950 had a uniquely distorted view of the free press that does not quite align with the somewhat naive optimism of his peers. Unlike Marshall, Parks, Collins, and others, MacArthur had become virtually a stranger to his own country and its public sphere, having last been in the United States in 1937. Throughout World War II, he and other field commanders were protected from the critical press by the censorship board and, as we have seen, by the diligence of Chief of Staff George C. Marshall in the Pentagon. As a consequence, they had grown accustomed to seeing only the right sort of story actually make it to print, and these stories were often personally flattering. But when the other commanders returned home to be confronted with the political logic of drawdown and reorganization, MacArthur stayed in the field. Since 1945, he had been serving as supreme commander for the Allied Powers, shifting from war hero to something more akin to warlord as the de facto head of the Japanese state and of military affairs throughout the region.

MacArthur was insulated from criticism and basked in praise. His large staff in Tokyo exerted all manner of pressures on the local press to ensure conformity. His attitudes to press freedom in Japan were complicated. Although he appears to have been largely oblivious to what was actually happening in his name, and despite repeatedly disapproving of censorship in his public statements, his staff believed that they were in fact expected to keep a very tight hold on any potentially negative media coverage.²⁷

And so MacArthur's personal expectations for a voluntary press censorship model were almost inevitably unrealistic in the extreme. Nevertheless, he committed to the course and maintained it for longer than many would have predicted. His mistake was, however, almost immediately apparent to him. Less than two weeks after instituting the voluntary model, MacArthur was loudly complaining about the press's overly critical portrayal of the war effort in Korea. On July 15, 16, and 17, 1950, he barred correspondents Tom Lambert of the AP, Peter Kalischer of the UPI, and Marguerite Higgins of the *New York Herald Tribune* for different reasons, none justified by operational concerns.[28] For months to come, MacArthur would find himself at odds with dozens of reporters and most of the major news organizations.

It is hard to imagine how positively the war would have had to be going for MacArthur to have read the sorts of reports he wanted and expected. The reality was that the war was not going well at all. Journalists had plenty of stories to tell about morale problems and dramatic battlefield reversals, and they were legally permitted to tell them. Their criticism was so intolerable to the Army command in the field and the Army's frustration with the press was so corrosive to the working relationship between the media and the military that the journalists soon came to want clear censorship standards imposed by the Army. After a turbulent five months, MacArthur rescinded the voluntary model and instituted military censorship through his Tokyo-based Press Advisory Division. The decision was accepted positively by the *New York Times* and other news agencies because it finally allowed their correspondents to report without fear of reprisal, even though it came at the cost of their autonomy.[29]

Despite MacArthur having initially stated that he did not want to reestablish wartime censorship, the form that censorship took in the Korean War was very close to the form it took in World War II. Indeed, the doctrine that guided Army press officers was the World War II Office of Censorship Press Codes established in 1942, apparently now supplied by an officer who happened to have a copy in his desk.[30]

At the time, the only relevant Army doctrine was Army Regulation (AR) 600-700, *Public Relations*, which had been introduced in 1928 and was revised continuously throughout the 1930s and 1940s. The most recent AR 600-700 was the 1946 edition, which merely directed that "impartial relations will be maintained with all information media" and otherwise described how commanders should send messages to the public rather than how the press should be managed by commanders.[31]

Interestingly, in the midst of the military censorship period, the Army in October 1950 released its first public-information doctrine, AR 360-5, *Public Information*, which superseded AR 600-700 and at ten pages long provided an unusually detailed guide to media-management issues.[32] AR 360-5 would be revised in 1967, 1975, 1986, and 1989; retitled AR 360-1, "The Army Public Affairs Program," in 2000; and revised under that title in 2011 and 2020. It is still active today. Accordingly, AR 360-5 of 1950 is a significant historical document, establishing the baseline doctrine for how the Army still manages the press.[33] And yet this doctrine limits itself to peacetime public information, making no reference to the dilemmas of managing correspondents in times of war. Typically for this era, the doctrine has an expansive vision of what the Army could accomplish in the information realm rather than what it risked. It stresses that the Army "has an obligation to report fully on its activities to the American people ... thoroughly and continually" and states that this active sharing of information should cover seven core topics: objectives, progress, cost and efficiency, teamwork within the Army, its role in war, its role in peacetime, and the need for an Army. However, little of practical value is offered about making the tough decisions on how to balance the media's right to information with the military's operational needs for secrecy. Rather, the doctrine highlights the need to emphasize the positive, that commanders and public-information officers should always stress "good human relations, good performance, and an individual code of honorable conduct."[34] Notably, then, the Army utopianism of the Pentagon transcended the growing anxieties of those on the information frontline in Korea.

For the remainder of the war, censorship of the press, critical reporting by journalists, and a general resistance by Army leaders to sharing information continued to mark Korea-based Army–media relations. The relationship was not all bad, of course, and Lieutenant General Matthew B. Ridgway, who replaced Lieutenant General

Walton Walker as commander of the Eighth Army, gained a particular reputation as a friend of the press. In a pattern that would be echoed in the conflicts that would come, Ridgway's positive reputation was built not on his deference to the press—he, too, demanded strict censorship—but rather on his personal relations with journalists, whom he treated courteously and with whom he discussed the war effort openly, although off the record.[35]

The period of voluntary censorship, June to December 1950, established narratives of organizational disorder and operational failures. MacArthur's response was strict press censorship, which stemmed the flow of new critical information but could hardly succeed in soliciting more positive stories. The period of military censorship, December 1950 through to the end of the war in July 1953, was not surprisingly characterized by more stories of disorder and failure. Significantly, however, the total amount of coverage (good and bad) declined fairly rapidly, so the issue of censorship ultimately became moot. This decline occurred not because of the Army's successful management of the war or because of improved relations with the press but simply because of the public's lack of interest. For Army leaders, the cultural and political factors that contributed to the Korean War becoming the Forgotten War also conspired to stall any serious interest in the lessons of media–military relations from this important but still-neglected theater.

OVERREACHING AT HOME

Back home, the spirit of Army utopianism exemplified in the Sidle-Notestein report was being expressed in a range of other utopian articulations of public-information policy. Chief of Staff Collins was replaced by General Matthew B. Ridgway, back from Korea. Like Collins, Ridgway, who had enjoyed unusually positive relations with the press in Korea, saw enormous potential in how the Army communicated with the public. On June 4, 1954, for example, Ridgway echoed the Page Report of 1945 and reaffirmed the spirit of Parks's creed in a letter to all major commanders in the Army, which essentially observed the importance of public affairs for Army life. However, he also focused his comments on an issue at the heart of the Sidle-Notestein report—namely, the equal importance of troop morale and local media relations to national media-management efforts. According to Ridgway, "Only by doing all these things thoroughly shall we be able to gain and retain the confidence and support of the American people."[36] This was not an idle concern on Ridgway's part. A few months earlier, on February 8, 1954, he had "disturbed" the chairman of the Joint Chiefs of Staff with his critical words to the House Subcommittee on the Armed Services, in particular his concern that the Army would lose too much manpower with President Dwight D. Eisenhower's New Look cuts.[37] Speaking before Congress was one way to pressure Secretary of Defense Charles Wilson and President Eisenhower; communicating to the public was another.

By 1956, then, there had been several important votes of confidence in Army public affairs, and a new understanding had emerged concerning just how extensive Army efforts in this regard could be. Most significantly, perhaps, was that both Collins and Ridgway in their successive turns as the nation's top soldier signaled the importance of the public-affairs field. At this crucial period of postwar Army reorganization, top leadership support would have been instrumental in allowing the two Army public-affairs offices, now called the Office of Public Information (successor to Collins's Office of the Director of Information) and the Office of the Chief of Information and Education (successor to Parks's Office of the Chief of Information), to continue their evolution. To this end, under the next Army chief of staff, General Maxwell Taylor, three Chief of Information and Education officers undertook a vast analysis of all Army public-affairs functions to develop a systematic approach to the Army's political strategy. The internal goal of the report was to coordinate what had thus far been four discrete fields of public-affairs work: public information (engaging with national media); troop information (informing, entertaining, and indoctrinating soldiers); troop education (courses and training for troops); and community relations (engaging with regional media and local governance).

The plan, reviewed by the now retired Parks, was innocuously titled *An Army Public Relations Plan*, but it is a truly remarkable artifact. At 250 pages, the plan systematically describes fifty separate platforms through which the Army can get involved in American domestic politics and everyday life. It describes itself as "aggressive public relations" and is perhaps better viewed as a blueprint for Army utopian thought. Its tenor can be gauged from an introductory section that describes the Army's audiences. Three main publics are identified in the plan: the general public, the troops, and Congress. But in the discussion that follows, these three are revealed to be in turn composed of multiple, distinct publics that require separate information strategies. Thirty publics in all are singled out as requiring special care, including the press, viewed as both audience and conduit; youth organizations; local chapters of national organizations; female members of Congress; veterans of other services; and many others. Notably, foreign publics, whether those of allies or enemies, are ignored entirely: according to this plan, the goal of Army public relations is to shape domestic and internal audiences.[38]

The spirit of the Smith-Mundt Act of 1948, which prohibited domestic propaganda, would have been sorely tested by this plan. The plan includes extensive discussion of slogans, marketing gimmicks (e.g., work with Zippo, Hallmark, Revlon, and toy manufacturers), major public events, and other obvious efforts to persuade the American public of the Army's merits. The plan is also pointedly oriented to the internal public of troops (with multiple subdivisions, of course), but here there is an important conceptual development. The plan reverses the traditional notion of troop information as concerned primarily with maintaining morale, instead viewing troops much as the press is viewed: as an audience that needs to be persuaded of the Army's message but also a conduit through which the Army message can be spread. In other words, troop information and education are intended to help encourage soldiers to spread positive messages about the Army to their civilian friends and family members, in effect to proselytize for the Army.

In an era of mass conscription, when UMT was still an Army goal, the utopian spirit of this expansive report is a reflection of a buoyant institution. However, there is no record of the report's fate, which reflects the more mundane reality of Army fortunes. As noted earlier, the postwar drawdown had sapped resources across the board, including in information activities, and defense budgets throughout the 1940s and 1950s had only further diminished Army resources.

Overt propagandizing was also coming under attack once again. On May 15, 1957, USIA chief Arthur V. Larson came under intense questioning by Senator Lyndon B. Johnson. The USIA's budget was reduced by $20 million, a major blow to the agency, in part on the grounds that Larson, in Johnson's estimation, had "stepped over the line" and begun using the USIA to support Republican Party interests.[39] For the Army's part, the budget of the Office of the Chief of Information and Education had been steadily declining even as the rhetoric of its value to the Army was heating up. In fiscal year 1952, its budget was $3,225,482, and so down about 44 percent from 1946, and in the year that *An Army Public Relations Plan* was written, 1956, the budget was only $832,000, down 75 percent from 1952 and only about a tenth of its wartime high. The authors of the plan refer to this far more modest budget as "totally inadequate, completely unrealistic, artificial."[40] Even if their plan was not ultimately passed, it remains significant as an attempt to reassert the importance of the field of public affairs to the Army and in turn the centrality of the Army to the nation.

OVERREACHING ABROAD

Dwight D. Eisenhower, retired five-star general, former supreme commander of the Allied Expeditionary Force in Europe, was on the campaign trail in October 1952, the Republican Party nominee with a surprising take on the Korean conflict. His stump speech began, "In this anxious autumn for America, one fact looms above all others in our people's mind. One tragedy challenges all men dedicated to the work of peace. One word shouts denial to those who foolishly pretend that ours is not a nation at war. This fact, this tragedy, is: Korea."[41]

Six months later, now president, Eisenhower contemplated survey findings from October 1952, November 1952, January 1953, and April 1953. To the question, "As things stand now, do you feel that the war in Korea has been worth fighting, or not?," respondents answered "not worth fighting" consistently across these four dates (56, 58, 52, and 55 percent, respectively).[42] For Eisenhower, peace was the goal of political life, and any projection of U.S. force abroad was a betrayal of that peace, no matter how small or contained the war. His principles and his survey findings agreed that Korea was not worth it.

How can the United States finally find peace? For Eisenhower, the answer to this perennial question lay in a reconsideration of the revolutionary potential of the nuclear arsenal. He began to think in earnest about how to use nonconventional weapons strategically to minimize the military instrument. Eisenhower was no Army utopian. His sympathies lay with the sleepy Army of the early 1930s. The New Look, as his defense doctrine came to be known, was in many ways a challenge to the endless optimism with which his former colleagues viewed the Army's role in American life. Conventional force was going out of style, and the Army—with its hopes of vast social influence—was faced with justifying its continued relevance to a commander in chief who was extraordinarily knowledgeable about military affairs.

At this time, military strategy was still coming to terms with the new place of civilians in war. Some strands of nuclear-deterrence strategy posited large civilian populations as the most likely target of Soviet aggression. That conceptual shift corresponded to a reimagining of conventional Army strength as a vestigial organ of state power, most powerfully exemplified by Eisenhower's New Look. Eisenhower was of course tapping into a strand of strategic reasoning that had emerged in the days following the bombing of Hiroshima. After passage of the National Security Act in 1947, the Army and Navy came to view the pro-nuclear approach as a means of advancing the Air Force's interests alone. Interservice rivalry reared its head.

In a lecture to the Naval War College on February 16, 1950, Rear Admiral W. S. Parsons dismissed what he viewed as the fallacious reasoning that led the public to assume that since nuclear weapons ended the war with Japan, they ended war as such and hence made conventional forces redundant.[43] On the same occasion, Vice Admiral Donald B. Beary spoke more plainly: "There is a vociferous, fanatical group of people in this country . . . who say that air power has sunk the Navy. . . . This is not true and all history refutes them."[44] Even though the Navy (unlike the Army) was responsible for an important element of the nuclear triad, Navy leaders feared that their fleets would wither in the face of failing executive support for conventional force.

For their part, Army leaders attempted to reassert the importance of the full spectrum of Army resources, justifying both conventional and irregular units as important front-line elements in the Cold War, in contrast to the New Look's preference for long-range missiles with nuclear warheads. These justifications hinged on making the case that limited wars could still be fought without tipping over into full-out nuclear war.

General Lyman L. Lemnitzer replaced General Maxwell Taylor as Army chief of staff. Taylor, who had been chief of staff when the utopian public-relations plan was written, was among the most pro-conventional of the Army utopians. He occupied an unusual role. After his retirement, he had campaigned publicly against President Dwight D. Eisenhower's New Look, in particular its orientation to massive retaliation as the key geopolitical pivot in a nuclear age. In 1959, he published a book advocating an alternative doctrine of "flexible response." In it, Taylor echoed Admirals Parsons and Beary, claiming that the New Look was premised on the "Great Fallacy" that the threat of nuclear weapons would prevent war. In Taylor's words, "While our massive retaliatory strategy may have prevented the Great War—a World War III—it has not maintained the Little Peace."[45]

Eisenhower's plan relied on nuclear deterrence and market tools to realize U.S. interests abroad, and Eisenhower was happy to get his country out of the business of warfighting. An added benefit of the plan was that the DOD, once modernized, could begin accruing savings by cutting "frills" and make do with a budget that was "a little leaner and tougher," in Eisenhower's own words.[46] It all hinged on the big question haunting military thinkers since 1949, when the Soviets broke the atomic monopoly: Would nuclear weapons prevent limited wars from being fought because of the risk of triggering what was then termed "general war," a third, nuclear world war? In contrast to Air Force and some Navy leaders, Army leaders rejected this notion and anticipated instead a broad space for what was in essence conventional-warfare brinkmanship.[47]

The Army's perspective can be gleaned in speeches by top soldiers during this period. On April 6, 1960, Lemnitzer spoke of Soviet expectations of a long nuclear war, one that might start with the exchange of devastating nuclear attacks on civilian populations but would still require conventional forces fighting on land to decide the issue.[48] He expanded this nightmarish vision in another talk in August, where he connected the long-nuclear-war scenario to the resulting decrease in the efficacy of deterrence. Enemies of the United States did not consider nuclear war a decisive event, and so nuclear power was not decisive. Indeed, Lemnitzer informed his audience that Soviet forces might launch a nuclear attack on U.S. soil simply to gain territory somewhere else. Accordingly, there should be no question of restraint when it came to conventional involvement in seemingly remote theaters; rather, a blend of U.S. forces would be needed that could go into any given area and "exterminate the rats without destroying the neighborhood."[49]

Lemnitzer was echoed by his successor as chief of staff, General George H. Decker, who spoke on the subject of "the army today" before an audience in New York on March 23, 1961. His comments supported the new ideas introduced by Eisenhower's successor, John F. Kennedy, who initially championed counterinsurgency ideas while hedging for the importance of maintaining conventional force. Decker noted that in this complex time, strategy "must be a flexible, pragmatic combination of all these [maritime, aerospace, and landmass powers], considered in context with political, economic, and other non-military factors."[50]

The struggle to preserve a conventional Army force would continue throughout the period. Three weeks after Decker's speech, Lemnitzer, now the chairman of the Joint Chiefs of Staff, responded to a request from Secretary of Defense Robert S. McNamara to provide joint doctrine that would minimize conventional force in a nuclear war and emphasize instead diplomatic solutions through the use of less force and scheduled breaks in fighting. Lemnitzer's response was in effect to reject McNamara's order, noting, "We do not have adequate defenses, nor are our nuclear retaliatory forces sufficiently invulnerable, to permit us to risk withholding a substantial part of our effort, once a major thermonuclear attack has been initiated. . . . [S]uch a doctrine, or to declare such an intent, would be premature and could gravely weaken our deterrent posture."[51]

The Army chief of staff (Decker) and the chairman of the Joint Chiefs of Staff (Lemnitzer) were risking their positions when they pushed back against McNamara, who had President Kennedy's support, but they did so because they believed the Army's monopoly on conventional ground force retained the Army's central place in legitimating U.S. foreign policy, even in the nuclear age.

During his presidential campaign, Kennedy had championed Maxwell Taylor's doctrine in particular and called him out of retirement to investigate the Bay of Pigs incident. And so it came to pass that Kennedy sent Taylor and the economist Walter W. Rostow to review the situation in Vietnam. In November 1961, Taylor and Rostow offered the fateful call for a "massive joint effort" to guarantee South Vietnamese freedom.[52]

There is no little irony that even as the Army withdrew (in part) from one Asian country, where it had met with consistently negative press coverage in a war viewed as "not worth it" by more than half the population, it immediately began to view another Asian country as the ideal showcase for its domestic political message of the relevance of the Army's unique capabilities in ground warfare. Army utopianism as a political strategy would soon enough crash against the realities of U.S. involvement in Vietnam, though.

Against the backdrop of Lemnitzer and Decker's thoughts on aggressive postures and Taylor's own notions of flexible response, U.S. involvement in Vietnam was a decision bred of confidence in the Army's ability to secure large-scale geopolitical ends. Taylor and Rostow's proposal included 8,000 American ground troops. Kennedy balked at the 8,000-troop request but approved a scaled-down version of the plan, which nevertheless signified such a significant increase in the U.S. role in Vietnam that a new headquarters would be needed.[53] With this force, the Army's top leaders began the difficult task of learning counterinsurgency while also establishing a conventional-force presence. Twelve years later, the Army would finally withdraw from the region, its relations with the public in a state of crisis.

LESSONS FROM THE ARMY'S OVERREACH

Following the end of World War II, the place of the Army in American politics underwent a dramatic transformation. At first, top Army leaders anticipated that they would retain a central role in public life and looked to journalists, then working under voluntary conditions of access and recently freed from censorship, to help the Army tell its story. Most importantly for many top Army officers (including a series of chiefs of staff), the Army had to justify its continuing monopoly on conventional ground force. This monopoly had been directly challenged by other services and governmental branches but was also indirectly challenged by a new emphasis on strategic deterrence (led by diplomats and backed by nuclear weapons).

In the words of Russell F. Weigley, one of the foremost historians of the Army, "To use—and restrain—its immense social, economic, and political influence wisely and effectively, the Army must obviously hold itself in close rapport with the people."[54] Some Army leaders in the post–World War II period quite reasonably pursued a strategy of close rapport, which I describe as "Army utopianism" and which, with the benefit of hindsight, can be see as a gross miscalculation. What this strategy revealed was that the relationship that Weigley sketches between "influence" and "rapport" is not straightforward and that simply amplifying the Army's presence in American public life can have the opposite of the intended effect. Accordingly, chief among the lessons of the turbulent period from 1945 to 1962 is to guard against the optimistic and expansive vision of the Army's role, of which Army utopianism is just the most extreme expression. But this lesson had yet to be learned in the early days of American involvement in Vietnam.

PART II
The Fall of the Political Army

3

OUTPACED

The Press and Public Affairs in Vietnam, 1963–1968

U.S. MILITARY involvement in Vietnam dates back to November 1955 with the creation of Military Assistance Advisory Group, Vietnam, commonly referred to as MAAG-V. MAAGs were headed by military officers but were ultimately part of country teams, headed in turn by ambassadors. In Vietnam, the military role increased gradually: Americans were in a shooting war as early as 1962, and the U.S. Army finally left in 1973. For two more years, a small number of marines remained in theater, now limited to guarding the embassy, and they left in spectacular fashion as North Vietnamese forces swept through Saigon and the last Americans scrambled aboard overladen helicopters, flying to safety with only minutes to spare.

Thus, for twenty years American officers served in Vietnam. More than 40,000 service members were killed in action, most of them soldiers. More than 3,000 Army officers were killed. Senior officers were not exempt, with two major generals, Keith L. Ware and John A. B. Dillard Jr., killed. It is little wonder that the significance of Vietnam remains profoundly and often bitterly contested within the Army and that it was an especially hard topic to debate for Army leaders in the 1970s and 1980s.

This chapter and the one that follows argue that of all the possible lessons learned from Vietnam, one lesson stands as the singularly most challenging and most important: operational success, winning on the battlefield, can nevertheless result in strategic failure. The lesson hinges on the work of war correspondents and combat photographers, on one hand, and the Army commanders and their public-information officers, on the other.

This chapter explores how and why Army leaders failed to effectively nurture the media–military relationship through their public-information officers, setting themselves up to learn the lesson of strategic failure despite operational victory. Recall that as a consequence of partisan conflicts at home in the 1940s and 1950s, the military was stripped of much of its legal authority over the flow of information in war zones by the early 1960s. Nevertheless, many of its leaders still operated with the same expansive understanding of the military's autonomy and its control over journalists, the Army utopianism described in chapter 2.

Entering the Vietnam theater, then, Army leaders expected a compliant press and viewed themselves as responsible to their civilian masters but not to the demands of their overseers in the media. Over time, a critical mass of journalists gathered in Saigon, gradually gaining the skills they would need to exert autonomy from military control. The first clear indication of this new relationship was during the Battle of Ap Bac in 1963. Following the shift of command authority from the U.S. ambassador to a military commander, a series of tense encounters occurred between reporters and senior officers that soured the relationship further. Only with the North Vietnamese Tet Offensive of January 1968, however, was the full scale of the Army's mistaken view of its own autonomy made apparent.

THE RECIPE FOR DISASTER

Just like MacArthur in Korea, American military leaders in Vietnam repeatedly fell victim to the temptation to corrupt the flow of information in order to protect operational goals. The formal U.S. presence in the region began in 1955 with the formation of a MAAG, but by the beginning of President John F. Kennedy's administration in 1961, mission creep had already set it. The first information policy for U.S.

forces in Vietnam, set by President Kennedy, was intended to deceive the American public as to the involvement of American troops in the region. Like Eisenhower before him, Kennedy had found himself with entanglements around the world, but he saw particular challenges in keeping South Vietnam out of the control of the recently victorious Viet Minh, now the governing body of North Vietnam.

In 1961, Kennedy began to promulgate a policy of downplaying U.S. involvement in the region, a policy that was largely successful.[1] Certainly, there was little sense at this time that U.S. forces were heading into a "quagmire" or "nightmare."[2] No calls were raised in the pages of the *New York Times* to reject the Kennedy administration's policy in the region. In this sense, at least, Kennedy found that some of the old tools that were so valuable in World War II were still useful in 1961: it was still possible to shape the supply of information to the public.

In November–December 1961, Kennedy, General Maxwell Taylor, Walt Rostow, and other leading figures in the administration began reassessing the U.S. mission. During this period, *New York Times* coverage came mostly from the Hong Kong–based correspondent Robert Trumbull, reporting from Saigon and Phnom Penh mostly on the diversity of issues confronting Vietnam (as well as Laos and Cambodia) as an allied sovereign state tackling the threat of global communism. In other words, at this stage Vietnam was for the most part a familiar but not exceptional topic of conversation in foreign-affairs circles, with interest centering on the conflict between North and South, not on the potential for U.S. involvement.

However, one voice, at least, was raised in alarm. On January 5, 1962, James Robinson reported on the region for NBC's news show *Projection '62*, the first television exposure of the Vietnam War. U.S. forces were still described strictly as advisers, and command was still held by the MAAG in Vietnam, so, in one scholar's words, "Robinson seemed to flabbergast his colleagues when he bluntly declared to anchorman Frank McGee, 'Well, Frank, like it or not—admit it or not—we are involved in a shooting war in Southeast Asia.'" In a discussion that followed Robinson's report, fellow reporter Bernard Frizell asked Robinson bluntly on air, "Is this going to develop into another Korea?" Robinson responded, "It already *has* developed into another Korea."[3] The report, having no accompanying footage or even stills, lacked impact but was an ominous introduction to "television's first war" and seems in retrospect to be fair confirmation of Daniel Hallin's thesis that Kennedy's downplay policy was fairly effective.[4] There was never a direct follow-up to Robinson's alarming report.

During this period, U.S. military policy was being shaped in response to both South Vietnamese preferences and U.S. State Department preferences. In refining Kennedy's information policy, Secretary of Defense Robert S. McNamara set out an optimistic but entirely unrealistic policy for MAAG information, instructing DOD information officers to declassify whenever possible "within their judgment," but only if doing so met with the approval of their South Vietnamese counterparts.[5]

Although it was becoming clear to the principals that the DOD would ultimately take on a larger role, the Department of State was jealous and not willing to cede control to the DOD until absolutely necessary. On February 8, 1962, the MAAG in Vietnam was formally redesignated Military Assistance Command, Vietnam (MACV), after extensive State–DOD negotiations. The key issue of chain of command was never entirely nailed down, but by informal agreement the U.S. ambassador to South Vietnam had final say in political and basic policy matters, and the military commander treated him as his superior in practice.[6]

Some historians view the end of MAAG-V as a tacit acknowledgment that State-led nation building had failed and militarization was inevitable.[7] The State Department still held the trump card, however, and the Army's conventional forces were not even in the country—the Army had 5,000 soldiers present, but they were mostly engineers, logisticians, and some Special Forces. State Department officials took the lead on further refining the information policy. In an ill-conceived move on February 21, 1962, an information policy was set for the theater that discouraged any criticism of the South Vietnamese leadership, a heavy-handed effort at public relations that convinced few seasoned reporters. In practice, reporters perceived the change as a hardening of policy, and historians now point to it as the beginning of the credibility gap.[8]

Journalists were already critical of President Ngo Dinh Diem and were growing distrustful of the U.S. government public-information officers who stressed Diem's virtues. To compound matters, relations between the press and the Diem administration took a sudden downward turn. The veteran correspondent Homer Bigart, fresh from covering the Adolf Eichmann trial in Israel, had been sent by the *New York Times* to join Jacques Nevard in Saigon. He saw little to admire in Diem's regime and began to criticize Diem and the U.S. mission. François Sully, a French correspondent reporting for *Newsweek*, had also taken to criticizing Diem. Between the two, their claims carried considerable weight. Bigart was viewed as a living legend. Sully, certainly less famous and a difficult personality, was nevertheless highly regarded by many of his peers. Peter Arnett, a Pulitzer Prizer winner for his reporting during the war, recalls that Sully was "far more knowledgeable about what was going on than most other correspondents."[9] In March 1962, Diem decided to eject both Bigart and Sully from South Vietnam. Ambassador Frederick Nolting intervened, arranging for them to stay until the end of their respective tours.[10] In the meantime, the pressure from Diem did little to intimidate Bigart, who wrote critically in the *New York Times* about the effects of the recent policy amendments (on June 3 and June 25, 1962), and when he did finally end his tour in July, he wrote a very critical summary of his experiences.[11]

And so even before the war began in earnest, the fault lines that would effectively destroy the media–military relationship were revealed. First, American political leaders struggled to control the supply of information about the region but in doing so had already discovered that the demand far outstripped their capacities for genuine control. Second, in part as a consequence of the first fault line, the interpersonal relationships between journalists and their official sources had already soured. On one hand, the relationship between Diem's administration and American journalists was eroded by Diem's illiberal attitudes and policies, a subject of journalistic interest. On the other hand, journalists' trust in American officials was eroded by the unreliability of American information officers, who were ultimately working to shore up the State Department's relationship with

Diem rather than thinking about the potential damage that unsympathetic war correspondence might do to both the current war and any future war. This unforeseen problem would compound because of the unprecedented skill and tenacity of the group of men and women based in Saigon who covered the war.

THE SAIGON PRESS CORPS GOES TO WAR

Among the first journalists to set up camp in Saigon was Malcolm Browne. He arrived in 1961 as Indochina correspondent for the AP. Browne wrote a pamphlet of advice on dealing with American and Vietnamese officials that would circulate among reporters for many years. In June, he handed a copy in person to Peter Arnett, who recorded the following sections of Browne's pamphlet in his memoir:

> Beware of claims of military victory; this is not the kind of war from which real victories turn up often on either side. . . . Beware the similarity of American reports of such things; Americans have occasionally had to make their reports on nothing more than the Vietnamese claims although this has been reduced as American advisers are reporting more effectively. Beware in particular of any information at all you get from certain officials who can be counted on to tell bald-faced 180-degree whoppers nearly every time; a list of these officials and their relative credibility is available at the AP office.[12]

As correspondents arrived in Vietnam, they read Browne's pamphlet or spoke with more experienced hands and were taught the norms of this new community of "Vietnam hacks"—most importantly, they were taught not to trust American or South Vietnamese officials.

Browne, Arnett, David Halberstam, and Neil Sheehan were leaders in the developing community of resident correspondents and combat photographers, or what would be called the "Saigon press corps."[13] When in 1962 Diem tried for a second time to kick François Sully out of the country, the nascent Saigon press corps gathered in Sully's defense—but failed to agree on a common course of action. Some signed a letter to Diem, while others signed a more moderate protest later.[14] In late October, Diem kicked out James Robinson, the NBC reporter who had produced the first television story on the war and who had claimed that it was already "another Korea," for a perceived insult.[15] The ejection of Sully and Robinson did not produce a Saigon press corps mutiny, but in Arnett's words it "convinced us that the American Embassy was indifferent to press freedom and unwilling to call the regime on its increasing paranoia. We labored on with an increasing sense of isolation, dismayed by a blanket of restrictions on news coverage that was aimed at freezing us out of critical war areas in the country."[16]

The general climate at this time can be gleaned in a meeting called by General Paul D. Harkins with three correspondents—Browne with the AP, Sheehan with UPI, and Halberstam with the *New York Times*—on New Year's Eve 1962. The general and his staff seemed to have clearly understood that the Saigon correspondents were not happy. Notably, his personal public-affairs officer (PAO) sarcastically referred to reporters as "the friendlies." In the meeting, Harkins angrily accused Sheehan of "giving information to the enemy"; the tempers of all four men were running high.[17] While the meeting gave Harkins the opportunity to dress down the reporters, they had attended in hopes that he would tip them on what was coming next. The meeting was not a success, so Harkins decided not to tip the journalists to a major offensive planned two days hence, the Battle of Ap Bac—an omission that was one of the great military blunders of the South Vietnamese and a turning point in media-military relations.

MACV advisers and South Vietnamese military leaders intended the Battle of Ap Bac as a set-piece battle through which the elusive Viet Cong irregulars would finally be forced to confront overwhelming conventional force. About 400 Viet Cong faced three South Vietnamese battalions, two companies, and fifty American "advisers," but the Viet Cong stood their ground, inflicted casualties, watched as South Vietnamese friendly fire inflicted many more casualties on the South, and finally disappeared into the jungle.

Opinions still differ on the quality of the South Vietnamese forces in this exchange.[18] There is, however, agreement regarding the effect of the loss. According to William Turley, the main conclusion drawn by reporters and military leaders was that the North Vietnamese military had founds ways to offset the South's greater numbers and better matériel, thereby proving "the inability of American support limited to advice, training and equipment to save the ARVN [Army of the Republic of Vietnam] from defeat." Hammond notes, "That failure presented the Saigon correspondents with just the *cause célèbre* they were seeking."[19] For their part, the North Vietnamese ruling council anticipated that the defeat would force the Americans either to step back and allow further South Vietnamese bungling or to commit ground troops.[20]

Because Harkins had decided not to alert Browne, Halberstam, and Sheehan to the expected battle on New Year's Eve, no correspondents knew about it, and none was present during the fighting. Sheehan appears to have been the first to find out. He was tipped by a friendly captain serving in the operation, who called him on *Time* magazine's telephone line. As usual, Sheehan followed this up with a call to a second source, a friend inside Harkins's public-information office, for confirmation. Sheehan arrived at the battle around the same time as Reuters' Nick Turner, who had heard about it from his own sources.

Tellingly, Halberstam was at the time feuding with his bosses in New York, complaining to them that in Vietnam, unlike in earlier wars, "there are no briefings to attend, no easy way of coverage."[21] He did get the tip fairly soon after Sheehan, however, and along with AP reporters and some others reached the battlefield in time to talk to many of the Americans, including Harkins. General Harkins provided an extremely optimistic assessment, which was then directly contradicted by a subordinate whom Harkins had tasked with advising the well-reputed South Vietnamese unit leading the offensive. In his memoir, Halberstam recalled the press meeting with Harkins, underscoring the Saigon press corps' sophistication even at this early date: "General Harkins and the public information officers seemed surprised at the extent of our knowledge about the battle; how they expected to keep such a disaster secret when it had taken place within fifty miles of Saigon is puzzling. . . . [T]hough we filed stories about Ap Bac for three days, none of the military or State Department information officers ever bothered to go down there; the reporters went every day."[22]

The historian William Hammond similarly finds fault with MACV information practices surrounding the Ap Bac Battle. He notes, "The

US mission in Saigon handled Ap Bac strictly according to policy. When questioned by the press, American spokesmen limited their comments to events directly involving American personnel and helicopters."[23] These comments offered much less information than what reporters already knew from traveling to the site day after day and repeatedly speaking with American and South Vietnamese witnesses.

Certainly, Halberstam, a New York–born Harvard graduate who could already boast a long career of covering progressive political causes in the southern United States, was an outlier among the Saigon press corps, and his critical perspective should not be taken as a general indicator of press attitudes. However, the frustration he felt at this early period and the steps he took to address his frustrations underscore that MACV's leadership was not prioritizing media concerns. The *New York Times* reporting and editorializing presented Ap Bac as a failure; its reporters presented MACV leadership as failing to recognize that failure; and they cited witnesses and advanced editorial lines that posited ways to better realize U.S. objectives. In response to this growing independence of press opinion, MACV leaders would soon move to develop a much more complex information-management system.

The Battle of Ap Bac provides a window into the development of both U.S. operational art and information policy in the first phase of the war. Regarding the former, we can see the gradual shift in the war effort from a State-led effort to a DOD-led effort, which still hinged on an unreliable ally in the South Vietnamese. Regarding the latter, we can see Army officers in the field who accorded little value to the work of journalists on South Vietnam's leaders and military, even as those journalists were clearly demonstrating their very high degree of autonomy from military control.

Significantly, this tension between officers and correspondents had not yet leaked back to Washington. Although the archival record is limited, it is possible to get a brief glimpse inside the Office of the Chief of Staff of the Army during this chaotic period. General Earle Wheeler had taken over as chief of staff upon the retirement of General George Decker. A list of Wheeler's suspense files (i.e., files listed under a future date when they will require attention or action) exists for the period from November 14 to December 14, 1963, and suggests that the chief of staff's role at this time was very much taken up with administrative decisions. There are fifty-four files for the month that required Wheeler's attention. Most of them concerned personnel, troop training, and logistics. Other issues included the racial integration of forces, the selection of corporations for Army contracts, and, pertaining to the fighting in Vietnam, persistent problems with the new Army rifle. The lack of impression left by either the U.S. mission in Vietnam or the continuing crisis in the South Vietnamese leadership in these files is striking. And so Wheeler's days were not cluttered with concerns from the field; rather, the chief ran the Army staff from the Pentagon, while combatant commanders such as Harkins remained fairly independent.

The Army's growing recognition of the importance of the media to the war effort can be charted over the course of three separate media-management paradigms. The first was Kennedy's request to downplay Vietnam, which was successful for a time but rested on the unstable premise that nothing newsworthy was happening. This may have been the case in 1961, but by early 1962 major news outlets were starting to staff local bureaus, and their reporters needed content. The second was McNamara's decision to allow maximum cooperation but with the major caveat that nothing negative be said about South Vietnam—although this arrangement rested on the equally unstable premise that Diem's regime would appear sufficiently legitimate to journalists that they would accede to these terms. The third arrangement, the State Department's policy in 1962, attempted to shore up the Diem regime's disastrous relations with the press by encouraging yet more openness—except on the subject of Diem, a contradiction considering that Diem's excesses were a very newsworthy topic in many journalists' eyes.

MILITARIZING THE MISSION

In early 1964, Secretary of Defense McNamara was growing convinced not only that the war was winnable but that South Vietnam could go on the offensive against the North rather than focus on Viet Cong insurgents within its own borders. Computerized plans detailing a bombing campaign predicted to defeat the North in only twelve days were presented to President Lyndon B. Johnson in May.[24] McNamara imagined that full mobilization of the South Vietnamese population in conjunction with a sharp increase in U.S. support in the way of matériel, covert action, and massive bombing would do the trick.

At this time, there were about forty foreign correspondents in Saigon. They knew that their interests did not align with MACV's interests, and they knew they were capable of gathering information from friendly sources. Assistant Secretary of Defense for Public Affairs Arthur Sylvester recognized the problem and requested more realistic and less strict rules for talking to the press. In turn, Army analysts recommended using experienced Army public-information officers but headed by a civilian (to encourage reporters' trust) and obtaining the assistance of leaders within the Saigon press corps in "correcting any problems that arose with the press."[25] A second prong would be to encourage regular informal conversations between commanders and the press.

The new U.S. mission was now composed of General William Westmoreland, formerly Harkins's deputy, as military chief, and Ambassador Maxwell Taylor as diplomatic and (in practice) overall chief.[26] A civilian named Barry Zorthian was the head of the United States Information Service (USIS, formerly the USIA), while Ambassador Henry Cabot Lodge Jr. and his staff in South Vietnam still held the reins of media relations. At the DOD in Washington, Arthur Sylvester was busy recruiting talented staff to help "manage news." On June 2, 1964, this team met in Honolulu to discuss the mission, with a special session dedicated to the issue of public information. It was eventually decided that an information czar was needed and that Zorthian, warmly recommended by the respected journalist Edward R. Murrow, was the man for the job. In addition to directing the USIS's psychological operations, Zorthian was thus also put in charge of setting information policy, liaising between Lodge/Westmoreland and the press, correcting misimpressions by the press, and encouraging journalists to cover positive stories.[27]

Zorthian's new command was the old MACV public-affairs office, now renamed the Military Assistance Command Office of Information (MACOI) to enhance its prestige. MACOI had three divisions: the

Press Relations Branch was designed to handle routine press issues; the Special Projects Branch was intended to "develop and place material designed to offset erroneous stories filed by the news media"; and the Troop Information Branch was used to buoy morale but was also intended "secondarily [to] indoctrinate" the public as troops explained their role to friends and family at home and to reporters in the field. Press relations were viewed as a supplement to rather than the focus of public-information activity. Zorthian, Westmoreland, and Colonel Rogher Bankson considered the Special Projects Branch to be the "catalyst in the development of a revitalized information program," a means of disseminating a sort of Army marketing rather than passive public relations.[28]

This active rather than passive attitude would manifest over the next few months. In late June 1964, Westmoreland began including journalists in his trips to the field; he recalled later that this was an effort at "improving relations, which had sunk to a deplorable low, between the US Army and the American press and television."[29] Zorthian, for his part, started up weekly background briefings, which together with the daily information briefings would become a central feature of mission–press relations for the remainder of the war. In early July, the term *maximum candor* was coined in a State Department message directing Zorthian to ensure that the mission promotes "maximum candor and disclosure consistent with the requirement of security."[30]

Military prognoses of the mission's success veered between McNamara's confident computer-based plan of attacking the North and the realities of simply keeping a U.S. presence in Vietnam at all. Information activities were gaining relatively higher standing in the mission but still had little impact on staff operations at the Pentagon. The policy of maximum candor had been adopted, but in practice it seems to have meant little change.

On August 4, 1964, President Johnson called a press conference that would reorder the priority of all these elements because now, finally, he would admit the reality of the mission in Vietnam: dramatic escalation of U.S. resources would be required to realize the administration's objectives. Johnson's press conference was responding to an incident that had begun two days earlier. By all reports, the

Navy destroyer USS *Maddox* had come under fire that Sunday, August 2, while off the North Vietnamese coast in the Gulf of Tonkin. On Tuesday, August 4, the *Maddox* returned to the region with the USS *Turner Joy* to rattle the saber. What happened next was not entirely clear, but military and government leaders believed that the two ships came under attack again on Tuesday, confirming the belligerence of the North Vietnamese.[31] Johnson announced that same day that U.S. forces would retaliate by bombing North Vietnam. On Friday, he would go much further and announce the Gulf of Tonkin Resolution. In Turley's words, "Broad in language, the resolution basically ceded to the president the authority to wage an undeclared war. With his approval rating jumping from 42 percent to 72 percent, Johnson claimed to have the support of the American people."[32]

The Tonkin incident separates the early stages of U.S. involvement in the Vietnam conflict from the more recognizable "Vietnam War" that would define a generation of Americans. Antiwar protests began in September 1964 at Berkeley.[33] Readers of the *New York Times* following the Tonkin incident would have expected an imminent and dramatic escalation of U.S. involvement, likely resulting in the presence of American soldiers on the ground.[34] But some top American officials still labored under the notion that North Vietnam would pose little challenge to U.S. conventional might. National Security Adviser McGeorge Bundy, echoing McNamara's earlier computer-aided predictions, presented President Johnson in November with a call for surgical bombing that he assured Johnson would so devastate the North that Hanoi would sue for peace in two to six months.[35] Because of the nature of Viet Cong–North Vietnamese supply routes, the plan would require extensive bombing in Laos. By mid-December, planes were in the air with payloads delivered (with questionable accuracy) in both Vietnams and in Laos.[36]

Amid this escalating and expanding violence, the U.S. Army finally took control over MACV's public affairs. In mid-February 1965, more restrictive ground rules for information officers were sent from the Pentagon's assistant secretary for defense for public affairs to the MACOI office in Saigon. The rules continued to allow information officers to supply with "maximum candor" factual reports on operations (time, location, participants) but "restricted the access of the press to information that might either embarrass the military service, help the enemy, or increase discussion of the war."[37] The latter category was in essence a directive not to release newsworthy information. MACOI knew this directive would not work in practice, and the resulting exchange between the offices led to yet another information conference in Honolulu, scheduled now for March.

Between the issuing of the new ground rules and the conference to fix them, the operational context changed dramatically. On March 3, 1965, Johnson launched Operation Rolling Thunder, a massive campaign that would last until the end of October 1968. Although Rolling Thunder was mainly an air-oriented strategy, Johnson had also decided to send 3,500 marines to Da Nang as part of an unacknowledged ground offensive. Television cameras captured the marines wading onto the beach (although journalists were not told the truth of the marines' role).

Troop levels continued to swell, with Johnson ordering an increase in mid-June from 51,000 to 116,000 and again in late July committing to 125,000, with the promise to send more if necessary.[38] These increases brought more scrutiny to the information policies, and so Zorthian's role suddenly became problematic. Zorthian had come to Saigon to head the USIS, the propaganda wing of the U.S. mission, but as information czar he had oversight over MACV's general (diplomatic) information, MACOI's military information, and the USIS's propaganda. The Joint United States Public Affairs Office was created for him. Journalists, however, questioned the appropriateness of mixing propaganda with public affairs. Significantly, in the end Taylor, a career Army officer who had been Army chief of staff and would later be chairman of the Joint Chiefs of Staff but was now the ambassador to South Vietnam, argued for Zorthian to retain his full scope of power, although MACOI was formally removed from his oversight. So Zorthian would stay both propagandist and press agent for MACV overall, thereby leaving press relations in the hands of civilians.[39]

Around this time, a yellow flag with a black horse's head was delivered to Fort Benning, just outside Columbus, Georgia. The flag was escorted from South Korea, where it had announced the presence of the First Cavalry Division of the U.S. Army. Called the First Team, the division had switched from a traditional horse cavalry to an infantry division during World War II. It was now becoming something quite different. The First Team was integrated into some of the existing elements at Fort Benning, where pilots and mechanics had dedicated themselves to mastering the intricacies of combat-helicopter tactics. The merged unit became the First Cavalry Division (Airmobile), called the First Air Cavalry. It was indeed the first of its kind, and the masses of suddenly reassigned troops were put to work rappelling out of helicopters, parachuting, and firing the Army's new rifle, the M-16.[40]

Among them was Marvin J. Wolf. Too small in stature to accept a position he had earned at West Point, Wolf had instead enrolled in the infantry, rising through the ranks of the peacetime Army to the level of sergeant. He left the Army when his tour was up and pursued various odd jobs. In a photography class run by Earl Theissen, he was shown proofs for an upcoming *Life* spread by Larry Burrows, who was among the most respected photographers in Vietnam. Of that moment, Wolf recalls, "It was very, very interesting and eye-opening experience for me to look at this photo-spread. Then and there, I decided, if I have the stones, I could do this."[41]

Although journalists had started to flock to Vietnam, there was little opportunity for an untrained amateur to be paid to join them. Wolf decided instead to reenlist. It was "suicidally naive" to do so: not only would he lose his rank and so would be starting over as a private, but he also had no guarantee that he would be assigned to a public-affairs position. He decided to go for it, anyway. At Fort Benning, Wolf was in for a nasty surprise: "I reported in at Fort Benning, and I went to the Public Affairs Office, and I talked to this Sergeant Major and told him what I was looking for, and he told me I was stupid—he was kinder than that: he said, 'You've fucked up, son.' He told me, first of all, all of their photo support came from the [Fort Benning] Post photo lab—they didn't have any photographers. And secondly, all of the photographer spots had been civilianized a year earlier. So much for the plan."[42]

After some wrangling, Wolf managed to secure himself a position with his division's public-information office, reporting on routine post life and taking photographs for command-information material. He had no training in public affairs, and there was no photojournalist role at the division level, so he was assigned as a general-information specialist. Although there was organizationally no formal place for him, his commanders viewed him as an asset because his stories could make their units stand out within the division.

Wolf's division became First Air Cavalry, and Wolf happened to be in the division's advance party when it was mobilized to go to Vietnam. He was flown to a rough runway in the Vietnamese jungle, near a town called An Khe. He was armed with a Speed Graphic camera, and his first mission as an Army combat photographer was to take pictures of his friends clearing a field in preparation to land the First Air Cavalry's fleet of helicopters. He was flown to Nha Trang to deposit the film for this and other assignments when, Wolf recalls, "a CBS reporter accosted me and asked me why my t-shirt was dyed green when all other Army t-shirts were dyed white. . . . I didn't know what to tell him, so I ducked him." Wolf called his commander, a Major Siler, for advice and was told what to do when he ran into the reporter again, which happened in short order:

> I said, "I cannot confirm or deny what unit I'm in." He [the reporter] kept asking me, "Are you in the First Cav? Where is the First Cav?" And I said I can't tell him where my unit, whatever it might be, is, but if he and his crew wanted to come with me, I was leaving the next day, and I would tell him where we were going after we were in the air. He agreed to that. And then we landed, and we met Major Siler, and he explained the new ground rules. The ground rules were that he [the reporter] and his people could interview anybody and they could talk to whoever they want, they could take any pictures they want, but they couldn't leave until he said they could go, and they couldn't send any film until he said they could.[43]

Wolf's story is entirely unique but is also indicative of several elements of Army public-affairs work in 1965. First, media management had only recently been integrated into the formal Table of Organizations and Elements, so there were obstacles to gaining public-affairs roles. Indeed, at this stage of U.S. involvement in Vietnam, units were shedding media work, outsourcing it to civilians. However, commanders sometimes recognized the advantages of information activities and could work around the system.

Second, the relations between the press and the Army at the level of actual newsgathering were often quite intimate and capricious. The reporter Wolf met was John Laurence, who also recalled the incident. He had been in Vietnam for a week when he noticed Wolf's green T-shirt. He and his team took Wolf up on the offer and soon found themselves taking pictures of soldiers chopping trees near An Khe. On August 31, 1965, two days after meeting Wolf and coming to the base, Laurence and his team were in assault helicopters watching soldiers exchange fire with Viet Cong, on the front lines and with a scoop—Laurence's first in Vietnam.[44]

The fighting that Laurence and his team recorded in early September 1965 would eventually build into a series of major engagements between the First Air Cavalry, supported by South Vietnamese montagnards, and a highly effective North Vietnamese force. At the Battle of Ia Drang in mid-October, First Air Cavalry combat losses were considered enormous, around 300. The response to these losses is indicative of the difference in perspective between journalists and Army leaders. The historian William Turley notes, "American commanders saw proof of the effectiveness of helicopter-assault tactics and the strategy of attrition."[45] In contrast, Neil Sheehan, at this point with the *New York Times*, had visited the command post at Pleiku ahead of Westmoreland and interpreted the exchange at Ia Drang as a costly loss. Westmoreland may have found Sheehan's interpretations vexing, just as Harkins had been vexed by Sheehan at Ap Bac, but on both occasions Sheehan was gathering news firsthand from participants.[46] By end of year, there were more than 250 members in the Saigon press corps, which in practical terms meant about 100 active reporters at any given time analyzing the battlefield, interviewing witnesses, and developing perspectives that often differed dramatically from those of Army commanders.

Perhaps inevitably, the option of press censorship in the field was raised in top Army circles. In December 1965, Colonel Winant Sidle, the same officer who had written the extremely optimistic public-affairs guidance described in chapter 2, was selected to join the Office of the Assistant Secretary of Defense for Public Affairs in the position designated to lead to the role of chief of MACOI. When his superiors' suggested censorship in Vietnam, though, Sidle balked. He wrote a report about how censorship would require such impractical expense that the chief PAO in the Department of State, Dixon Donnelley, was convinced that it would simply not work in Vietnam. Donnelley was a powerful ally, and, as Hammond reports, "with that, all consideration of field press censorship in South Vietnam ended[;] . . . the press corps would report the war as it saw fit, under only the lightest official scrutiny."[47]

The next year, 1966, began on a mixed note for MACV. Westmoreland was named *Time*'s Man of the Year in January. This was the moment when the Army utopians finally had a chance to breathe and feel confident in the direction of the war. In the words of one historian, "The new 'big unit' campaign was beginning to look invincible, and for once the military had few vociferous critics."[48] The pattern of MACV resilience to critique continued through 1967 as well. In late April 1967, Westmoreland gave an impressive performance before Congress when called upon to explain MACV's performance in the war. He received warm reports from both parties in Congress, but this overtly political arena may ironically have polluted Westmoreland in the eyes of journalists. Hammond notes, "Suspecting that Westmoreland had become a tool of the Johnson administration, newsmen replaced their favorable coverage with more skeptical appraisals."[49]

In December, a mixed delegation of reporters and members of Congress visiting the Vietnam theater would encounter what David Snow calls "the rosiest picture" of the war yet prepared by MACV public affairs: "American troops were ordered to secure the entire highway during the trip, and as soon as the delegation passed, US troops were withdrawn. Enemy forces quickly resumed control of many sections of the highway. Reporters exposed this charade through leaks from their sources inside MACV."[50] Even as the operational side of the war was starting to yield successes, the information side continued to suffer from unforced errors and clumsy efforts to persuade journalists of falsehoods that they could easily dispel. In this sense, despite the enormous churn in policy and staffing over this complicated period, in Army media management there was a consistent pattern of misguided expectation that the message transmitted by reporters to the American public could in some fashion be dictated by the Army's leaders if only reporters would play along.

LESSONS FROM A FREE PRESS

From an operational perspective, the transition from MAAG to MACV in February 1962 marked a turning point, signifying that military rather than diplomatic tools would define U.S. involvement in the region. From an information perspective, the Battle of Ap Bac in January 1963 is arguably a more significant turning point because it was at this moment that the Saigon press corps recognized that its newsgathering capacities significantly outstripped American officials' efforts to shape the corps' message.

By December 1967, the relationship between press and military leaders was ridden with tensions and conflicts. Many of the bureau chiefs and leading correspondents had lived five years of this relationship, had five years of contacts and background knowledge to draw upon when confronted with calculated but ultimately amateurish dissembling by PAOs following the official line. Conversely, for the Army, five years of advising and then fighting had consistently affirmed the "Big Army" logic of conventional force, which held that the goal of war is to compel the enemy forces to bend to your will, while resisting being compelled in turn.

At times, Army leaders took to viewing the press as another tool to help in the task of forcing the enemy to bend rather than as an autonomous institution with its own interests and resources. At other times, they viewed the press as another enemy that needed a little bending. This lack of precision in relating to the press gave rise to a schizophrenic public-affairs doctrine in which periodic and provisional maximum candor gave way to indignant silences and, more troubling to reporters, thinly veiled attempts to indoctrinate the press.

December 1967 became January 1968, and in the new year forces beyond the control of the Army were hard at work, aiming a spear at the heart of the U.S. mission. On January 30, 1968, the North Vietnamese regulars and the South Vietnamese insurgents united in a major offensive. Now, the war correspondents would become active participants in the U.S. war effort, shaping large-scale outcomes through their reporting and altering the facts on the ground through their very presence.

4

THE TET PARADOX

Media-Management Regimes in Vietnam, 1968–1975

THE MEN leading America's war effort in Vietnam at the beginning of 1968 had reason to feel confident. General William Westmoreland, the combatant commander, was literally Man of the Year, at least according to *Time*. Public accolades and operational successes alike seemed to legitimize the heavy focus on conventional warfighting—back to Army basics—championed by Westmoreland and his team. Politically, Westmoreland may have felt he had bought himself some breathing room with the charade around securing the highway during the congressional visit to Vietnam. Militarily, he was laser focused on the siege at Khe Sanh, which was superficially reminiscent of the French disaster at Dien Bien Phu in 1954. If he could avoid disaster there, the North Vietnamese might finally sue for peace.

THINGS FALL APART

The Khe Sanh siege had been underway for ten days when the yearly Tet (Lunar New Year) festival occurred on January 31, 1968. The North Vietnamese leadership saw an opportunity. They had come to believe that Westmoreland was both obsessed by the Dien Bien Phu analogy and deluded with the idea that the North would never attack during the Tet holiday.[1] They saw the festival as the perfect opportunity to surprise their enemies. According to MACV records, they were both right and wrong: Westmoreland foresaw a sixty-forty chance of a major assault around Tet but was nevertheless "preoccupied" by Khe Sanh.[2] At 2:30 a.m., a very small group of Viet Cong assaulted the U.S. embassy in Saigon. Simultaneously, North Vietnamese troops attacked all major South Vietnamese cities, although they took only Hue. Westmoreland may have been preoccupied by Khe Sanh, but he was hardly unprepared, and the offensive was by and large crushed.

Westmoreland had spent the day of January 30, 1968, contacting senior commanders throughout Vietnam. He was awoken at about 3:00 a.m. with reports that a wide-ranging series of attacks had indeed been launched. He sat out the drama unfolding at the U.S. embassy until finally, at about 8:00 a.m., he was informed that U.S. airborne troops had landed and cleared the site. He drove to the embassy: "Like any battlefield," he wrote later, "the compound was in disarray, bodies of Americans and Vietnamese still lying about. Yet unlike most battlefields, American reporters and television cameramen were seemingly everywhere. Their faces mirrored dismay and incredulity, as if the end of the world was at hand."[3]

Westmoreland recalled that Barry Zorthian then asked him to hold a press conference: "I took the opportunity to try to put the Embassy raid and the countryside attacks into perspective. . . . I had no hesitation in saying that the enemy was inviting defeat. My efforts at perspective went for nought."[4] In the *New York Times*, Charley Mohr, one of those "dismayed and incredulous" journalists, reported Westmoreland's comments rather blithely, quoting him as saying that the enemy had sought "to cause maximum consternation in South Vietnam."[5] Forty-five years later, NBC's Don North, who was also on the scene, recalled Westmoreland's comments with rather more emotion:

> I will never forget: I was at the U.S. embassy that morning of the Tet attack when the sappers went in there, and after the smoke cleared and most of these guys had been killed or injured, . . . Westmoreland [was] standing there in the rubble saying, "Don't be deceived, this is a minor incident, they've all been killed, and we've thrown them out of Hue," which wasn't true. In light of this incredible

surprise, Westmoreland was still talking positive spin.... [W]e were hearing Westmoreland and [President] Johnson tell us that we're winning the war, and here we have this incredible, intense offensive. Even though thousands of the enemy were killed, and it was a military defeat [for the North], it made everyone realize that this was not a war that was near to being won.[6]

In fact, behind Westmoreland's bluster there were moments of despair. An aide recalled him at perhaps his lowest when he said, "Everything I have worked for is lost. It's all been a failure."[7] Despite his private doubts, though, Westmoreland's instinct was to rattle the saber.

This is the paradox of the Tet Offensive. It is true that the U.S. and South Vietnamese forces repelled the North Vietnamese and Viet Cong forces, realizing a significant victory on the field of battle. Yet it is also true that in the course of achieving operational success, they experienced political failure. This singular truth, that operational victory and political victory are fundamentally decoupled, would take years to be fully absorbed into Army doctrine, but it is in certain respects the most emblematic development of war in our age of mass-mediated democracies.

Meanwhile, Westmoreland's deputy, General Creighton Abrams, was also being pressured to talk to the press. Whereas Westmoreland thrived in and often sought out the spotlight, Abrams was press shy. His biographer records Abrams telling his closest aide that "the best way to hold a press conference is to remain silent," and, indeed, this meeting was likely his only "mass encounter" with the press.[8] It attracted little attention, positive or negative. He spoke frankly and acknowledged the cost of the offensive in American lives, and then he went to work. This difference in command styles, Westmoreland's insistent positivity versus Abrams's relaxed sincerity, would be institutionalized in due course, reflecting a growing awareness that public oversight is a military problem of the first order.

The fight to regain land lost during the offensive would last until February 24, when U.S. forces would finally retake and hold Hue. But grim news would come on the heels of this success: "South Vietnamese government intelligence units employed the confusion to send out 'black teams' of assassins to eliminate some of those believed to have aided the enemy," raising serious moral questions about Saigon in the minds of many.[9]

February 24 was a busy day for other reasons as well. It had begun for Westmoreland with an early message from Army chief of staff Harold K. Johnson, who told him to "stop talking" to the press in the hope of quelling chatter in the press regarding a possible expansion of the draft.[10] Later in the day, Admiral U. S. Grant Sharp, commander of the naval effort, told Westmoreland to stop reporters from publishing exact counts of enemy rounds hitting bases and to stop giving exact American casualty numbers, a directive that would set in motion the next major development in media-management policy. At this moment, there were 636 accredited reporters in the country. Competition had reached new levels of intensity. Westmoreland acted on Sharp's orders by revising the ground rules such that reporters could describe casualties only as "light," "moderate," or "heavy." Somewhat surprisingly, reporters accepted this rule (as well as a separate directive not to count shells) as a reasonable security amendment. But, as William Hammond notes, this was but the "first indication that the Defense Department was reassessing its relations with the news media."[11]

As it happens, Defense Secretary Robert S. McNamara had already planned his resignation before Tet, and with the end of fighting in Hue it was made public. He was replaced by Clark Clifford, who once again called upon Maxwell Taylor (among others) to assess the future of the war. The report produced by this task force would eventually leak a request by Westmoreland and Army chief of staff Earle Wheeler for 206,000 more men, resulting in much public outrage, but coincidentally at this time another event occurred that would shape the future of warfare in another, equally unexpected way. On March 16, a company of soldiers from the Twenty-Third Infantry Division (the Americal Division), under the command of Captain Ernest Medina, was ordered to destroy Son My village and its various hamlets. The platoon under the command of Lieutenant William Calley raped and murdered the villagers of one of these hamlets, identified as "My Lai (4)" on Army maps. Hugh C. Thompson, a warrant officer, saw what was happening, landed his helicopter, and saved sixteen children. Thompson and everyone else present failed in their duty to report the atrocity, but importantly it was recorded by an Army journalist. As one historian notes, "My Lai-4 might never have been known—or at least never proved—except for the fact that a *Stars and Stripes* reporter on the operation took photographs of the Belsen-style bodies piled in the ditch."[12]

This report had not yet been made public when Army leadership underwent another shuffle. Westmoreland was fired upward to Army chief of staff, replacing the retiring Harold K. Johnson. His friend and deputy, Bruce Palmer, was named vice chief of staff. Westmoreland's second-in-command, Creighton Abrams, was promoted to commander of MACV. None of these choices was a surprise, but President Johnson did manage to shock the nation four days later when he announced a series of unexpected decisions: he would freeze the troop level, limit air war, seek negotiated peace, and not run for reelection.[13]

THE ABRAMS APPROACH

Although the president's decisions reflected his commitment to bow to broad public dissatisfaction with the direction of the war, it was not simply a reactive position. Behind the limitation of the troop levels and restriction on air war was a purposeful strategic pivot from Westmoreland's strategy of attrition to a new strategy that would come to be called "Vietnamization." It was predicated on the successful shedding of command responsibilities, transferring them from American to South Vietnamese hands in an orderly and graded process, first freeing the U.S. forces from worrying about the insurrection of the Viet Cong and then exiting the war against North Vietnam as well. Abrams's biographer, Lewis Sorley, notes that as of early April 1968 "Abrams was effectively exercising command," instilling the mission with his vision of Vietnamization and instructing his staff on the strategy and tactics needed to realize that vision. General Frederick C. Weyand, future chief of staff but at that time commander of Second Field Force, told a reporter that MACV tactics "changed within fifteen minutes of Abrams's taking command." Abrams was not reinventing the wheel; rather, he was largely implementing the findings of a study from 1966 titled *A Program for the Pacification and Long-Term Development of South Vietnam* (appropriately spelling out the abbreviation *PROVN*), which Westmoreland had long ignored in favor of search-and-destroy tactics and attrition. Now, Sorley points out, "population security, and not body count, was going to become the measure of merit."[14]

The truth that slowly emerged after the war is that Westmoreland's attrition strategy would never have worked. Estimations of Vietnamese war deaths from 1965 to 1975 show that although approximately a million Vietnamese men, women, and children were killed, the attrition never occurred. Simply put, the death rate of about one percent of military-age men never matched the demographic replacement rate of approximately 2 percent per year—in other words, every year twice as many young men aged into recruiting than were killed.[15] Westmoreland could not have known the specific numbers involved, but his strategy did require an enormous death toll to succeed. The reality is that Westmoreland and everyone else involved sought a political victory—the North's surrender—even as they prepared for and executed a policy purportedly seeking an operational victory alone—namely, to attrite the enemy to a state of no longer being capable of fighting. Just as Westmoreland and many others were vague on how the operational effects they were producing would feed into a North Vietnamese political surrender, they were equally vague on how the domestic American political context would support or undermine their own efforts. These relationships, domestic public to military to enemy public, were vital to the war at every level but never clearly understood or integrated into the mission.

Creighton Abrams, Westmoreland's replacement, sought to simplify the operations–politics link through cutting out the confounding effects of the press. After Tet, an approach to fighting in Vietnam that diminished press interest appealed to military and political leaders alike, and Abrams was by temperament and experience ideally suited to run it. He had joined the cavalry when sabers were still in style, but his preference for tanks over horses sidelined his career until World War II. He soon distinguished himself as a top commander, competing with General George S. Patton for headlines. His career following that war was less remarkable, a slow climb through moderately desirable postings. Eventually, however, he transferred to the Pentagon as an assistant to the deputy chief of staff for operations and found himself charged with heading the Civil Affairs Branch, the branch of doctrine ordinarily concerned with liaising with local governments in occupied territory. The placement of Abrams in this position became critically important when Civil Affairs was called upon to manage civil disobedience, those military affairs concerned with disturbances within the United States. In a series of tense encounters in Mississippi, where the military was called upon to manage potential riots, Abrams distinguished himself again, this time for his understated political savvy. In his first test in this role, he intervened in a tense confrontation between an African American lawyer and the Mississippi State Police by arriving in person with an Army lawyer and three PAOs. Together, they defused the situation.

Abrams had been considered as a candidate to take over MACV when Westmoreland was given the job, and it is tempting to imagine this counterfactual scenario. It is of course impossible to know what effect Abrams's command style starting in 1964 rather than 1968 might have had on the failing media–military relationship. What is certain is that Abrams's style of leadership prioritized low-key press relations to a very high degree, and this priority was matched by shifting press interest away from the U.S. campaign. Abrams's biographer describes his change in public-affairs doctrine as "one of the clearest and most unequivocal" of his new command. On June 2, 1968, even before the MACV job was formally his, he directed that, "effective now, the overall public affairs policy of this command will be to let results speak for themselves." On June 10, Abrams took command of MACV, removing the "luxurious executive-type furniture that Westmoreland had installed in the office. . . . What Abrams wanted instead, and got, was some regulation GI-issue gray steel furniture."[16]

What precisely did Abrams change in the actual management of war correspondents? As we have seen, the first round of post-Tet revisions preceded Abrams's taking office. Those revisions were concerned with ending reporters' use of body-count numbers. Abrams's June revisions required PAOs to stop propagandizing and start being forthright with potentially negative information. In July 1968, Abrams sent a memorandum to senior commanders and PAOs with clear and precise amendments to the existing policies. He listed five points, which are worth considering at length:

> 1. Let our accomplishments speak for themselves. . . . a) [W]e should abstain from the "hard sell" or any publicity or promotion schemes; b) we should not try to impress the media with our plans and what we are going to attempt to do but rather with what we are doing and have done; c) there are two problems which preclude discussions of plans with the press. The first is security. . . . The second is that many plans do not turn out as well as we expect and, if we pump up the press in advance about how well we are going to do, we inevitably receive a public black eye when implementation falls short.
> 2. Ensure that unauthorized information is not provided to the press.
> 3. "Bad news" will be made public.
> 4. Ensure that "good news" is correct before public release.
> 5. Do not become angry with the press. We cannot afford to react to criticism that we consider unfair, non-objective reporting by succumbing to the temptation to refuse to meet the press or by barring them arbitrarily from our areas. Such opportunity not only encourages more criticism but, more importantly, denies the press the opportunity to report on our accomplishments.[17]

Breaking in spirit and in form with much of the guidance that preceded it, the new policy would be tested by the revelation of the failure to come forward with the "bad news" in the My Lai affair, precisely the kind of thing it was intended to prevent.

THE ARMY'S ATROCITIES

The events at My Lai became known to Westmoreland, at the time still Army chief of staff, when a former soldier wrote to the Department of the Army with allegations of war crimes: the rape and murder of the villagers near Army map coordinate My Lai (4). The soldier, Ronald

Ridenhour, heard rumors and realized some of his friends might have been involved. When pressed, his friends confessed. One historian notes that by this point such rumors had spread through the division and beyond, supported in part by the sudden and otherwise inexplicable collapse of morale in the guilty company.[18] Although Westmoreland found such allegations "beyond belief," to his credit he nevertheless pushed forward an internal investigation.[19]

Early reports of a court-martial at Fort Benning, Georgia, received little attention, although it did pique the interest of Seymour M. Hersh. An experienced freelancer, Hersh finished his investigation by November 11, 1969, but was turned down by *Life* and *Look*. He then offered it through a news service, ultimately managing to sell it to thirty papers across the United States and Canada for release on November 13. Widespread coverage would not begin until November 20, when he published a follow-up that included more detailed descriptions.[20]

My Lai was reported at a critical moment of the war, when the meaning of the Tet Offensive was still consolidating. For some reporters, it provided an opportunity to question the morality of U.S. involvement abroad. For others, it was a launching pad for reflections on America's relative standing in the world and the effect of the war on U.S. interests. My Lai soon became an American story rather than a Vietnamese story because most journalists who covered it did so in the United States, focusing on the intricacies of trials and investigations. And so even as My Lai helped to solidify the narrative of U.S. military failure in Vietnam, it also reflected and reinforced a media pivot away from the war itself. The public, weary of front-line stories from battles that failed to win an endless war, would buy newspapers that described the corruption and disorder within the United States Army.

If Tet forced Army leaders to rethink the place of the American public in their strategy in Vietnam, My Lai had a less obvious strategic significance.[21] My Lai eroded public support for American fighting in Vietnam, but in some quarters it seems to have generated support for American soldiers. As with the Abu Ghraib prisoner-abuse scandal in 2004, there was a conceptual disconnect between press interpretations of the atrocity and Army and government responses. In both cases, reporters accused the Army of corruption and moral bankruptcy, and in both cases the Army responded by symbolically isolating the perpetrators as aberrant and unrepresentative of the institution. But where the perpetrators in Abu Ghraib never enjoyed significant public support, Lieutenant Calley, despite his horrific crimes, found himself a sort of folk hero, and he would eventually be pardoned on an appeal of his life sentence.

Accordingly, My Lai stands as an ambivalent milestone in the evolution of the media–military relationship in Vietnam. My Lai did invite Americans to pay close attention to the horrors of the war, but the story was ultimately about the military itself, not about the war it was fighting. This refocusing fed into a new story looming on the horizon, perhaps the most damaging of all for the Army: the story of an institution amid collapse. With My Lai acting as proof of concept, reports would now be filed continuously on Army morale, discipline, drug use, and racism. The increased public scrutiny of the military as an institution (rather than simply of its role in fighting the war) would also give rise to congressional interest, and although testimony in hearings failed to effect legislative change, it offers much illuminating material about public affairs after Tet.

In the first quarter of 1970, matters would begin to spiral out of control. While the Army's leadership was now hoping to offload the war onto the shoulders of its longtime South Vietnamese allies, U.S. political leadership was still looking for a silver bullet that could mortally wound the North Vietnamese war effort and force a negotiated peace. Like Truman with the bombing of Hiroshima and Nagasaki and Eisenhower with the New Look, President Richard Nixon looked to strategic airpower as the perfect political solution. The target was, however, not in Vietnam at all but in bordering Cambodia, where North Vietnamese supply lines could in principle be utterly destroyed. Prince Sihanouk of Cambodia was deposed in March, which together with diplomatic reversals encouraged President Nixon to "go for broke" in this Cambodia policy: 15,000 U.S. troops and 5,000 South Vietnamese troops descended in separate strikes. American antiwar activists were outraged. As one historian describes the effect of the attack in Cambodia, the protests that followed "brought confrontational tragedy unknown since the Civil War."[22] At Kent State University in Ohio, four students protesting the new air campaign (among other matters) were killed by National Guardsmen called up by the governor.[23]

THE WAR FROM ABOVE

Army leaders were not alone in failing to untangle the meaning of Tet, the paradox of operational victory leading to political and strategic failure. Four days after the Kent State killings, President Nixon was listening peacefully to Rachmaninoff's Second Piano Concerto when he happened to notice a group of young people gathered in protest at the nearby Lincoln Memorial. His hope, he wrote later, was to "lift them a bit out of the miserable intellectual wasteland in which they now wander aimlessly around." According to Nixon, one of the young people thought Nixon was "tired and dull and rambled aimlessly from subject to subject."[24] Nixon's assistant John Erlichman would later quote one of the students: "Gee, this guy is just not on our wavelength."[25] Between the president and the protestors lay a generational and cultural gulf that neither would bridge.

Although Nixon, like Truman and Eisenhower before him, viewed strategic airpower as a silver bullet that could avoid the politics of land power, airpower in fact triggered its own political challenges. The apparently illegal bombing in Cambodia, which now included bombing in neighboring Laos as well, was undermining public support for the entire war effort. Abrams was aware of the increasing domestic unrest and that the bombing in Laos and Cambodia was contributing significantly to that unrest. The bombing itself was above his paygrade, a decision made by President Nixon for his own purposes. Abrams's conclusion was that U.S. involvement in those countries could nevertheless be largely shielded from the press.[26] He was heading toward a full-scale press embargo, and although this embargo would not be enacted until January 1971, his low-key press style was already shifting the character of Saigon correspondents' newsgathering. One historian notes that MACV's reluctance to engage with reporters began pushing correspondents to backchannel sources, allowing rumors to take the place of official statements and forcing the reporters to set out on new investigative pathways.[27]

The war in Cambodia was still news, though, and reporters would cover it. Competition by this point was very fierce, and even veteran correspondents might find themselves risking their lives for a minute (literally) of footage. The correspondent Don North remembers two respected colleagues who made this mistake while covering Cambodia:

> [George] Syvertsen [CBS] often started taking really bad risks that he knew were not wise to compete with [Don] Webster [CBS] and also to compete with Welles Hangen [ABC]. And Hangen was doing the same thing, looking over his shoulder, "Where's George"? In fact, he followed George this day [May 31, 1970] to this area, which was a floating occupation of the North Vietnamese and Khmer Rouge. Syvertsen approached a break in the road that was manned by Cambodian government troops, who said, "Don't go ahead, it's too dangerous"—but he went anyway, and Hangen followed him down this very dangerous road. They were both ambushed, killed—Hangen was captured, killed later. That's what competition can do.[28]

Although reporters varied in their risk thresholds, the correspondents who worked for major news outlets were well aware that their jobs were based on producing competitive content, and this meant taking the same risks as or even greater risks than their competition. North notes: "I felt competition. We were always looking after our shoulder, and we would often get rockets on the cable from New York saying, 'North, why you no have combat in Delta, CBS having 2 minutes leading news last night?'—this sort of thing. The New York office would always say, 'Be careful, don't take any unwise chances, blah blah blah,' but if you missed a story or missed some particular combat, they weren't very forgiving."[29]

The carrot was minutes of airtime or inches of column space. The stick was losing your job, and life itself hung in the balance. On another occasion, North befriended two Army Mohawk pilots, only to be shown pictures of their corpses hours later: "I was really spooked about going out in the field again for quite a while because I could just see these mangled bodies of my friends, and I just had an intuition that I would be next." At the time, he was a freelancer and could avoid the field by filing stories about Vietnamese politics or daily life in Saigon: "If I were with ABC [which he joined later], . . . and I said, 'I can't go out in the field right now, I'm afraid I'm going to be killed,' they'd have said, 'OK, bye-bye, that's the end of your job.'"[30] In this context, the media industry's demand for content was a nontrivial element of the battlefield, and MACV's low-key position on press communications exacerbated professional competition in such a way that more journalists died.

One of the appeals of bombing is that it is relatively easy to hide. Although planes leaving tarmacs may be observed, it is hard for reporters to know where the bombs will land. It is certainly easier to keep a lid on bombing operations than on missions involving thousands of soldiers and officers with friends in the press corps and family at home. Nevertheless, in January 1971 Abrams would institute a highly unpopular embargo on reports of fighting, an effort that would end in failure within days. Why did Abrams take this step?

While the national traumas of My Lai and Kent State were responsible for considerable anger toward the Army, a new series of reports on the social problems facing the Army were perhaps more destructive of the institution's credibility. These stories addressed the decline in morale and discipline as well as greater drug use and racism. Army leaders knew about the existence of these problems, and we know that officers in Vietnam did inform their superiors at the Pentagon of the scale of the problems, even at great personal risk to their careers.[31]

In April 1970, a month before Syvertsen, Hangen, and their crews were killed, Jack Laurence was once again embedded with the First Team. Gone was the esprit de corps he encountered while chatting with Marvin Wolf in 1965. The First Team of 1970 was a veteran force with embittered soldiers, at least the ones Laurence met. In a report for CBS, he presented footage of men resisting orders on a route chosen by a new commander, a scene he described at the time as a rebellion. Hammond, in his authoritative study of media–military relations in Vietnam, stresses the contrasting character of Laurence's report with what had come before: "He suggested that the war had taken on a new dimension that kept 'normally brave and obedient' American fighting men from risking their lives without reason."[32] The report first aired as a long five-minute piece introduced by Walter Cronkite and consisting of conversations with two soldiers Laurence described as a "hero-pacifist" and a "peacenik."[33]

The story was a major news item and was reproduced prominently in print by *Newsweek*. Within days, while still embedded with the First Team, Laurence and his crew were informed by the First Team's new public-information officer, Major Melvin Jones, that there were new ground rules for covering the division, requiring the CBS crew to endure lengthy check-in processes and close supervision: "In effect, Jones was making it impossible for us to complete the documentary" they had decided to make. Although friendly with the junior public-information officers, the CBS crew were distrustful of Jones and resolved to "test the new ground rules" immediately. They flaunted the new rules by chartering a plane to avoid checking in. Unsure what to expect, they headed off to resume their story but en route were given some advice. A friendly junior public-information officer called over the radio to warn them that their next meeting with Army brass, this time a colonel in the division, would be bugged. "So watch your ass, Jack. And be cool." The meeting, complete with an ineffectually hidden recording device, went poorly, and Laurence resigned himself to leaving the First Team and finding a new story to cover. A final exchange was emblematic of the difference between officer and soldier with respect to the press: "One of the enlisted men in the PIO [Public Information Office] shop appeared with a bunch of tiny red wildflowers. He put one of the flowers in the lapels of each of our fatigue jackets. He and the other soldiers seemed sincerely sorry we were going away and not coming back."[34]

The sociological insights that we can draw from Laurence's experiences here and Marvin Wolf's in 1965 concern the contingency of the media–military relationship. Although our primary traces of this relationship are contained in command decisions, and although these decisions did have direct impact on the journalists (Laurence and his crew did leave the First Team, after all), nevertheless the relationship was most meaningfully enacted face-to-face. These direct encounters were negotiated in countless ways, and formal command structures were often simply incapable of interfering with them. The bonds connecting journalists to public-information officers, embodied here in the potent cultural symbol of the wildflowers stuck in

Laurence's lapel, were predicated on much broader cultural structures cutting through the indoctrination and professionalization so central to the military. In this context, it is little wonder that commanders made increasingly desperate attempts to reassert institutional control.

THE EMBARGO EXPERIMENT

The immediate context for Abrams's news embargo of January 1971 was the planned South Vietnamese invasion of Laos, for which U.S. forces could by law serve only in a supporting role. Abrams's ideal outcome would be for journalists to embed with South Vietnamese units, ignore the U.S. support units, and file stories about South Vietnamese successes—but only after the battle was done. In consultation with Admiral John S. McCain Jr., who now commanded the Navy side of the mission, Abrams decided on a total embargo of stories about the buildup and execution of the mission until after it was over. There would also be an embargo on reporting about the embargo. In order to discourage reporters, Abrams directed public-information officers to tell reporters to travel in press pools and thus restricted individual access. And, finally, he also required journalists to fly on South Vietnamese helicopters.[35] Admiral McCain worried that a blackout would backfire, but Abrams went ahead with the plan.[36]

The announcement was met with frustration by reporters who felt betrayed by the sudden restrictions, but it also triggered intense speculation about the reason for the blackout (and for the blackout about the blackout). MACV stayed the course, but the organizational logic of a highly competitive global-media landscape quickly ended it as London papers began to publish stories about the embargo on the embargo, justifying reports in New York papers about the British coverage (in other words, American stories about British stories about the lack of stories coming from Vietnam and lack of stories about the lack of stories coming from Vietnam). The embargo had started on January 29; the first English report came out on January 30. On February 1, "little semblance of the embargo remained."[37] The three-day embargo was a failure.

This ordeal was compounded by the failure of the operation around which MACV was hanging its hopes for successful withdrawal. Operation Lam Son began on February 8, 1971, and constituted a major offensive by South Vietnamese forces crossing into Laos with the goal of destroying the Ho Chi Minh Trail, the supply lines connecting the North Vietnamese to the Viet Cong insurgency. As dictated by law, there were no U.S. infantry, but 10,000 Americans provided artillery, air, and helicopter support.[38] During the battle, the U.S. support came from Khe Sanh, while South Vietnamese troops marched down Route 9, making their way ten kilometers into Laos before their attack stalled. One historian notes, "What MACV-ARVN spokesmen called an 'orderly retreat,' newsmen captured in images of terrified ARVN troops dropping from the skids of overloaded helicopters."[39] This failure was only compounded by a public-affairs gaffe: "During the battle, public affairs officers attempted to illustrate Lam Son's success by holding up a piece of pipe during a press conference. The briefer claimed that the pipe was seized from North Vietnamese petroleum supply lines during the invasion. However, reporters discovered that the pipe was not actually seized during the invasion."[40]

The battle would last more than a month, with heavy losses on both sides. The North Vietnamese surprised the Americans and South Vietnamese with the skill and resources of their air capabilities, but they also slowed the South Vietnamese by virtue of the enormous casualties the northerners were willing to accept. A paradigmatic encounter saw 27 South Vietnamese soldiers killed for 1,130 North Vietnamese—and still the North Vietnamese fought.[41] The North Vietnamese won on account of their superior resolve: Abrams attempted to rally the South Vietnamese command in early February, but only days later President Nguyen Van Thieu called off the offensive.

Operation Lam Son was MACV's last sustained battle, and the U.S. presence in the region was rapidly diminishing. The highest point of U.S. military involvement was early 1969, with 554,000 members of the armed services in the country; the highest point for the number of accredited journalists was February 1969, with 636 correspondents and photographers on the books. Following Lam Son, the numbers for both groups fell dramatically when 141,000 members of the armed services and about 200 reporters left in early 1972.[42] Vietnam was decreasingly newsworthy, but those 200 reporters still had to produce content.

President Nixon was now talking ceaselessly about ending conscription and withdrawing from the war, which led Army planners to begin focusing not on the war but on the withdrawal. The experience of one general is typical. General William B. Rossom was transferred from the Planning Division in Washington to serve as a deputy at MACV, moving in effect from a desk job to a field position amid war—exactly what most generals would prefer. At the time, however, redeployment was the "hot account," and so Rosson left with mixed feelings but upon arrival discovered to his relief that the MACV staff were deeply immersed in planning withdrawal.[43]

The Pentagon-based Office of the Chief of Information's (OCI) annual report in late June reflected this mixed year of Army accomplishments. The Public Information Division report summarized the confusion of the time: the year was "characterized by an increase in the already fast pace coupled with a decreased capability to plan and implement actions in an orderly fashion. Public, Congressional and media interest in the Army rose sharply during the year, media and Congressional criticism of Army activities was at an all-time high."[44]

The public was interested in the Army. The OCI handled 29,544 total press queries, with 4,008 requests for appearances by Army personnel, 382 for performances of the Field Band, and 133 for parachute jumps. But the issues interesting the public were rarely connected directly with the fighting in Vietnam.

Two weeks after the end of the reporting period, on July 14, 1969, a truly bizarre press event unfolded and can be taken as an indication of the complex moral narratives of the war that were circulating in the public at this time. Abrams informed General Wheeler (chairman of the Joint Chiefs), Admiral McCain (commander of the naval component of the war), and General Westmoreland (chief of staff of the Army) that he had launched an investigation into the possible assassination of a South Vietnamese double agent by U.S. Special Forces. The officer in charge, Colonel Robert Rheault, would later assert in an official oral-history interview that "agents were being eliminated right, left and sideways by a lot of programs," including the Army's Special Forces and the CIA.[45] Strangely, *Newsweek* and other liberal media organizations would side with Rheault and the other accused (and indeed confessed) killers, openly questioning Abrams's decision to waste time charging soldiers with murder.

VIETNAMIZATION AND WITHDRAWAL

The drive to Vietnamization was now in full force, and perhaps the callous attitude of some reporters and members of the public reflected a sense that with just a little more violence and disorder, the United States would finally be rid of Vietnam. At the end of July 1969, Nixon personally visited Saigon to direct Abrams "to allocate full responsibility for the security of South Vietnam to ARVN forces"—meaning complete the first phase of Vietnamization by ending the U.S. role in fighting the Viet Cong and focus only on fighting North Vietnam.[46] A week later the secret Paris talks began at Sainteny.

Making sociological sense of this spectrum of activities is challenging. On one hand, stories of abuse and law breaking by the U.S. president and by Special Forces triggered little anger at the war effort; quite the opposite, there seems to have been an impatient acceptance of these dark deeds. On the other hand, stories of military success, with their inevitable casualties, were met with anger at the waste of soldiers' lives. We may interpret this contradiction as indicative of a context in which the sacred center orienting political debate had lost focus. Soldiers' lives remained sacred things, but the hard calculation of lives lost in the present for lives saved in the future was resisted—a reasonable reflection of the credibility gap, perhaps. Law and common morality were also somehow infected by this malaise.

This infection was not inconsequential. Within this cultural and political setting, the world once again skirted near the edge of nuclear war as Nixon considered the use of nuclear weapons for Operation Duck Hook. Although he would ultimately reject this option, he "settled instead for a worldwide nuclear alert in the last half of October to signal resolve and preserve his 'madman' reputation."[47] We may take the consideration of this option as a signal of how much geopolitical risk is associated with a political moment when an unpopular war is being executed with increasing secrecy and decreasing moral accountability.

Nixon's next move was to refocus debate and regain broad support for the war, and he was surprisingly successful at snapping the public out of its malaise. On November 3, 1969, he gave his famed "silent majority" speech. In the speech, Nixon warned that only lack of political will, not foreign aggression, could defeat the U.S. war effort: the silent majority must now voice its support. He justified this request on the promise of Vietnamization: "In July, on my visit to Vietnam, I changed General Abrams's orders so that they were consistent with the objectives of our new policies. Under the new orders, the primary mission of our troops is to enable the South Vietnamese forces to assume the full responsibility for the security of South Vietnam."[48] The speech was likely his most successful, and polling suggested broad public support for his Vietnamization timetable.[49]

PIVOTING AWAY FROM VIETNAM

Withdrawal from Vietnam marked the beginning of a new mission facing a select group of top Army leaders: the rebuilding of the force and the prevention of another Vietnam. This group certainly included Abrams, who was promoted to Army chief of staff. It also included Abrams's MACV assistant, General Frederick C. Weyand, who was brought along as vice chief of staff. In a speech given in October 2000, Weyand would explain the perspective the two shared on their responsibilities to the Army as it exited Vietnam: "In the aftermath of Vietnam, for Abe and me, our watchwords were 'Readiness' and 'Stability' for the Army. Because readiness was a given. Abe and I believed that to build a truly ready Army, we needed a stable force. You've got to have that. We both believed with stability, cutting out all the historic ups and downs of Army strength, we could build a good Army."[50]

But Abrams would not live to achieve this goal. In the spring of 1974, a tumor was found in his lungs. By the fall, he was dead. Weyand agreed to follow Abrams as chief of staff to help realize Abrams's vision of readiness and stability. In this he was aided by Secretary of the Army Howard H. Callaway. Writing to Weyand, Callaway proposed "the Secretary of the Army's Top 5" priorities for "building a better Army in [fiscal year] 1975." The priorities were: (1) reduce the officer corps to minimal essential strength; (2) upgrade overall quality of the Army while keeping it representative of the population; (3) increase combat capability in Europe and attain a sixteen-division active Army; (4) improve Army management of matériel acquisition; and (5) enhance the role of Congress as a partner.[51]

At first glance, these goals may appear to be the sort of budget slashing one would expect from an unsympathetic civilian chief. Points 1, 2, and 4—the reduction of the officer corps, the mandate to ensure "representativeness" (of African Americans and women), and the commitment to matériel acquisition—were political considerations intended to avoid accusations of Army shirking. In fact, Callaway was aligned with the Abrams–Weyand contingent. I advance this claim based on points 3 and 5. The commitment to increasing the Army to sixteen combat-ready divisions was one of Abrams's goals and marked a significantly more optimistic vision of what Congress would permit than was generally shared in the Army. Abrams's biographer describes his commitment to sixteen rather than fourteen divisions as a "bombshell" that left his staff "thunderstruck[;] . . . most of them thought it was an objective that just could not be achieved."[52] Callaway would nevertheless pursue it, and to do so he needed the fifth point to be in place as well: the support of Congress. Weyand, a former chief of legislative liaison, was well matched in Callaway, a career politician, and together they charted a nuanced political strategy for rebuilding the U.S. Army. The legacy left by these three Army leaders—Abrams, Callaway, and Weyand—was a particular way of thinking about the stages connecting the Army to the public and then to Congress through the press.

THE FALL OF SAIGON

The Army had almost entirely withdrawn from Vietnam by the end of 1973, and so the last phase of American news coverage of the Vietnam War was not particularly shaped by the insights of Abrams, Callaway,

Weyand, or their teams—their influence would be felt later, as we will see in subsequent chapters. Nevertheless, the fall of Saigon in 1975 was big news. This tone could be sensed on the front page of the *New York Times* on April 30, where three rows of text above the fold screamed,

> MINH OFFERS UNCONDITIONAL SURRENDER;
> 1,000 AMERICANS EVACUATED FROM SAIGON
> IN CHOPPERS WITH 5,500 SOUTH VIETNAMESE.

Where these refugees would go and what this unconditional surrender would mean for Americans would become the through-lines for subsequent reporting on the region, with the role of the Army diminishing quickly from view.

But what of the war? Millions of Americans served in Vietnam, and about 57,000 of them died. Around one million Vietnamese people were killed, with approximately 150,000 killed or abducted during the final North Vietnamese offensive in 1975 alone. And, of course, this Second Indochina War, an outcome of the First Indochina War and its hundreds of thousands of war deaths, would give rise to war with Cambodia (and briefly China), famine, forced-labor camps, and untold human suffering. Anticipating this dark future, many South Vietnamese and virtually all the remaining journalists scrambled to leave the country as the city was falling to North Vietnamese forces.

This epochal moment when Saigon finally fell was recorded by several reporters working for American news organizations. Fox Butterfield recalls being herded by marines through the Defense Attaché's Office building, his own press colleagues mimicking the relentless official U.S. optimism they had listened to for the past ten years: "'We've just turned the corner in Vietnam, and there's light at the end of the tunnel,' a newsman said. In fact, at the end of the corridor were the green helicopters in the Defense Attaché's Office parking lot, their rotors whirling." Butterfield filed the report from aboard the USS *Blue Ridge*, but he was first brought to the USS *Mobile*. That ship was soon overrun with refugees, so much so that the helicopters used to bring them to the ship and so instrumental in transforming Army tactics were simply pushed into the sea (at an estimated cost of $25 million). After four days aboard the *Mobile*, Butterfield and the other thirty-two reporters were transferred to the *Blue Ridge*, the flagship of the evacuation fleet. There, they finally relaxed, listened to live soul music, and ate "hamburgers, baked beans, macaroni salad, Coke and root beer. For dessert there was chocolate cake.... Vietnam seemed far away, if you didn't stop to remember."[53]

Several reporters stayed in Saigon, most famously George Esper, Matt Franjola, and Peter Arnett. Arnett had been there the longest of the three, arriving in 1962. He recalls the flood of reporters arriving in the days before the fall, sent by bosses who knew the story would sell. AP would not be outcompeted: "In a war where his guys had won five Pulitzer Prizes, [AP chief Wes] Gallagher was determined to maintain the competitive advantage until the end."[54]

Although most reporters, such as Butterfield, dodged rockets to escape as North Vietnamese overran the city, Arnett was determined to stay, sending a message to Gallagher to inform him, "Because I was in Vietnam at the beginning, I felt it worth the risk to be there at the end."[55] Matt Franjola was also set on staying. He had covered the war first for UPI and then the AP and later admitted "he used to bribe the U.S. military signal operators in Khe Sanh . . . with fresh loaves of French bread so they would relay his stories back to the U.S. ahead of competing news services."[56] Perhaps this competitive zeal kept him in the city. It was not a sure thing. Franjola and Arnett did drive with the convoy to the airport with the other reporters but at the last minute recognized a South Vietnamese Information Ministry official standing with his son, desperate to escape. Arnett and Franjola ceded their places to them and returned to the office to see George Esper.

Esper, the AP bureau chief and one of the leading figures in the Saigon press corps, refused to leave if the younger Franjola was staying. Esper was perhaps the ideal figure to cover the end of the war, given his extraordinary productivity and constant challenges to the Army public-affairs office. Don North notes in his obituary of Esper that "one retired public affairs officer included Esper in a wall montage of 'all the commanders I served under.'" North describes the events that followed Arnett and Franjola's return to the AP office:

Esper wrote his most memorable Vietnam story as the AP bureau chief on April 30, 1975, the day Saigon fell to the North Vietnamese. . . . It wasn't long before two North Vietnamese soldiers walked into the AP office. Esper offered them Cokes and stale cake—and he interviewed them. "They showed me photographs of their wives and children," Esper recalled. "Vietnamese, South and North, Americans, we're all the same, it seems. That's how the war ended for me." Hours later, AP communications were cut, but not before the story got out and landed on the front page of *The New York Times*.[57]

Butterfield's Coke and cake on the *Blue Ridge* were for him a symbolic act of returning home, of putting the war behind them. The Coke and cake Esper shared in his Saigon office with North Vietnamese soldiers served perhaps the same function, cutting through the decade and more of violence to a shared moment of tranquility, shared not just with the people in the room but with the million or so readers of his report. A very brief moment in the lives of the Vietnamese soldiers and a final turn away from the region by the American public.

THE LESSONS OF VIETNAM

What lessons about democratic oversight and military autonomy are revealed by this long and complex war? From the journalists' perspective, Vietnam tipped the balance of power all the way back from military dominance to something approximating journalistic control. The doctrine and customs in place at the beginning of the war set journalists up to have exceptional depth of field and organizational penetration, while technological developments combined with broader cultural upheaval meant that some journalists, such as Halberstam, Sheehan, Arnett, Browne, and many others, produced copy that was quickly and broadly disseminated to an eager audience. The years of U.S. involvement in Vietnam were also years of an American press discovering a new idiom of critique and new justifications for inquiry that constitute the birth of a new form of democratic oversight.

At the level of military high command, a very different story has been told. Although some media-savvy individuals recognized the need to court the press, Army leaders tended to be dismissive of journalists and were instead concerned with navigating the often dysfunctional dynamics of civilian (i.e., formal political) oversight. Only after the Tet Offensive was there a consensus among military leaders that domestic political concerns must be integrated into operational strategy and organizational grand strategy, but this integration was still on an ad hoc basis and imperfectly conceived.

Finally, it is important to note that the Vietnam War was "good" for Army public affairs. Despite the Army's old pattern of closing down public-affairs offices at the end of hostilities, despite the considerable pressures to downsize facing every Army unit, the OCI kept its doors open, shed only one component, and continued to offer myriad services in its three fields of responsibility: community relations, command information, and public information. With the death of Abrams, the Army lost a leader who held strong convictions concerning one vision of Army–media relations, honest rather than propagandizing but also jealous of Army secrets and wary of the power wielded by journalists. The paradox revealed by Tet, political failure despite operational success, would loom large in the minds of Abrams's successors for decades as they struggled with suspicions that the Army had been betrayed by its political masters, by journalists, and even by the American public it existed to serve.

5

TET SUPPRESSED

Army Doctrinal Innovations, 1976–1982

MAKING SENSE of Vietnam, including the paradox of the Tet Offensive, was a contested, protracted, imperfect process within the Army. Ultimately, it would require a generation of professional soldiers not only to look hard and long at the institution to which they had dedicated their lives but also to pass judgment on their own careers and their own biases. Much, of course, had changed by the close of the Vietnam War. Growing from George Marshall's personalized media management during World War II, a vast network of media-management organizations had taken root. The compliance of the press during World War II and the Korean War was now a distant memory, replaced by a highly professional and competent media profession that had lost its faith in the Army to support its coverage of American wars. And, operationally, the role of the media had by now evolved in the eyes of the Army's leaders from a helpful amplifier of the Army's message to a vulnerability that could eclipse any effects the Army achieved on the ground. What remained unclear in the mid-1970s was how to fit the pieces together—in other words, how commanders should draw upon their expansive media-management resources to mitigate risk and potentially once again draw benefits from the work of independent journalists while also meeting all their other obligations on the battlefield and in the political arena. The meaning of Vietnam and the significance of Tet were up for grabs.

This situation was not made easier by the fact that the Army was led by men who had direct personal experience with Army warfighting in Vietnam but who tended to split into two camps as to what this experience meant for the future of the service. A long sequence of chiefs of staff, combatant commanders, and chairmen of the Joint Chiefs were Vietnam partisans of one stripe or another. General Maxwell D. Taylor, the Army's chief of staff from 1955 to 1959 and chairman of the Joint Chiefs from 1962 to 1964, was followed in both positions by General Earle Wheeler. Both Taylor and Wheeler championed Big Army conventional warfare in the face of the New Look preference for strategic deterrence, and in William Westmoreland (MACV commander from 1964 to 1968 and Army chief of staff from 1968 to 1972) they found a Big Army practitioner who could demonstrate the enduring value of the Army's unique capacities.[1] But Taylor, Wheeler, and Westmoreland failed to integrate democratic oversight into their operational thinking and were left with the messy paradox of Tet—operational success, political failure.

Meanwhile, General Harold K. Johnson, who replaced Wheeler as Army chief of staff and served from 1964 to 1968, viewed Chairman Wheeler and MACV combatant commander Westmoreland as part of a toxic mixture of personalities who together were losing the war.[2] Johnson retired to allow Westmoreland to be fired upward and replace him as chief of staff, clearing the way for Abrams to take command of MACV.[3] While Westmoreland's influence as chief of staff was limited by his public failure in Vietnam, Abrams was empowered by his successful implementation of the Vietnamization policy. He died as Army chief of staff at the height of his influence in the service and was replaced by his friend and ally General Frederick C. Weyand.[4] Weyand finished Abrams's term and worked to fulfill Abrams's vision while doing so. But Weyand was the last of this generation. He retired in 1976, replaced by General Bernard W. Rogers, who had served in Vietnam from 1966 to 1967 but who had occupied mainly staff positions subsequently.

The significance of this sequence was that from about 1962 to 1976 the Army's top staff officer, its primary combatant commander, and the chairman of the Joint Chiefs were men whose personal reputations were tied to operational success in Vietnam, either as a showcase for conventional force (Taylor, Wheeler, Westmoreland) or as proof of the limitations of conventional force that needed to be corrected by adapting new strategic principles (Johnson, Abrams, Weyand).[5] Vietnam loomed very large indeed for these men, and all of them recognized the role of the media, but in two different ways. Taylor, Wheeler, and Westmoreland viewed democratic oversight as yet another obstacle exogenous to the war that needed to be overcome, while Johnson, Abrams, and Weyand recognized it as endogenous to the war and so a strategic concern of the first order.

These two perspectives on democratic oversight were reflected during the war in a series of media-management innovations. For the most part, these innovations were located organizationally in MACV and included attempts to censor or court, downplay or mislead. At home, too, the Army's expanded OCI in the Pentagon found much to occupy its attention, responding to a constant stream of public inquiries, managing promotional activities, and reacting to scandals. Public affairs (especially media management) had evolved during the war to become a central element of the Army's domestic political strategy as practiced by combatant commands and the Army staff, reflecting a recognition that democratic oversight had supplanted civilian oversight as the primary political concern.

In the background of these efforts loomed the paradox of Tet. More Tets—more operations that trigger unexpected political disasters regardless of the battlefield outcome—might well lead the Army back to the state of existential crisis it had experienced in the New Look era. Back then, the Army had sought to dispel the growing sense among civilian leaders that a conventional ground force was a destabilizing and potentially disastrous use of state power. Now, it faced a new legitimacy crisis in the notion that a conventional ground force was politically toxic.

And yet in the very period that MACV and the OCI were redoubling their public-affairs efforts, some Army leaders set themselves the task of renewing the Army's commitment to an operational culture purified of politics, in essence downgrading the importance of the Johnson-Abrams-Weyand strategic developments while also recognizing the problems of the Taylor-Wheeler-Westmoreland paradigm. The two major waves of doctrinal innovation following the Vietnam War took their lessons primarily from the Arab-Israeli October War of 1973, lessons intended to be applied to war in Germany. This chapter accordingly explores the peculiar mixture of endogenous cultural assumption and exogenous strategic concerns that led an important faction of Army leaders directly away from the political lessons of Vietnam and back toward a robustly autonomous organizational posture.

After Vietnam, the Army was yet again facing the double pressures of drawdown and pivot (this time to face a possible Soviet invasion of Europe). One might expect that its leaders, badly wounded by the Army's experiences in Vietnam, would have focused first on the lessons from that war. Instead, focus shifted elsewhere, indeed almost in the opposite direction. Why, then, did the Army leaders of the mid-1970s reject the lessons of Tet and refuse to integrate political concerns into their new operational doctrines?

THE PIVOT TO EUROPE

The Army's pivot to Europe can be traced back as early as January 1972, when Lieutenant General William E. DePuy, assistant Army vice chief of staff, set in motion a plan to reorganize the Continental Army Command (CONARC). CONARC was created in 1962 to organize activities within North America, including all the tasks associated with training, supplying, and transporting soldiers to other regions. In 1972, CONARC was busy with both the Vietnam drawdown and the anticipated end of conscription, and to DePuy's mind it was badly bungling the drawdown.[6] His solution was to bisect CONARC into two functional units, Force Command, managing the departure of troops for combat, and Training and Doctrine Command (TRADOC), charged with training troops and crafting doctrine. By July, TRADOC was activated, and DePuy was named its first commander.

DePuy fully recognized the power of his position as the chief of the Army's doctrine and would skillfully navigate the bureaucracy to craft a sweeping doctrinal revision that reflected his personal experience of war and belief about what wars would come. Although he had been the chief of staff of operations at MACV and had then commanded the famed Big Red One, the First Infantry Division, in combat in Vietnam, he oddly would take his cues from his experience with tank warfare in Europe during World War II.

Why did DePuy turn away from the lessons of Vietnam? Certainly, he was not alone in wanting to avoid the issues that marked the Army's time in Vietnam. Several exogenous factors are important to note. Most obvious were two major structural changes: the withdrawal from Vietnam, which included force reduction, and the end of conscription, which required masses of volunteers. Both drawdown and the end of conscription tended to eclipse the war in the daily affairs of the Army staff leaders in the Pentagon. In DePuy's own words, this was "an inward looking time."[7]

In addition to these obvious structural changes, both the goals and capacities of the Army of the future were changing quickly. President Nixon had reset the DOD's long-standing defense posture in his Guam Doctrine of 1969, which now planned for a one-and-a-half contingency posture, meaning the DOD should be capable of fighting one major war and one minor war at any given moment. Few polities in history have held such ambitions, but this was in fact a major limitation of post–World War II American ambitions, which had established a two-and-a-half-war contingency posture throughout the 1960s.[8]

The more modest requirement would naturally lead to budget cuts, but at the same time Army planners were growing convinced that the budget needed to be increased to secure the Army's capacities. They specifically set their sights on procuring the "big-five" weapons systems: tanks, mechanized infantry combat vehicles, attack helicopters, transport helicopters, and antiaircraft missiles.[9] While still assistant vice chief of staff, DePuy recognized the organizational dilemma of asking Congress for more resources to achieve a smaller goal. In the words of one Army historian, "DePuy believed that the Army could not convince DOD or Congress that these weapons were needed unless the Army could demonstrate clearly that they would improve the Army's overall combat capabilities."[10] TRADOC was accordingly set the task of proving this requirement. And, in fact, it succeeded. Operation Desert Storm would showcase all five systems, making each momentarily a household name: the M1 Abrams tank, the Bradley fighting vehicle, the Apache attack helicopter, the Black Hawk assault helicopter, and the Patriot air-defense missiles.

The pivot to Europe also reflected endogenous, cultural forces. Most importantly, the Big Army mentality that manifested itself as Army utopianism in the 1950s was once again ascending, this time with a nostalgic eye to the battlefields of World War II. As early as 1979, Army historians were diagnosing "a feeling of malaise engendered by the complexities of the Vietnam War and relating to ongoing problems with personnel and morale."[11]

For DePuy in the early 1970s, at any rate, the major operational innovations of the Vietnam War held little interest. His mind kept returning to the power of the tanks he had witnessed as a battalion commander with the Ninetieth Infantry Division racing across France in 1944.[12] Suddenly in early October 1973, though, DePuy's memories were brought to life as Egyptian forces swiftly crossed Israel's Bar Lev Line along the Suez Canal, while Syrian forces descended from the Golan Heights in what would be called the Yom Kippur or October War.

The Egyptian strategy was based on political rather than military goals and came about through the unique geopolitical configuration of the era.[13] President Anwar Sadat of Egypt wanted to puncture Israelis' faith in their military because doing so would encourage domestic political pressures on Israeli leaders to make peace with their Arab neighbors and relinquish claims over the Sinai Peninsula. He also knew that U.S. and Soviet diplomacy could be called upon to keep the war from becoming too large. Accordingly, a quick psychological victory over the Israeli public, even if it were based on precarious operational footing, could achieve his ends—either through Israeli citizens asking their government for a long-term peace treaty or through American diplomats demanding Israeli settlement because of the threat of Soviet interference.

Sadat's strategy could not have been more familiar to the U.S. Army fighting in Vietnam. Indeed, it was based on Sadat's assessment of the Tet and Easter Offensives.[14] Yet DePuy and other Army leaders were focused on his tactics, which combined effective air-defense and ground maneuver in ways that were startling in their efficacy. DePuy was shaken by what he read about the war, and he quickly reordered

TRADOC's priorities to build a doctrinal foundation for countering Sadat-style offensives.[15] What TRADOC analysts saw when they analyzed Sadat's force posture was a substantial improvement in Soviet military technology combined with new tactical uses of airpower and artillery; in their eyes, this combination eroded the force advantages that Americans had enjoyed thus far in the Cold War. More troublingly, Sadat's forces revealed a serious weakness in how the United States had used tanks in combat, indicating that now tanks would need support from other arms to retain their tactical value.[16] This meant that the allied democracies in Europe were suddenly at far greater risk than had been imagined. While Sadat's strategy was less interesting to DePuy than his tactics, one political lesson was drawn from the October War: a Tet scenario could trigger a sequence of political concessions that would lose a European war. And so DePuy cannot be said to have ignored the lessons of Vietnam entirely. Rather, he learned one lesson, drawn not directly from his own experience in Vietnam but rather indirectly from Anwar Sadat's analysis of Tet. The singular lesson was really quite simple: the Army must win the first battle of the next war. The doctrine would provide combatant commanders guidance on how to win the first battle in a major land-based surprise offensive launched by Soviet forces across the fields of Europe.

APOLITICAL DOCTRINE: *ACTIVE DEFENSE* (1976) AND *AIRLAND BATTLE* (1982)

Given these pressing geopolitical fears, what did DePuy hope to achieve by focusing on doctrinal revision? Doctrine, after all, needs to be enacted by human beings, and so a different sort of leader might have focused on making his case directly to his fellow generals. Indeed, the Army's organizational culture had long made commanders particularly resistant to radically changing their behavior to adhere to a new piece of doctrine.[17] To understand why doctrine came to the forefront of military affairs in the immediate post-Vietnam era, we must consider first what *doctrine* meant to officers; second, how DePuy personally mobilized TRADOC's new publications; and finally, the content of this doctrine and the responses it provoked.

First, then, it is necessary to clarify what *doctrine* means in this context. Foreign-affairs scholars tend to use *doctrine* to refer to broad institutional preferences in strategy and tactics.[18] In doing so, they follow Barry Posen, who in the mid-1980s described doctrine as the immanent logic of a military service that may be detected by the careful observer: "Force posture, the inventory of weapons any military organization controls, can be used as evidence to discover military doctrine."[19] In other words, doctrine for many scholars is an academic reconstruction of how a country thinks about and prepares for war, something akin to an ideology of war or a culture of war.

But *doctrine* has another meaning, and this second meaning is inferred in virtually all internal military discussions of the term.[20] The DOD uses the following narrow definition: "**Doctrine**: Fundamental principles by which the military forces or elements thereof guide their actions in support of national objectives. It is authoritative but requires judgment in application."[21] I depart from the scholarly custom and preserve the use of *doctrine* as a folk category, referring narrowly to the written documents of a service intended to guide agents in their official duties. DePuy and his colleagues had this narrow, specific definition in mind when talking about doctrine.[22] They envisioned doctrine as both joint publications defining DOD-wide policies and Army publications, which included training manuals, technical manuals, and, most importantly for our purposes, field manuals.

DePuy believed that official Army doctrine, if written effectively and if given the active support of Army leaders, could bring about real change in how the service worked.[23] Whereas Army manuals had traditionally been written in bureaucratic language by boards of officer-authors, now DePuy tasked TRADOC with writing a new form of doctrine that would excite the reader and energize the force. Whereas earlier doctrine was prone to be read (if read at all) without being acted upon, DePuy wanted his manuals to be studied and admired, and he had enough experience with the inner workings of Pentagon bureaucracy to know what not to do.

This optimistic assessment of doctrine reflected DePuy's pessimistic assessment of American soldiers and officers, whom he considered prone to making worse decisions when they acted independently than when they simply followed the orders from a unified command.

For this belief, Paul Herbert credits DePuy's own experiences with a poorly led unit in World War II, and the personnel crises of the Vietnam era would likely have further diminished his faith in the American soldier's abilities.[24] Training, instilling lessons deduced from what DePuy considered to be objective analysis, was a better use of resources than education, the attempt to improve inductive reasoning.[25] When creating TRADOC, he very much had in mind rigorous training rather than merely abstract education; doctrine would guide that training and coordinate it across organizational contexts, creating basic standards rather than inspiring innovative new solutions.

Ultimately, his faith in training and doctrine inspired DePuy to tackle the core regulations of the service. DOD doctrine is hierarchical within and across services and is often described in near-mystical terms by the writers tasked with synchronizing new doctrine to the existing complex frame. At the highest level are the field manuals, stating rules and providing guidance for the management of personnel, intelligence, operations, logistics, planning, and communications; each of these topics has many narrow occupational categories governed by their own field manuals. DePuy directed TRADOC to begin its work by rewriting the keystone manual for the Army's operational tasks. Given the political lessons of Tet and Sadat's implementation of those lessons in the Sinai, one might expect DePuy to have integrated political concerns at the core of his revision. However, other than enshrining the political importance of the first battle, DePuy did quite the opposite.

DePuy's perspective on the problems confronting the Army was clear. Regarding tactics, he believed that the October War had revealed shortcomings in how U.S. forces combined airpower and land power.[26] Regarding strategy, he was focused on winning the first battle, a concern enshrined on the first page of his masterpiece, the completely rewritten edition of *Field Manual 100-5: Operations*: "The first battle of our next war could well be its last battle: belligerents could be quickly exhausted, and international pressures to stop fighting could bring about an early cessation of hostilities."[27] Regarding organization, he believed that a mental shift was needed to pivot Army thinking to Europe. In his talking points for a presentation on the field manual on July 8, 1976, he stated this belief unequivocally: "The entire

United States Army, from Private to General needs to focus on a form of combat in which the Army of today has had no battlefield experience. In a sense, this manual takes the Army out of the rice paddies of Vietnam and places it on the Western European battlefield against the Warsaw Pact."[28] How would he bring about this change?

DePuy's leadership style was characterized by choosing a small number of motivated juniors to tackle a problem and then to present their findings (with his edits) as a final product to his own commander. The goal was to side-step the time-consuming work of having every interested party weigh in with their ideas, while the risk lay in overlooking certain areas of concern and in generating animosity among those who are ignored. He had done this successfully with his plan to reorganize CONARC and did so again with the keystone operations manual. His responsibilities as chief of TRADOC included canvassing the opinions of the intellectual hubs of the Army: Fort Leavenworth, which housed both the Command and General Staff College and the Combined Arms Center; Fort Benning, the home of the Army Infantry School; and Fort Knox, which housed the Army Armor Center. The natural home for the sort of combined air–land doctrine DePuy envisioned would have been the Combined Arms Center at Leavenworth, but it was new and unproven, so DePuy decided to place his bets instead on the dynamic leader of Fort Knox, General Donn A. Starry, and let the Army Armor Center take the lead.[29]

This decision was fateful for two reasons: first, it set Starry on a course that would lead him to head the next major revision to the keystone operations manual in 1982; and second, it made an enemy of the Infantry School chief, Lieutenant General John H. Cushman. Starry would later characterize Cushman's resistance to DePuy as "probably the greatest act of institutional and individual disloyalty I have ever had the chance to observe."[30]

Although Starry and others were involved in its writing, the 1976 version of *Field Manual 100-5* was shaped primarily by DePuy and his focus on air–land tactical solutions, first-battle strategic preparation, and a symbolic break with Vietnam. This edition came to be known as *Active Defense* after the main concept developed in its pages. As Herbert notes, "No officer on active duty in 1976 could fail to identify its author as General William E. DePuy[;] . . . the 1976 edition [would be] known as the DePuy manual."³¹ Historians still debate the manual's insights, although they readily acknowledge its many innovations.³² Herbert lists the key insights as the already-mentioned need to win the first battle; a new insistence on being able to fight when outnumbered alongside a new belief that attack should occur only with a six-to-one force advantage, while defense should always strive for a three-to-one advantage; the insistence that the tank remain the "decisive weapon" but must be used as part of a "combined arms team"; a renewed commitment to classical principles of cover, concealment, suppression, and teamwork; and, finally, a recognition of the "new lethality" of war because many international states now had exceptionally powerful weapons.³³

Together, these insights form a constellation of military thought that prioritizes maneuverability. *Maneuverability* in a very specific sense here means the ability to draw one's forces together quickly to launch a six-to-one force-ratio attack or to consolidate a three-to-one force-ratio defense. It also means the ability to bring together different types of arms to provide suppressive fire and rapid attack. And, finally, it carries the political insight that the perception of rapid advance, even if thinly supported, can devastate an enemy's morale. DePuy was almost immediately successful in his basic task of producing a field manual that would be read and debated, and he was very successful in shaping the conversation to come. His key principle, maneuver, was accepted widely (and has remained so ever since), but the specific guidelines and conclusions he drew from those principles would be subject to intense criticism. From within the Army, Leavenworth chief General John H. Cushman and others raised enough doubt about the new manual that it was subject to serious scholarly scrutiny in military journals. Civilians such as Edward Luttwak (who called it "a doctrine of pure attrition") and William Lind (who, among other criticisms, questioned the logic of DePuy's "winning the first battle" prerogative) also added their voices to the criticism.³⁴

The dissatisfaction with DePuy's *Active Defense* was sufficiently intense that following DePuy's retirement, the new head of TRADOC, General Donn A. Starry, would be tasked with rewriting the keystone operational manual yet again. Starry, under DePuy, had contributed to the original, but he had left Fort Knox in the interim for command of Fifth Corps, stationed in Germany. There, on the frontline of the anticipated next war, he had cause to ponder the criticisms of DePuy's manual, and so he came to TRADOC with a more experienced and critical perspective. Starry approached the task of writing the manual in a more conciliatory and collaborative fashion than his predecessor and benefited from all that had been written critically and supportively of the earlier manual.[35] A first draft was prepared by January 1981, and within a year Starry's staffers were briefing members of Congress and top Army and DOD officials, including Vice President George H. W. Bush in March. By August, the final edit was approved, and it was published in 1982 as *Field Manual 100-5: Operations* but was often referred to by its key conceptual innovation, *AirLand Battle*.

Because DePuy's manual had already redefined doctrine as a subject of operational value and intrinsic interest rather than as an exercise in bureaucracy, the *AirLand Battle* manual found an immediate audience. Most of its revisions addressed tactical concerns such as weather and terrain, adding nuance and sometimes revising DePuy-era assertions entirely. The concept of "air–land battle" was first articulated in DePuy's manual but emerged now as the key concept for the Army, indicating an ever-tighter connection between aviation (both Army and Air Force) and ground forces than envisioned by DePuy. Overall, the 1982 manual charts a new course in several key respects, emphasizing the offensive, focusing even more on maneuver, and elevating the importance of leadership, in particular lower-level autonomy in decision making, in ways DePuy would have rejected out of hand.[36]

More importantly, however, the 1982 manual made some effort to reintegrate political concerns into Army doctrine.[37] The manual opens with a brief paragraph warning its readers that "defeating enemy forces in battle will not always insure victory. Other national instruments of power or persuasion will influence or even determine the results of wars." Throughout the text, there is a more pronounced concern with "moral factors" such as deception, misinformation, psychological operations, special operations, and civil affairs. Notably, however, public affairs warrants only one mention as the ninth in a list of components of the new Combat Service Support Personnel system (other elements include "chaplain activities" and "health services").[38]

A keyword search reveals that *the press, media, journalist, news, reporters, correspondent*, and related terms appear nowhere in DePuy's 1976 manual. Only the word *press* is given once in Starry's 1982 manual, where it appears critically in a subsection of an appendix describing the operational value of surprise, which is worth quoting at some length: *"Strategic surprise is difficult to achieve. . . . This problem is compounded in an open society such as the United States, where freedom of press and information are highly valued. However, the United States can achieve a degree of psychological surprise due to its strategic deployment capability."*[39] An open society creates problems, from this viewpoint, because a democracy's military is burdened with a free press that makes operational secrecy harder to achieve. Nowhere is there a sense that freedom of the press is a good in its own right or can have operational benefits. Although Starry and his colleagues worked hard to revise DePuy's manual in response to the many trenchant critiques it had received among officers and civilian intellectuals alike, they had mostly forgotten the role of the media, the power wielded so clearly by war correspondents and newspaper editors throughout the Vietnam War, and only in this one moment acknowledge it begrudgingly.

How do we account for the omission of media concerns from Army doctrinal development in the period from 1972 to 1982? I have already offered a few explanations. This was a busy time, and structural changes and geopolitical concerns may have overshadowed the immediate lessons of Vietnam. The culture of the service—preferring conventional war, reflecting a deep unease about the Vietnam experience—encouraged that obfuscation. A more obvious and more troubling explanation can be found in Starry's oral history, recorded on September 18, 1991 (seven months after the end of Operation Desert Storm), where he compares his own perspective on the role of the media with that of his colleague Lieutenant Colonel Larry Icenogle, then the Army War College's PAO: "I think Larry has a pretty good handle on that. I am more inclined to run the press off, just because I don't think you can trust them. But Larry has a much more rational, and I think mature, viewpoint on that than I do. My resentment comes from Vietnam; I can never forgive them for what they did."⁴⁰ From our historical vantage point, it seems clear that Starry's anger led in part to the internalization of combat principles that would undermine the democratic character of contemporary warfighting.

PEACETIME PUBLIC AFFAIRS

Although the *Active Defense* and *AirLand Battle* doctrines gave rise to considerable debate and organizational change across the service, Army public affairs maintained a steady but only linear growth untroubled by those conflicts.⁴¹ Much of the Army was searching for its future identity everywhere but in its collective memory of Vietnam; public-affairs offices, however, appear to have been untroubled by the memory and to have moved ahead optimistically.

In an expansive manuscript commissioned by the Army but never published, Jack Pulwers interviewed the three public-affairs chiefs who served from 1973 to 1980, Major Generals L. Gordon Hill, Robert B. Solomon, and Robert A. Sullivan. All three viewed themselves as having presided over a period of expansion and growing confidence in the field of public affairs. Hill, chief information officer from 1973 to 1977, recalled of his own first encounter with public affairs, "I took every lousy job that could be offered to me. I was also a Public Affairs Officer on several occasions, and that was considered the pits. . . . I'm glad to say that in my time of office, I did much to change that feeling."⁴² Most of Hill's tenure concerned the drawdown from Vietnam, but he was still the chief when on July 1, 1976, the OCI was transferred from the Office of the Chief of Staff of the Army to the Office of the Secretary of the Army. The term *information* was dropped across the board in favor of *public affairs*, and so the OCI became the Office of the Chief of Public Affairs (OCPA). The move was reflective of an increased sense of the importance of the field because the chief of public affairs now reported directly to the civilian secretary of the Army rather than to the uniformed chief of staff.

Hill was replaced by his deputy, Major General Robert B. Solomon, in June 1977. Elsewhere in the Army, the battle over *Active Defense* was then reshaping the basic notions of Army readiness, but the OCPA seems to have had little involvement. In the next few years, two developments in Army public affairs should be noted. The first was the growing declaratory commitment to openness and honesty in the Army's relation to the public, which sometimes mimicked the language of Vietnam-era "maximum candor" but was not necessarily embraced at a deep organizational level. The second development was a growing integration of public-affairs concerns at the level of Army leadership training. Solomon's tenure as public-affairs chief exemplified the first, while Robert Sullivan's subsequent tenure exemplified the latter.

Solomon took over from Hill while a new presidential administration was still settling in. President Jimmy Carter took office in January 1977, appointing Harold Brown to replace Donald Rumsfeld as secretary of defense and appointing Clifford Alexander as the first African American secretary of the Army. Brown was a child prodigy who had obtained a PhD in physics at twenty-one and was recruited as one of McNamara's "whiz kids" by age thirty-three. Charles A. Stevenson, who has written the history of U.S. secretaries of defense, considers Brown to have had "more high-level prior experience inside the Pentagon than any other secretary of defense," up until the war-on-terror era.[43] Carter appointed him for his detailed technical understanding, which would allow Brown to challenge the Joint Chiefs on the specifics of the different branches' weapons programs and dig deep into their nuclear arms posture. Carter also assigned the president of Coca-Cola, Charles Duncan, as Brown's deputy and de facto chief of the DOD's administrative issues. Both Brown and Duncan were loyal Carter supporters, so the arrangement allowed Carter to micromanage the department at a very fine grain. Speaking from this position of knowledgeable civilian command with full presidential backing, Brown revised the DOD's policy on press relations on June 22, 1977, to embrace "a new openness in government." The three criteria for releasing information to the press stood firmly in the maximum-candor school of public affairs. In Jack Pulwers's words, "Information would be made fully available unless precluded by statute; information would be withheld when disclosure would adversely affect national security or threaten the privacy and personal safety of the men and women of the Armed Forces; and . . . information would not be withheld to protect the government from criticism and embarrassment."⁴⁴

As with maximum candor in Vietnam, the limits of this idealistic declaratory policy would be sorely tested almost immediately. On May 17, 1977, the *Washington Post* ran a story that quoted Major General John K. Singlaub, chief of staff of U.S. forces in Korea, criticizing President Carter's decision to withdraw forces from the region, which had been a campaign pledge. Singlaub was removed from his post and retired. Although in retrospect Singlaub's criticism of his president would strike most civil–military relations scholars as highly unprofessional, at the time the combination of criticism and apparent muzzling cast the administration in an unflattering light. Assistant Secretary of Defense for Public Affairs Thomas Ross worked damage control in early June by "announc[ing] that the Pentagon is advising its military and civilian leaders not to let the disciplining of Singlaub dampen the publication of their own opinions."⁴⁵

Major General Robert A. Sullivan replaced Solomon in 1979 and oversaw a rapid expansion of the OCPA. He had been trained in Scott Cutlip's graduate program at the University of Wisconsin and so was a product of the public-affairs institution in a way that his predecessors were not. Where Solomon had viewed his role in moral terms, Sullivan possessed a more strategic sensibility and described to Pulwers his method of withholding information: "This is not censorship. By doing this we are not trying to censor the news at all. What we would do is simply hold back the information until we could get the complete story and provide full information for the reporter. Then you get the story out *in full* but not before it's completed."⁴⁶

The general posture of Sullivan's OCPA was closer to the low-key approach embraced earlier by Winant Sidle and Creighton Abrams than the more open approach of Barry Zorthian and Robert Solomon. Sullivan noted, "If the press person would ask me a question I would certainly answer it. But where people get into trouble in the Public Affairs business is when they try to tell too much. . . . If the reporter is quiet, then you be quiet." Rather than petition the press to pay attention to the Army, Sullivan's focus was on promoting public affairs' wares to Army commanders. And he was successful. During his time as chief of public affairs, the role was integrated into the daily business of top Army command. He would meet with fellow department heads four days a week. During these meetings, "important matters which were of great interest to [public affairs] were always brought up at the top of the list." He would also meet with the secretary of the Army and the assistant secretary of the Army twice weekly.[47]

Pulwers's interview with Sullivan is particularly valuable as a window into what aspects of public affairs were being integrated into command concerns. Above all, the change appears to have involved the sensitization of general officers to media logics. Sullivan worked with top officers to guide them to be able to talk directly to reporters rather than have their PAOs do the talking for them. In addition to formal training programs at key professional education moments, Sullivan developed a "murder board" system where his staff would grill top officers with the most challenging questions they could think of in preparation for a press conference. Because the Army has not maintained (or perhaps did not record) the annual reports for the OCPA in the years from 1979 to 1986, it is not clear whether the subtle difference in style between Solomon and Sullivan was reflected organizationally.

THE SUPPRESSED LESSON

By 1972, Army leaders had understood that despite the extraordinary latent power that they commanded, their forces would not resolve the Vietnam conflict operationally. Focus shifted to leaving the theater and pivoting to a new security posture, while in theater the goal was to offload all responsibility onto the South Vietnamese. For all Army leaders, the media played a critical role in the war, and this meant that the Army's way of war had to evolve. For some, the men who came to control the Army's internal doctrine, this meant that the Army needed to find a way to avoid public oversight. For others, men whose voices would be heard increasingly in the coming years, a different solution needed to be found, a way of fighting war that integrated publicity concerns at a deeper level.

And so the immediate post-Vietnam period was marked by the suppression of a critical lesson: the media matter. Public affairs was systematically downgraded and removed from operational concerns through the doctrinal revisions made by DePuy in 1976 and by Starry in 1982, even though it was (contradictorily) increasingly an element of top commanders' daily lives. The period thus marks a divorce between operational and political strategic concerns but not a wholesale rejection of the political lessons of Vietnam. As the U.S. military confronted new operational challenges over the coming years, lingering doubts about the role of the media would continue to raise doubts in many senior officers' minds that the Army had learned the right lessons from Vietnam.

PART III
The Rise of the Political Army

6

RECOVERY

Small Wars and Organizational Renewal, 1983–1989

THE MEANING of Vietnam and the lessons of Tet were institutionalized during the 1970s through the principles of avoiding quagmires and minimizing exposure to media criticisms. The doctrine guiding the Army toward these goals were the *Active Defense* and *AirLand Battle* revisions of *Field Manual 100-5*, published in 1976 and 1982, respectively.[1] These manuals promised that quagmire could be avoided and exposure to negative publicity could be minimized by focusing on maneuvering forces and targeting fires. The logic here is quite simple. The manuals promised that if wars were fought in this new way, the first battle of the next war could be won so supremely that any such war would be fought with the Army on the offensive and ultimately concluding the war on its own terms.[2] There would thus be nothing much to criticize and not enough time for criticisms to affect the war.

Some aspects of this new thought would quickly be tested. Two small operations, one fought by the United Kingdom in the Falkland Islands in 1982 and the other by the United States in Grenada in 1983, allowed senior officers and military thinkers to reflect on the direction that the Army was moving in managing the press. Ultimately, despite the successful resolution of these small operations, Army leaders began to guide their institution away from the antipress bias of the DePuy–Starry era and toward a more nuanced balancing of operations and (mediated) politics.

The preceding chapter asked, Why did the Army of the mid-1970s pivot away from integrating political concerns into their operational doctrine despite the lessons of the Vietnam War? With this question answered, we can now ask virtually the opposite question: Given the success of this apolitical operational doctrine in Grenada, why did the Army turn back to the question of politics in the mid-1980s? Echoing Tet, Grenada's operational success would come to be viewed as a flawed model for the Army of the future. Political strategy, in particular media management, came to be recognized as a necessary component of the way wars of the future should be fought.

LESSONS FROM THE SOUTH ATLANTIC: THE FALKLANDS WAR, 1982

The turn away from democratic oversight as an operational concern was deeply integrated in the Army's doctrine in the early 1980s. Starry's comments about his distrust of the media mentioned in the preceding chapter suggest that feelings of betrayal led Army leaders to willfully ignore the media's latent capacities to affect military affairs. This is of course an incomplete story, and many other factors were also drawing attention away from the lessons of Vietnam. Regardless, DePuy's *Active Defense* and Starry's *AirLand Battle* reaffirmed the belief that the media had no place in war. In 1982, the same year that Starry published his revised manual, the Army received an unexpected object lesson in media management by way of the British Ministry of Defence's treatment of the press during the brief but high-profile Falklands War.

British media management of the Falklands campaign was highly restrictive, upending that country's long-standing tradition of a voluntaristic press model and mimicking at times the most repressive forms of censorship employed by the U.S. military in Vietnam.

Why did the British adopt this restrictive form of press control? In his official, two-volume history of the Falklands War, Lawrence

Freedman argues that press management had simply not been worked out, and although complaints by journalists were indeed recognized as an operational problem, the government's response was sluggish and ineffectual.[3] The point, of course, is that the Ministry of Defence discovered that its lack of preparation for managing the press worked out nicely for the war effort, despite journalists' discontent.

For readers of the *New York Times*, the war had already been covered extensively from the time that Argentine forces had landed on the Falkland, South Georgia, and Sandwich Islands on April 2–3, 1982. The British military response, with amphibious landings on the beaches near San Carlos on May 21, followed the cycle of reporting that had been established for major military operations during the Vietnam War. The day of the attack included multiple front-page stories along with explanatory stories deeper in the paper covering a variety of related issues. The front page featured a large-point banner stating, "BRITAIN SEIZES A BEACHHEAD IN FALKLANDS; CLAIMS 16 PLANES, REPORTS 5 OF ITS SHIPS HIT."

Although everything seemed normal enough on the front page, *New York Times* readers were offered criticisms of the British press controls in a short article on page 9. The unnamed author complained that "Britons given only 2 official reports during day" and described the press coverage as "a few scattered reports." Four days later, William Borders followed up this story with a long piece titled "British Journalists Voice Complaints Over Being 'Used' by the Government." Buried deep in the paper, the story described the "official secrecy and the arcane briefings system under which British journalists reporting on the Government work, complicated by the distaste the Defense Ministry has often shown for the press."[4] The criticism of press control was thus a minor note in a major story.

There is some debate on the degree to which strict press controls were either accidentally or deliberately restrictive. One historian notes that "the navy and the military were determined not to make the same mistakes as the Americans in Vietnam and sought to impose strict controls on media reporting. . . . Only 202 photographs were transmitted, most of these contrived by the military for propaganda use."

Unfortunately, the historian gives no source for this claim, and the accident hypothesis seems more likely. The Royal Navy allowed twenty-nine war correspondents and combat photographers (all British) to join in its fleet in its initial military response.[5] The journalists were reliant on the Navy's communications equipment to transmit their stories. Based on the example of the HMS *Invincible*, this restriction still allowed about 4,000 words of copy to be sent per ship per day, but so much material was being produced that this ship soon ran up a 1,000-message backlog, and the Navy soon limited the journalists' transmissions.[6]

This lack of preparedness served as a sort of natural experiment in censoring war correspondence in a mediated age. Did U.S. military leaders take their cue directly from the Falklands when preparing for Operation Urgent Fury, the invasion of the small island state of Grenada, the next year? The record is not clear. In an issue of the *Naval War College Review* published in late 1983, Lieutenant Commander Arthur A. Humphries of the U.S. Navy described archly the "unconventional wisdom" revealed by the public-affairs work of the British government in the Falklands: "Control access to the fighting, invoke censorship, and rally aid in the form of patriotism at home and in the battle zone."[7] Although later scholars view this mantra as evidence of the U.S. military's happy rediscovery of censorship, Humphries's article is rather more complicated.[8] For Humphries, the British approach to information was no better than the authoritarian Argentinian government's policies, and both were "two routes to the wrong destination."[9] Humphries acknowledged the moral concerns, criticized the means and ends of both nations, but then failed utterly to provide any contrary guidance—a good reflection, perhaps, of the ambivalence toward public affairs spreading throughout the U.S. military.

Although there are no clear indications that the Falklands War inspired the U.S. military's public-affairs approach directly, it seems likely that American PAOs would have recognized in the Falklands a sense of military authority that they had lost during Vietnam and might well have envied the British forces their illiberal press control. At any rate, similarly illiberal policies would indeed be enacted by U.S. forces with Operation Urgent Fury, the strange and sudden invasion of Grenada.

GRENADA AND THE AMERICAN EXPERIMENT IN PRESS CONTROL

The U.S. invasion of Grenada, despite its short duration and relatively small size, has given rise to considerable commentary. Both the Army's Center of Military History and the Joint History Office of the chairman of the Joint Chiefs of Staff have published detailed monographs on the topic, and several scholars have provided rich academic perspectives. From these sources, several points of consensus have emerged.

The invasion was intended to serve two goals. The first goal was to "rescue" the 600 or so American medical students and 400 or so other foreigners believed to be stranded in Grenada following a bloody coup.[10] The coup was led by members of a Marxist-Leninist revolutionary party against their own leader, Prime Minister Maurice Bishop, who had taken power four years earlier in a bloodless coup. Bishop was executed on October 19, 1983, at which time the party declared a "shoot-to-kill" curfew; however, it also claimed that the medical students were not in danger.[11] Fifty people were killed, the airport was closed, and foreign journalists were forced to leave the country.[12] The students told their parents they felt safe, and some of their parents telegrammed President Reagan to request he not take "precipitous action" against the new regime.[13] However, American spies had determined that armed Grenadians had confined the American students to their dormitories and that armed troops were guarding them (or keeping them hostage).[14]

The second goal was to check Soviet and Cuban influence in the Caribbean because these two countries had been involved in supporting the revolutionary Marxist-Leninist government of Maurice Bishop (and Cuba denounced the killing of Bishop).[15] Hundreds of Cuban workers were in fact in the process of building an airstrip and became entangled in the revolutionary operations.[16]

U.S. involvement was fairly rapid, although slow enough that approximately 600 reporters were able to gather at the jump-off point in Barbados.[17] U.S. forces (1,200 marines and 600 Army Rangers) departed Barbados on October 25, 1983, with soldiers from six Caribbean countries but without any journalists.[18] After forty-eight hours, hostilities had ended, and a pool of fifteen reporters were escorted to Grenada. Each subsequent day, more journalists were allowed into the pool to visit the island, until the ban was lifted entirely by the fifth day.[19] By December 15, 1983, all U.S. combat forces had left the island. Casualties included 18 killed and 116 wounded among U.S. forces; 45 killed (24 civilians) and 116 wounded among Grenadians; and 24 killed, 59 wounded, and 638 captured among the Cubans.[20]

RAND researchers Christopher Paul and James Kim attribute the restrictions to animosity toward journalists by the top military officers, who, they note, "had a strong dislike for the press and declined to take press coverage into consideration at the planning stage of the operation."[21] The media scholar Jacqueline Sharkey argues that the decision to block press access was made jointly by the White House and Pentagon before the operation was launched, citing a report published by Lou Cannon and David Hoffman in the *Washington Post* on October 27.[22] Cannon and Hoffman's report in fact suggests a deeper conflict within the White House. They claimed that the Pentagon pressured the president's staff not to inform the White House's own communications staff, including Larry Speakes, the White House spokesman, of the initial invasion by marines and Rangers on October 25. Speakes accordingly denied reporters' suggestions that the attack was underway, leading to the initial conflict with the press and then, when he discovered he was indeed wrong, leading him to complain in a memo to the White House chief of staff and to discuss possibly resigning.[23]

The Joint History Office, part of the Office of the Chairman of the Joint Chiefs of Staff, produced a ninety-page history of the operation that draws upon the records of that office. This source is particularly valuable because, rather bizarrely, the Grenada invasion was managed directly by the chairman of the Joint Chiefs of Staff, General John A. Vessey, who had been given operational control by Secretary of Defense Casper Weinberger. On October 22, 1983, Vessey imposed special restrictions on all planning-message traffic "to ensure maximum operational security." These restrictions were perhaps too little, too late because reporters had already revealed the previous day that U.S. warships were on the move. Vessey, channeling the theories of maneuver at the heart of *AirLand Battle* that stressed the need to attack with overwhelming force, responded to this loss of strategic surprise by moving even more quickly to strictly limit the circle of those informed about the operation. The result was that the relevant experts in logistics, civil affairs, and public affairs were left entirely in the cold. Ronald Cole, the Joint History Office historian, notes, "Their absence was felt."[24] All of this would tend to support Cannon and Hoffman's belief that Pentagon operational concerns somehow overcame normal White House protocol with very divisive effects.

How then should we characterize the relationship between the Pentagon's operational art and press policies for Grenada? Cole takes seriously the notion that Vessey's restrictions on the press were based on justifiable concerns for the safety of the marines and soldiers in the force. Vessey, for his part, defended the exclusion of reporters on an episode of *Meet the Press* on November 6, 1983, noting "we kept reporters out and a whole lot of other people out of that operation because we needed surprise and secrecy to have any chance of having the operation be a success under the terms we'd set for ourselves, and those were minimum casualties, not only for our own people but also for the people of Grenada."[25]

Although the Army historian Richard Stewart agrees that concerns about operational security were "a continuing theme" throughout the Cold War, in this case he characterizes it as an "obsession" and argues that by the time journalists were allowed to visit the island on October 27, "the damage to the media–military relationship had been done."[26]

In pursuit of an offensive art unencumbered by political concerns, Vessey made decisions that led to intense criticism from the press, which in turn created precisely the sort of political friction that had undermined operations in Vietnam. The difference, as Vessey, Starry, and everyone else knew, was that high-tempo operations could keep ahead of the political consequences and did so for the length of this short war. Nevertheless, in their RAND study Paul and Kim describe the Grenada invasion as "the low point in press–military relations to date," and forward-thinking generals might have anticipated that the political costs would eventually have to be paid.[27]

These critical perspectives might suggest that there was less coverage of this invasion than the previous military operations we have considered, but in fact Grenada received far more press attention. The fall of Saigon was mentioned in 135 reports in the *New York Times* in the two weeks following the event (more than Ap Bac, Tonkin, Tet, My Lai, or the Easter Offensive); Grenada was mentioned 442 times. It earned a full-page banner headline for two days after it occurred (October 26 and 27), then a three-quarter page banner (October 28), and then a half-page banner (October 28). It remained on the front page until November 9, a total of fourteen days. The sheer quantity of coverage, much greater than coverage of earlier Vietnam operations, was driven in part by the levels of competition among media outlets. Sharkey argues that reporting about press restrictions became a competitive news story in its own right, with evening news anchors on ABC, CBS, and CNN reporting on the public's support (or lack thereof) for freedom of the press in this situation.[28]

Several stories published in the *New York Times* forthrightly addressed the issue of press restrictions. On the first day of the invasion, October 25, 1983, the banner announced, "1,900 U.S. TROOPS, WITH CARIBBEAN ALLIES, INVADE GRENADA AND FIGHT LEFTIST UNITS; MOSCOW PROTESTS; BRITISH ARE CRITICAL." The front page included a detailed map of the offensive, a story by Michael T. Kaufman filed from Bridgetown, Barbados, a story by Hedrick Smith filed in Washington, DC, and a story by Barnaby J. Feder filed from London. As with the Falklands War, the front page looked normal enough for a crisis, but by the second day a critical story appeared (deep in the paper) concerning press restrictions. This story, by Jonathan Friendly and titled "Reporting the News in a Communiqué War," observed, "No reporters were allowed to accompany the invasion force . . . so the major stories were written by reporters in Washington, based on information given to them by State Department and other Government sources." Drawing a direct connection to the Falklands War and other foreign wars with no press coverage, Friendly also noted that his supervising editors were "wary of efforts by a government to minimize reports of its casualties."[29]

On October 28, a longer story reported that fifteen reporters were allowed to go the island but noted that the "furor continued over the limitations imposed on the coverage. . . . The Reagan Administration's policy on coverage has caused considerable consternation and suspicion among editorial writers and commentators."[30] A report deep in the paper on October 30 noted that *Newsweek* was barred from further trips to Grenada because one of its photographers had failed to return on the appointed return trip, prompting the editor of *Newsweek* to declare, "The Pentagon's policy of trying to hold an off-the-record war [is] totally outrageous and unnecessary."[31] Two days later, the *New York Times* carried an AP story announcing that "the American Society of Newspaper Editors protested to the Defense Department today over its refusal to permit reporters to cover the first stages of the invasion of Grenada."[32] In a long editorial published on November 4, Bernard Weintraub described the way the war was experienced by the correspondents, calling it "probably the most difficult conflict to cover" since Vietnam: "Long delays, canceled flights and frayed tempers were common." He described the daily schedule of waking up at 4:00 a.m. on Barbados, waiting around to board an 8:30 military flight to Grenada, only to rush back to the airport in Point Salines in the early afternoon to wait for hours for often delayed return flights.[33]

Although military control over logistics meant severe restrictions on newsgathering, journalists have also been assigned blame for what has subsequently been viewed as very poor quality of coverage. Greg McLaughlin, citing Peter Braestrup and Mark Hertsgaard, notes in his history of the war correspondent that journalists, despite their complaints about access, tended to accept press briefings and press releases on face value.[34] Restrictions on access, however, were very real; not only was *Newsweek* banned because of an itinerant photographer, but reporters attempting to access the island by sea were also turned back, with some claiming that U.S. Navy aircraft fired shots at them.[35]

When journalists are under intense professional pressure to produce content, and where their original newsgathering is blocked by their own military, it is hardly surprising that their critical perspective on the information they can access is diminished. Since this limited access aligns so precisely with military operational interests, only political pressures will be likely to convince military leaders to relinquish their press restrictions. A more complex and intriguing possibility is that these political pressures would be integrated into military doctrine, thereby preventing the cycle of operational planning obsessed with secrecy, followed by poor-quality coverage of the war, followed by press attempts to generate scandal over restrictions. The military interest here is based on the unpredictable public response to journalists' efforts to generate scandal as well as the unpredictable political responses to public outrage. Politicians and vocal members of the public hold enormous sway over the military's capacities through the yearly process of allocating funds to each service. For competent, professional Army leaders, however, the lives of their soldiers are of much more pressing value than the money the Army may forego in some hypothetical future. For press relations to exit the Grenada scenario, democratic oversight would have needed to be reintroduced as an operational, not just political, concern, a factor of contemporary war that could cost soldiers their lives.

THE SIDLE PANEL REPORT, 1984

The Office of the Chairman of the Joint Chiefs of Staff, empowered by order of Secretary of Defense Weinberger and occupied by the long-serving General John W. Vessey Jr., initiated an investigation into the military-media relationship following Operation Urgent Fury. The panel would be headed by a veteran press officer, the now retired Major General Winant Sidle, who as a young man had proposed a utopian press policy for the Presidio and who later was a leading figure in MACV's press office. His group released its report in August 1984.

Why did the chairman investigate press relations? David Kiernan attributes the immediate cause to a letter of protest sent to the DOD in January 1984 and signed by ten press groups, including two major wire services (AP and UPI) and the major professional organization for publishers, editors, broadcasters, and journalists.[36] Yet although this unusual expression of press solidarity and animosity surely increased the temperature of military-press relations, it may not have been necessary because Vessey had already set Sidle the task—or at least told the press he had done so. In his appearance on *Meet the Press* on November 6, 1983, he told columnist Joseph Kraft, "I have asked retired General Si Sidle, whom some of you may know—long in the public-affairs business—to try and head up a panel for me of experienced newsmen to help us decide how we can conduct military operations and protect the operation—protect our own people—and still inform the American people—how to do it in this modern age of the television camera and instantaneous communications around the world."[37]

In making its determinations, the Sidle Panel solicited opinions from the top press organizations and former war correspondents, and Vessey's office uniformly endorsed its report.[38] The panel met February 6–10, 1984, at Fort McNair in the District of Columbia. Although it had the full cooperation of the key news organizations, it did not include any working journalists because the media groups considered it inappropriate for a reporter to serve on a government panel. The panel did have several civilians, including three retired war correspondents (Keyes Beech, A. J. Langguth, and Wendell S. Merick); Richard S. Salant, the president and CEO of the National News Council; the scholar Scott M. Cutlip, long involved with training Army PAOs; and Barry Zorthian, the MACV information czar. The rest of the panel comprised officers representing the major public-affairs offices of each service.[39]

In addition to the experience and expertise of the panel members, the panel met for three days of public presentations from twenty-five "senior media representatives" as well as from the chiefs of the Army, Navy, and Air Force information organizations. The information chiefs of the Marine Corps and the Office of the Joint Chiefs of Staff as well as the assistant secretary of defense for public affairs presented informally during the two-day closed sessions that followed the public comments. About seventy reporters covered the open sessions.[40]

The panel came to eight recommendations, which I paraphrase here for the most part:

1. Public-affairs planning for military operations should be "conducted concurrently with operational planning."
2. In cases where press pools are considered "the only feasible means of furnishing the media with early access to an operation," the largest pool possible should be supported, and full access should be allowed as soon as possible.

3. The secretary of defense should investigate the possibility of maintaining a preestablished pool with up-to-date credentials and notifications.
4. The voluntaristic model of compliance should be brought back, with the minimal number of "guidelines or ground rules established and issued by the military," and violations should be subject to exclusion from further coverage of the operation.
5. PAOs should be granted sufficient resources to work effectively with the press.
6. Communication requirements should also be carefully considered by the military, although "these communications must not interfere with combat or combat support operations."
7. Operational planning should include provisions for transporting journalists in the field.
8. Top military PAOs should meet with news organizations "on a reasonably regular basis"; public affairs and especially media participation should be taught in service schools more effectively; commanders and line officers should visit news organizations more regularly; the chairman of the Joint Chiefs of Staff and the secretary of defense should meet with top broadcast-news representatives to prepare for the future scenario of "real time or near real time news media audiovisual coverage of a battlefield."[41]

All of the points quite directly reflected public-affairs failures of Operation Urgent Fury, but they also struck to the theoretical core of the maneuver-focused strategic paradigms of the day. By insisting on public-affairs involvement in planning (point 1) and requiring heavy operational investment in managing the media (points 2, 5, 6, and 7), the panel called for the military to fight slower, less secure battles whenever possible. The panel also called for the department to take steps to assure increased structural autonomy for the press (points 3 and 4), backed by a cultural shift to embrace the work of journalists as an operational concern (point 8).

It is impossible to say how much actual consensus was shared among the panel members and how much their eight recommendations were viewed as valuable insights into the new character of war—or instead as irritating distractions with possibly deadly consequences.

Having been brought out of retirement by Vessey personally and having served in Vietnam and in many of the top Army information roles to general acclaim, Sidle would have had considerable clout, and, accordingly, his views should be of special interest to us.

Although Sidle had retired in 1975, he had always remained involved in Army information concerns to some degree and had participated in a Senior Public Affairs Officer Course at the Defense Information School at Fort Benjamin Harrison, Indiana, in 1983. The Defense Information School published the speeches from that course along with questions and answers in a booklet titled *Vietnam 10 Years Later: What Have We Learned?* (1983). There, Sidle noted, "I'm not sure we learned too many lessons. They were there for the learning, but I haven't noticed any great change in how we are operating public affairs at the top level of government. We're still making the same old mistakes we made in Vietnam." For Sidle, the key lesson of Vietnam for the Pentagon was that the government's press officers, from the assistant secretary of defense for public affairs on down, should view their role as representing the views and interests of the press to their commanders rather than fighting the press on behalf of the government.[42]

Along with the failures in public-affairs leadership, Sidle observed general bias against the field of public affairs throughout the military. He noted, "The point is having an adversary relationship does not mean having an antagonistic relationship, and one of the problems since Vietnam that I've seen in a lot of the public affairs officers is that they hate the press and their commanders hate the press."[43] Even though the Sidle Panel Report, backed by Vessey, offered a clear vision of the centrality of media management to future U.S. military operations, it would be a tough sell to a department still deeply distrustful of the media and unconvinced of media as a genuine operational rather than simply political concern.

THE ARMY'S DOMESTIC POLITICS, 1982–1986

While journalists and press-oriented military insiders were signaling that there was a crisis in media–military relations, there were also gestures by the Army's top officers toward the importance of good relations with the public and of media management as a means of achieving those good relations. Despite DePuy's *Active Defense* manual and Starry's *AirLand Battle* manual, and despite the operational successes of Grenada, the importance of public support had not been forgotten entirely by the Army's chief of staff. During his tenure as top soldier, General Edward C. Meyer stressed on a few occasions the Army's great need to maintain positive relations with the public. As reflected in his collected works, the first occasion was on October 21, 1981, when in a speech to the Association of the United States Army he told his audience that "this has been a great year for the United States Army. . . . We have an Army today that's off of its backside and moving out smartly. Moving beside us are many others who are not in uniform: a firm civilian leadership, a supportive Congress, and a concerned public." However, this sense of solidarity would be lost later in the same speech when he sounded the refrain of irresponsible and operationally damaging press criticism: "Much of our self-criticism and that of civilian pundits which aims to correct legitimate deficiencies, instead targets unfairly the Soldier who's doing his damnedest with what he's been provided—and in the past that's been too little."[44]

Meyer would note his concerns about military–media relations again at the AirLand Battle 2000 Symposium on May 10, 1982, an audience more engaged with operational concerns than the Association of the United States Army community. At the symposium, he warned his audience that the Army's public-affairs offices were in a poor state: "The support of the American public is my greatest concern, for our support base is fragile, to say the best. And it is the one area I am least able to do a great deal about. It's certainly not that Defense [the DOD] hasn't got its share of attention lately. Quite the contrary. But it's been a little like the three-year-old at the TV set—the channel portraying the great need for national defense grows tiresome, so some are switching to another channel."[45] The three-year-old with the remote control may be the American people in this metaphor, but there is also implicitly a criticism here of the structure of journalism, which allows for enough choice that by implication viewers can ignore what really matters.

Meyer's replacement, General John A. Wickham Jr. (Army chief of staff from 1983 to 1987), was no stranger to public affairs. He had been the chief of the Eighth Army in Korea during the Ingman Range shooting incident, which received significant press interest and accordingly had conferred with the other senior officers on key investigative decisions. One division-level PAO, Colonel Michael Sullivan, recalled that there had been a "strong inclination on the part of Wickham and others to minimize the attention on the division."[46]

As Army chief of staff, Wickham appears to have been largely buffered from serious political concerns and was focused instead on restructuring the Army's personnel, maintaining morale, and investigating quality-of-life issues for soldiers and their families. The political buffer that shielded him was a result of a close professional relationship with Secretary of the Army John O. Marsh. Wickham recalled in an oral history that the two men would frequently walk through the door separating their two offices, meeting several times a day: "I would seek his opinion on matters of politic-military nature. . . . [We] had an excellent relationship." The close collaboration also extended to their two staffs. Likewise, the various joint chiefs enjoyed a good rapport in this period.[47]

Perhaps of equal importance to what Wickham did in his role as Army chief of staff was how he did it. He came to embody a new style of Army leadership that would prove influential in years to come as leaders sought to reconcile the uncivil character of a profession of arms with the changing dynamics of the public and civil spheres. Wickham stressed family values in place of militarism or Big Army machismo. He recalled in his oral history, "I don't believe in this old myth, 'if you aren't a whoring, hard-drinking, profane individual, you aren't a good warrior.' I think a good warrior need not have those attributes. So I tried to make a difference in terms of moral values."[48] Although Wickham was hardly the first mild-mannered general, he was perhaps the first to adopt a technocratic habitus with intent.

The *Annual Historical Review* of the Office of the Chief of Public Affairs for 1987 provides yet another window onto Army media management. The chief of public affairs in 1987 was Major General C. D. Bussey, who oversaw an active year. The top issues of media interest were typically diverse: the Army's antismoking campaign was first, followed by a scandal concerning NW Ayer, the Army's advertising agency. Other topics of interest were the experiences of African Americans in the military; the quality of personnel; the restructuring and reorganization of the Department of the Army; and reports of child abuse at West Point and the Presidio. Occupying center stage in the office's busy year, however, was the Worldwide Public Affairs Conference in October. As noted in the *Annual Historical Review*, "Many suggestions were made to improve the Army's public affairs program to include broadening career opportunities, improving professional development for PAOs, diminishing printed material in favor of a faster form of communication—DIALCOM, disseminating the 1988 Army theme in the PA [public-affairs] plan, establishing a research capability within OCPA and finally, emphasizing professional job performance commensurate with the PAO's position as a key member of the commander's staff."[49]

Also present at the conference was Wickham's replacement as Army chief of Staff, General Carl E. Vuono, who gave a long address. Vuono told his audience of public-affairs workers (active and reserve, military and civilian, officer and enlisted) that they were a central part of the Army team: "Public Affairs Officers are not a lot different than a guy running point in a squad somewhere. Think about it. You are all the point men[;] . . . you need to know what the boss is thinking, what his goals are, and what his vision is." However, the role of the PAO on the team was not always happily acknowledged, Vuono admitted: "Most commanders will give you the stiff arm because they say they are very busy. . . . There is also a natural distrust of the media on the part of a tremendous number of commanders." Vuono not only recognized this bias in other commanders but admitted that he used to hold it as well, although he had recently grown to respect PAOs. Accordingly, he assured his audience, "I will do my part and am doing my part to bring the commanders into a more comfortable feeling in dealing with external audiences. That takes time, because we have not worked at it as hard over the years in the Army as we should have."[50]

Having committed himself to the importance of media relations in particular and public affairs more generally, Vuono ended his speech with five priorities for PAO messaging in the coming months and years. First, he wanted them to help the Army recruit and retain higher-quality soldiers, in part by overcoming the World War II–era image of soldiers as Willie and Joe huddled in a foxhole. Second, he asked PAOs to make the case of the balance of forces—in other words, help move away from the Big Army heavy-arms and heavy-infantry bias. Third, he asked them to train harder, to gain practical experience in their fields. Fourth, he requested they promote Army modernization as equally important as the modernization of the other services, likely an attempt to align the Army with the technological symbolism associated with the Air Force in particular. Finally, he asked PAOs to help leader development: "We want to build and nurture selfless service, bedrock integrity, and an absolute, clear, unequivocal understanding that leaders set the example and that leaders know and enforce standards."[51] The five points reflect a clear movement away from the traditional symbols of the Army—the massing of infantry and heavy artillery on a conventional field of combat. Vuono encouraged PAOs to project in the place of these symbols a vision of a "modern" Army, adaptive, collaborative, and technologically sophisticated. This modern Army would be led not by the "whoring, hard-drinking, [and] profane," in Wickham's terms, but rather by media-friendly technocrats.

LESSONS IN MEDIA SENSITIVITY

From 1974 to 1988, the United States Army underwent two major doctrinal revisions (written up in the field manuals *Active Defense* in 1976 and *AirLand Battle* in 1982) and fought one successful operation (Urgent Fury, the invasion of Grenada in 1983). The doctrinal revisions suppressed awareness of and concern with the news media as a strategic actor, even though that strategic position had become obvious to many Army leaders during the Vietnam War. Meanwhile, the success of Operation Urgent Fury seemed to confirm the wisdom of these acts of suppression, at least on the battlefield. Nevertheless, Army leaders set about assessing the political problems associated with Urgent Fury. Surprisingly, they allowed themselves to be guided by a panel of public-affairs experts and ultimately concluded that media management needed to be reintroduced to Army doctrine as a high-level operational command concern.

Why did the Army initially suppress these lessons, and why did it decide to regain them? As we have seen, the suppression was obscured in part by overwhelming concerns with balancing new budgetary realities and new geopolitical forecasts. It was also likely caused by officers confusing their personal biases against journalists with their objective assessments of journalists' impact on the field. With these blinders in place, some Army leaders saw the Arab-Israeli October War not as a replaying of Tet, which was precisely how Egyptian planners saw it, but rather as an irresistible call to reinvest in conventional force. The political dimension of war was not entirely forgotten, however. Rather, it was collapsed into a single imperative: to win quickly before the chaos of domestic politics neutralizes military power. Although this perspective was at first unique to one individual, William DePuy, his effective bureaucratic maneuvering, his central bureaucratic position, and his canny promotion of his ideas allowed this vision of war, defined in his revision of *Field Manual 100-5: Operations*, to trigger intense debate and discussion. Although DePuy's shortcomings undermined the success of his manual, he did succeed in defining the debate to a large degree, and as a result the next revision was not only headed by DePuy's former collaborator, Donn A. Starry, but also stayed closely within the conceptual frame developed by DePuy. Observations of British press management during the Falklands War and failures among journalists to signal clearly from the outset just how tight those restrictions were surely gave guidance to some officers as to the possible extent of an apolitical operation.

Given the factors that contributed to the suppression of politics in the Army's operational art, it may seem surprising that the invasion of Grenada so quickly turned the tide. One counterbalancing factor that must be acknowledged is that this suppression was never absolute, and, indeed, many PAOs found plenty of work to occupy them and to justify their place in the force. Similarly, the chiefs of staff, in daily if not hourly contact with the politics of military affairs, were far less antipathetic to media management than their combatant commander counterparts. In addition, although the bias against reporters and the near obsession with maintaining security through speed led the planners of Urgent Fury to ignore press concerns, the outcry from journalists was sufficient reminder that these concerns were real. In compiling an expert panel to review the failures of Grenada, the Army naturally called upon several of MACV's leading figures, who duly restated the primacy of public affairs to the Army's operational future, which had been so obvious to them for so long.

The dilemma facing combatant commanders at the end of this period was whether to accept the increased costs (in time, money, and possibly lives) associated with following the Sidle Panel's recommendations or instead to adhere to the principles of rapid maneuver. Iraq would prove the testing ground.

7

THE TEST

Media-Management Regimes in the Gulf War, 1990–1991

T**HE EIGHT** lofty principles crafted by the Sidle Panel were presented to the Department of Defense in 1984. There, at the Office of the Secretary of Defense level, with its important assistant secretary of defense for public affairs role, the eight principles were distorted and diminished, whether through bureaucratic indifference or some more concerted effort at misunderstanding. By 1986, the Sidle Panel Report became little more than an imperative to make use of press pools (recommendation 2). This simplified version was then subject to testing over a period of five eventful years. The result was a series of lawsuits from media organizations, legions of outraged reporters and editors, and a popular new term for the media's influence over military operations, the *CNN effect*. Most importantly from the DOD's perspective, however, this version also worked as part of a massively successful operation, one that would stand as proof of U.S. military dominance from the end of the Cold War in 1989 to the shock of the terrorist attacks of September 11, 2001. Yet it would also provide a blueprint for pivoting from the pool system to a system at once better for the military and more appealing to reporters.

The "test" at the center of this chapter cannot thus be mapped directly onto the Sidle Panel's eight recommendations. Nor was it a test of the media's satisfaction with the rules. Rather, Army and other DOD leaders should be understood here as testing the effect of their new approach to media management (a far cry from what Sidle promoted) on short-term political pressure on the operation. The critical periods run from 1986–1987, when press pools were first used (domestically in Honduras and in Operation Earnest Will in the Strait of Hormuz), through 1989, when the pool was used (imperfectly) in Operation Just Cause in Panama, then from 1989 to 1990–1991, when the pool model was used to cover Operation Desert Shield in Saudi Arabia and Operation Desert Storm in Kuwait. Together, these periods can be viewed as a time of probing the effect of the press pool on the political sustainment of each operation.

THE FIRST DEPLOYMENTS OF THE NATIONAL PRESS POOL

The Sidle Panel Report made an immediate impact, but its standard interpretation was a far cry from what the panel members advocated. A student paper written by Major Kenneth S. Plato of the Marine Corps for his operations course at the Naval War College in 1991 is suggestive of how Sidle's eight recommendations were interpreted by the DOD public-affairs community. Written at the height of combat operations during Desert Storm, Plato's paper states simply that "the most prominent recommendation" of the Sidle Panel was to create a national media pool.[1] Tellingly left unsaid are the other recommendations, which were largely ignored by virtually everyone leading up to Desert Storm. In its original formulation, the development of a standing press pool was the second recommendation, one clearly flagged as appropriate when deemed "the *only* feasible means." The first recommendation was that "public affairs planning for military operations be conducted concurrently with operational planning."[2] In other words, operations planning should also be public-affairs planning, including the search for and development of alternatives to the use of press pools. This important distinction reflected journalists' strong dislike of the pool model, which they were willing to live with only when necessary to gain early access to an operation.[3] Indeed, the journalists who shared their insights with the panel were "unanimous in requesting that pools be terminated as soon as possible."[4]

The mere existence of the standing national press pool seemed to act against the spirit of the Sidle Panel recommendation to plan for alternatives. The pool system was simply there, ready to use. Notably, it had clear benefits from the Army's perspective, including the fact that it allowed the Army to control the framing of stories and closely monitor access.[5] We see evidence of military leaders experimenting with the compliance of the press pool as early as 1986, when a young officer named Larry Icenogle (then serving in the Pentagon's Defense Public Affairs Office) was sent with the newly formed national press pool to cover a yearly airborne exercise called Gallant Eagle.[6] An exercise in coordinating air and land units in a simulated conflict, the Gallant Eagle series was known to be quite dangerous. In 1982, a mass-casualty event had occurred when nearly 10 percent of all participants were reported as casualties, including six deaths.[7] This incident had naturally drawn much internal Army scrutiny and must have been viewed as a source of potential risk from a public-affairs perspective.[8] The exercise in 1986, viewed by the pool reporters who had been briefed extensively by Icenogle, also featured casualties (one death and several severe injuries), but the reporting by UPI and the AP was neutral in tone and implied no fault on the Army's part. The UPI report was particularly positive toward the Army perspective, quoting the Army spokesman at length, including the unchallenged statement that "everyone generally feels happy and satisfied"—notwithstanding the maimed participants or the family of the dead soldier.[9]

Scholars have failed to reconstruct the full early history of the national press pool and tend to erroneously place the first use of it in Operation Earnest Will on July 24, 1987. Even the most comprehensive studies miss many of the minor deployments scattered in the oral histories of PAOs.[10] Icenogle, for example, remembered multiple deployments in 1986 (none of which has previously been described in the secondary literature) to Honduras and domestically to Camp LeJeune (North Carolina) and Fort Campbell (Kentucky), in addition to Gallant Eagle.[11] These brief deployments likely contributed to normalizing the use of the pool in senior DOD circles. Those paying attention might have noticed that the pool reporting, shaped as it was by constant (if brief) socialization within a military environment and exclusive framing according to a military perspective, tended to go easy on the military.

Nevertheless, scholars are right to stress the importance of Operation Earnest Will, the first international deployment that led to major press coverage of a military action. In 1987, near the close of the Iran-Iraq War, Iran had significantly increased its attacks on Kuwaiti oil tankers as retaliation against Kuwait's support of Iraq. The U.S. interest was in supporting its ally, Kuwait, and in maintaining the global flow of oil. A quick solution was to reflag Kuwaiti ships under the U.S. flag and provide them a U.S. Navy escort through the Strait of Hormuz. Because this solution brought U.S. naval forces under risk of direct fire (albeit with a very small risk of actually coming under attack), the Office of the Secretary of Defense saw another opportunity to test the national pool in a highly contained environment and did so by sending a ten-person pool to cover the first escort mission on July 24, 1987.

Titled Operation Earnest Will, the mission was placed under the command of Rear Admiral Harold Bernsen, and the reporters would be stationed on his flag ship for the duration. Navy perspectives about the media at this time were not so far from the views of Army officers shortly after Vietnam. Both Bernsen and Chairman of the Joints of Staff Admiral William James Crowe Jr. were strongly against hosting journalists and skeptical of the potential effects of media coverage of the operation. It was Assistant Secretary of Defense for Public Affairs Dan Howard who fought to enact the pool and to place reporters closest to the firing line.[12]

To everyone's surprise, there was blood in the water after all, something to report. The *Bridgeton*, one of the reflagged vessels, hit a sea mine within sight of the reporters (who were reporting from Bernsen's bridge). The journalist Richard Pyle reported on the incident in an uncredited AP wire, which was followed up quickly by UPI and others. Despite their sometimes caustic tone, these reports were well received by the Navy, which was relieved to find no operational risk associated with the stories. For their part, the reporters were happy to have been in the exact right place at the right time.[13]

OPERATION JUST CAUSE

Less successful for all involved was the use of the press pool in Operation Just Cause, the brief U.S. invasion of Panama. The origins of the conflict lay in the clash between Presidents Ronald Reagan and George H. W. Bush, on one hand, and the Panamanian leader Manuel Noriega, on the other. During the Reagan era, U.S. Southern Command had pressured Noriega through a slow buildup of U.S. forces in the country. This strategy, headed by General Frederick F. Woerner, failed to impress Reagan's successor, Bush, who replaced Woerner with General Maxwell ("Mad Max") R. Thurman, known for his aggressive approach. Bush had brought in a new secretary of defense, Dick Cheney, in March and a new chairman of the Joint Chiefs of Staff, General Colin Powell, in October. Cheney's first task as secretary of defense involved debating how to get Noriega to retire. Powell, meanwhile, was already a familiar face, having worked closely with Bush on Panama issues when they had served together in the Reagan administration. The Panama problem was a constant concern at this highest of levels throughout much of 1989, triggering frequent interagency meetings and planning processes.[14]

Ultimately, Bush favored a small, quick, but decisive intervention. Thurman accordingly shifted from a pressure strategy to an operational footing intended to rapidly increase the forces in the country in order to launch a strike against Noriega. To that end, he assigned Lieutenant General Carl W. Stiner, U.S. Army, the task of leading a joint task force in a combat operation. The task force was mostly Army (22,000), but also included large detachments from each of the other services, 3,400 airmen, 900 marines, and 700 sailors, making it truly joint from an organizational perspective. The casus belli was provided by the killing of First Lieutenant Robert Paz, a marine, by Panama Defense Force soldiers, on December 17, 1989. Bush quickly announced Operation Just Cause. December 20 saw Stiner's Special Forces units attacking key installations throughout the country before dawn and land forces securing the U.S. embassy and capturing the Panama Defense Force headquarters by dusk.[15] Thus, the operation became an example of a successful joint operation achieving quick results, the template for Desert Storm.[16] However, these results, though quick, were not decisive, and the poor handling of press matters proved deeply troubling to many in the public-affairs community.

The quick tactical success reflected a years-long process of planning to undermine Noriega and remove him from power. Despite how this process had occupied U.S. military and civilian leaders' thinking so completely for so long, no one appears to have thought about the role of reporters. The operation fundamentally rejected the spirit of the Sidle Panel recommendations: planners failed to produce any public-affairs plan at all by the beginning of combat operations, completely ignoring the panel's first and most important recommendation.[17] Remarkably, the question of how to involve the press was not brought up until December 17, when the president raised the issue during final deliberations over launching the operation.

Equally significant was how the national press pool was used, another major transgression of the Sidle Panel guidelines. It was intentionally activated four and a half hours *after* the beginning of operations on December 19, timed specifically to avoid tipping off reporters until after the seven o'clock news. This decision was taken by Secretary of Defense Cheney, which he justified on the grounds of operational security.[18]

More broadly, the press pool model was irrelevant in Panama, which at the time was one of the few places in the region with a large resident U.S. press corps, already well established and capable of reporting accurately on events on the ground. Indeed, reporters in Panama had already begun filing stories about unusual U.S. military activity by mid-December, signaling the potential for an invasion, but journalists back in the United States mostly ignored those stories. Rather than pull the local reporters into the deployed joint task force and provide the missing pieces to those stories, Cheney preferred to pull in fresh reporters who would be reliant on the framing and access offered by their government public-affairs escorts.

The inappropriate use of the national pool had a cascade of negative consequences. The local chief of public affairs for the task force, Colonel Ron Sconyers, U.S. Air Force, first heard about the plan to invade on December 18, the day after the president gave the go-ahead. Sconyers assumed that he would be responsible for supporting the work of the Panama-based reporters and that the local reporters would be able to arrange their own transportation throughout the theater. As a consequence, he failed to book dedicated press helicopters. Sconyers also erred in how he managed the media center, which he set up to accommodate a handful of locals. The small number of phone lines proved a major limitation as the size of the pool swelled.[19]

The national pool was activated after the evening news on December 19 through calls by the deputy assistant secretary of defense for public affairs and staff, who anticipated that the pool reporters would receive notification from their employer more or less immediately and then have two hours to drive to Fort Andrews in Boston to catch the plane, observing total secrecy throughout. Unfortunately, several of the news bureaus were in the middle of their Christmas staff parties when the calls came, which contributed to both confusion and a wildfire of gossip. As a consequence, the reporters who assembled at the plane were often ill-equipped and in some cases were last-second replacements for colleagues not able to make the short turnaround.

Two thousand miles due north of Panama, in Chicago, the journalist Peter Copeland was one of the pool reporters unable to make the first flight. He was visiting family for the holidays when he received the call alerting him that the press pool was activated. Copeland was an exceptionally good candidate to cover the invasion, having previously acted as Scripps-Howard's first Mexico City–based Latin America correspondent and subsequently as a Pentagon correspondent. Copeland had developed particularly good relations with Army leaders when he had first arrived in Washington the previous year. In his autobiography, Copeland describes how the Army "cultivated" him, or "greened" him up, and, embracing the opportunity, he undertook a short tour of Army installations in the fall of 1989.[20] When his editor called him in Chicago on December 19, there was no chance he would make the press pool flight, so he set about considering alternatives. A Spanish speaker who had spent time covering related stories in Panama in previous years, Copeland would have a leg up if he could manage to get to the country. Sources at the Pentagon, however, informed him no flights would be allowed in for at least a week.

Down in Panama, the pool reporters chaperoned by Sconyers soon discovered the problems caused by a lack of helicopters and phone lines. Indeed, they were effectively stuck at a base far from the fighting, unable to follow the task force to the battle or get to Panama City to see the story through the eyes of the locals. In the days that followed, they traveled together in a group, accompanied by Sconyers, visiting places where there was no danger of enemy fire and where they were informed that they would not be allowed to photograph the dead, the wounded, or even caskets that would hint at American casualties (policy decisions that would prompt a lawsuit in 1991). These decisions appear to have been made independently by Sconyers acting as chief of public affairs for the task force.[21]

Copeland, meanwhile, flew to Costa Rica, where he met up with a group of equally frustrated reporters prevented from flying into Panama. The land border, with unknown parties holding the other side, was the only way in. This ad hoc press pool rented a bus and driver and drove across the border. On the Panama side, the bus eventually ran into a U.S.-held checkpoint, and Copeland, "speaking both Spanish and US Army lingo," was chosen to approach the checkpoint and bargain a way through. Copeland used his Pentagon press corps pass to convince the young lieutenant on the barricade to let them through, based on the lieutenant's mistaken belief that Copeland was a DOD civilian official of some sort acting as a public-affairs escort. Once through, the bus drove to Panama City, where the reporters scattered.[22]

Copeland explored the city on his own, filing stories by phone. He eventually decided to make his way to the U.S. base where the press pool sat cloistered. On the way in, he met a young female soldier and asked her about her experiences over the past three days of fighting. To his surprise, she indicated that her unit had a rather intriguing story to tell and directed him to her commanding officer, Captain Linda Bray. Knowing that a junior officer would expect a reporter to be escorted by a PAO, Copeland found a PAO and asked for an interview with Bray. Approval was granted, and he drew from her an unexpected story. The event revolved around a kennel for police dogs. Bray, a Military Police officer, was instructed to secure the kennel. Her unit soon discovered that the kennel was inside a Panama Defense Force military barracks and thus heavily protected. The subsequent firefight, commanded by Bray and including twelve other female soldiers, is today widely credited as the first instance of American women service members in a combat operation, and Bray is remembered as the first American woman to lead troops into combat. This story of women in combat—totally unexpected for most Americans, who generally believed female soldiers were excluded from combat roles—became a front-page feature in the *Washington Times* and probably the most significant story of the brief invasion.[23]

The story was, however, unwelcome in the eyes of senior leaders, both military and civilian, who were eager to prevent the invasion from becoming a debate over women in combat. Reflecting and reinforcing this view, the *Los Angeles Times* reporter John M. Broder wrote a follow-up that relied on Army general Bill McClain's assertions that Copeland's story exaggerated the incident, which then generated further stories about the dispute.[24] This critical reporting, which barely touched on the core issues Copeland reported upon, nevertheless was enough to cast a pall over Bray's efforts and the work of women fighting on the front lines.[25]

Operation Just Cause, enacted by Bush on December 17, 1989, ended on January 31, 1990. The planning process for the operation, which took years and involved many of the most senior people in government, ignored the Sidle Panel's first recommendation to plan for public affairs alongside planning the operation (see table 7.1). Military planners failed to develop a public-affairs annex for the operation, and the civilian leadership failed to think through an appropriate role for media to cover the invasion. Reporters already in place in Panama were ignored in favor of a hastily deployed national press pool from

TABLE 7.1 Eight Recommendations of the Sidle Panel Report (Paraphrased)

1	Public-affairs planning should be "conducted concurrently with operations planning."
2	News pool should be used when it is the "only feasible means" of reporter access.
3	News pool activation list should include either individuals or organizations.
4	Ground rules should be few, worked out for each operation, and followed voluntarily.
5	Public-affairs planning should include sufficient equipment and personnel.
6	Public-affairs planning should establish media communications capacities as soon as feasible.
7	Public-affairs planning should include provisions for journalists' intra- and intertheater transportation.
8	Media–military understanding and cooperation should be improved.

the United States. This pool deployed late; its members discovered that their access would be severely limited and that they were expected to follow arbitrary and excessively narrow ground rules of what could be reported upon. The few reporters who managed to access the field independently of the military did so through bluster and guile. Their reports were nevertheless largely positive, and yet when Copeland revealed an important new development in U.S. military affairs to the public as a result of his original and ultimately quite lucky reporting, senior officers worked to silence his story and undermine his credibility. These factors collectively pointed to civilian and military leaders viewing the press pool in instrumentalist terms as a tool that could be controlled by PAO escorts and press pool systems. Rogue reporters were a problem because they could not be controlled.

Much of the preceding information is known to us because of a nineteen-page report filed by Fred S. Hoffman to the new assistant secretary of defense for public affairs, Pete Williams (a former journalist).[26] Hoffman painstakingly pieced together the decision making of all the principals involved in the operation, revealing the lack of public-affairs planning, the decision by Cheney to stall the pool until four and half hours after combat operations began, and the poor facilities and limited access given to members of the pool. His report ended with seventeen recommendations for future operations, listed in table 7.2, which should be read in relation to the Sidle Panel's eight recommendations, given in table 7.1.

Although more focused on the mechanics of the pool, Hoffman's recommendations echo Sidle's in that both argued for public-affairs planning to take center stage and for senior officers to signal to the force their commitment to supporting reporters through the work of PAOs. Hoffman believed "excessive concern for secrecy" was to blame for many of the problems.[27] In 1992, Major Colleen L. McGuire of the U.S. Army wrote a thesis at the U.S. Army Command and General Staff College in which she agreed strongly with Hoffman that the Panama press pool simply "didn't work well" and that there remained a lot of work to do in educating the military on "how to talk to and manage the press" upon entering Desert Storm/Desert Shield.[28] In the overlap between the Sidle Panel and Hoffman report recommendations lies

TABLE 7.2 Seventeen Recommendations of the Hoffman Report (Paraphrased)

1	Secretary of defense should issue guidance supporting public-affairs efforts.
2	A public-affairs annex should be added to all operational plans.
3	Deputy assistant secretary of defense for public affairs should closely monitor all public-affairs plans.
4	Chairman of the Joint Chiefs should issue guidance supporting public-affairs efforts.
5	Assistant secretary of defense for public affairs must be prepared to challenge the secretary of defense and the chairman of the Joint Chiefs on public-affairs matters.
6	Chairman of the Joint Chiefs should be informed of status of media pool throughout operations.
7	Assistant secretary of defense for public affairs should consider use of two pools.
8	The national media pool should never again be herded as a single unit.
9	The pool should be exercised once per quarter with units most likely to deploy.
10	Senior operations officers should brief pool members.
11	Assistant secretary of defense for public affairs must ensure adequate staffing.
12	Assistant secretary of defense for public affairs should consider adding an editor slot to the pool.
13	The pool should not be escorted by the chief of the Plans Division but by appropriate officers.
14	Pool members should share all pool products with all elements of the industry.
15	News organization costs should be shared by pool members.
16	All pool-assigned reporters should attend quarterly sessions to discuss rules and responsibilities.
17	PAOs from unified commands should meet with pool-assigned reporters.

the singular dilemma facing PAOs—namely, the challenge of changing the minds of the Army's senior leadership and creating a serious command-level commitment to getting media management right.

TRAINED AND READY: THE ARMY AS STRATEGIC INSTRUMENT

Army leadership in the late 1980s was well aware that the geostrategic environment and hence the Army's own role in providing security were undergoing rapid change. Even before the end of the Cold War, the possibility that the Army would be involved in a major combat operation was viewed as remote. Although Army leaders often congratulated themselves on having steered the Army back into the good graces of the nation (reflected in ever-rising confidence polls), they clearly recognized that the goal of a seven-division, 718,000-soldier force was politically unsustainable. Quick, decisive engagements were called for under the Army's own *AirLand Battle* doctrine, a model that seemed to have been successfully tested (despite some minor press complaints) in Grenada and Panama.

For Army chief of staff General Carl E. Vuono, what was needed was evolution, not revolution. Speaking to Leavenworth students in 1987, his first year in the position, he described two "major responsibilities" guiding his efforts at change: combat readiness and modernization. The two had more than a little overlap between them. Combat readiness was broadly conceived as including getting better at jointness; getting doctrine, especially joint doctrine, right; contributing to strategy; and making the job more rewarding to improve retention. Meanwhile, modernization was less about hardware and more about working differently. Under this umbrella, he placed downsizing, increased reliance on the reserves, as well as improving command and control. Both aspects of his thinking stressed the Army's anticipated future reliance on its sister services in conducting joint operations. The message was fuzzy: the future would include joint operations, a smaller force, and a smarter set of policies to make the most of what remained after downsizing. Unclear was what those future operations would look like, but many of Vuono's contemporaries assumed they would be small wars. Vuono was quick to minimize the importance of contributing to small-scale operations such as Earnest Will in the Persian Gulf, which he dismissed as "something in a contingency area," and reasserted the Army's duty to be ready for large, conventional operations. The students, however, were less sure, and possible Army involvement in Earnest Will and the Persian Gulf region attracted most of the questions.[29]

Outside observers began to question why the Army was needed at all, given that the Marine Corps was already around to conduct small, quick operations. In a widely discussed *Washington Post* editorial on November 15, 1988, one respected military thinker, Jeffrey Record, predicted the end of the Army in the coming decades. Record, then a senior research fellow at the Hudson Institute, argued that an Army geared toward "high-intensity mechanized combat" was no longer relevant and would be superseded by the Marine Corps, which had "a more active political constituency."³⁰ Vuono responded in a letter to the *Post* that flatly rejected Record's suggestions, ignored the question of the Army's political constituency, and stated instead: "The challenges of low-intensity conflict also are complex, and we have prepared our Army to meet them. . . . We have learned the lessons of the past. We have fielded an Army able to meet the challenges of today."³¹ The challenge for the Army was to acknowledge the importance of low-intensity operations while refusing to concede that the other end of the scale was not still equally important.

Although Record and Vuono's exchange was fairly civil, it did shake Vuono enough that he felt it necessary to write a letter immediately to all Army general officers expanding on his thinking. This letter, dated the day after his *Post* piece was published, underscored the political stakes as he saw them and the need for generals to get out and actively promote the Army's public image: "Now is the time to ensure we portray a fully accurate image of the Army's current trained and ready status. . . . I expect Army leaders to provide the facts to the American public in a straightforward and timely manner."³² "Trained and ready" was Vuono's personal slogan for an Army capable of matching Marine Corps competencies at the small end of the scale, while retaining its deterrent and conventional capabilities at the large end of the scale, something for everyone, with nothing critical sacrificed for the sake of downsizing (evolution, not revolution). His force would have to do more with less, which would be made possible by a much-increased reliance on the reserves as well as smarter doctrine, better training, and better collaboration with the other services.

Given Vuono was pursuing a reform mandate based on guiding the Army through difficult choices in its organizational structure, it is not surprising that he focused on shoring up the perception of the force domestically. The message had to be that the Army was an unparalleled strategic tool, not only critical for deterrence and security in Europe (which justified a large force) despite a crumbling Soviet Union but also newly competent at things as varied as disaster relief, emergency assistance, drug interdiction, and peacekeeping—all the sorts of exotic operations the Marine Corps was eagerly conducting. Vuono naturally focused on the importance of public affairs to convey this difficult message, and he repeatedly stressed public affairs to commanders throughout his time as chief of staff. In an address to the Army's public-affairs community in October 1989, he told the assembled PAOs, "It is no overstatement to say that what you do in the next several years will help determine the shape of the Army in the next century." Of course, the traditional Army aversion to media matters was still a problem. Recognizing that many of his audience members' bosses were probably still skeptical of public affairs and wary of the media, he concluded by directing the PAOs to "develop for your command and your commander a comprehensive communications strategy.... Public Affairs cannot be a passive activity.... You must reach out and press ahead with programs to convey the Army message and to confirm the realities of our strategic role."[33]

In his most significant policy program as chief of staff, Vuono synthesized his thinking in a White Paper, which was distributed in January 1990. He argued, "The Army is assuming increased prominence in U.S. national security strategy," exactly the opposite of what the report by Jeffrey Record had claimed two years earlier.[34] For Vuono, the Army needed to excel at both small- and large-scale operations if it were to continue to justify its existence. When the White House began to talk about a direct confrontation with Iraq and its enormous, million-man force, Army leaders saw an ideal opportunity to sell the policymakers and the public alike on the new, hyperprofessional Army force, "trained and ready" for everything from Panama to Kuwait.

OPERATION DESERT SHIELD: THE FIRST POOL

The media management of Operations Desert Shield and Desert Storm began in earnest with the deployment of the national press pool on August 11, 1990. Desert Shield, the operation designed to bring U.S. forces to the theater, and Desert Storm, the combat operations that followed, were born from the same regional tensions that had pulled the press pool into the Strait of Hormuz during Operation Earnest Will. At that time, the Iran-Iraq War was in its final stages. A cease-fire had finally ended open hostilities between the two nations in mid-1988, but peace was fleeting. For a year, Saddam Hussein busied his forces with plans for an invasion of the oil-rich U.S. ally Kuwait, previously the target of Iranian attacks. Then 100,000 Iraqi troops crossed the border into Kuwait on August 2, 1990.

Desert Shield was conceived as a means of staging a U.S. force in bordering Saudi Arabia without risking direct engagement with Iraqi forces in either Iraq itself or Kuwait, effectively buying time to transition to combat operations with a coalition of partner states. Thus, Desert Shield was fundamentally reliant on Saudi hospitality for the reception and staging of forces.[35] This critical partnership took four days to hammer out, but by August 6 U.S. forces began to deploy to Saudi Arabia on a mission to protect the Saudi state and its oil fields. Operation Desert Shield was officially announced on August 8, by which point 15,000 soldiers were already deployed to Saudi Arabia.

Chief of Staff Vuono, speaking to the Army Operations Center staff in the basement of the Pentagon on the day of the announcement, typically stressed the information aspects of the coming conflict: "Coordinate, anticipate, and verify—make sure of your information; make sure you have the complete picture, and keep the forces in the field informed."[36] Nevertheless, members of the press saw yet more proof that the military was not taking press needs seriously as forces deployed because the pool remained inactive. On August 9, the *New York Times* reporter Michael Wines evoked memories of Panama: "For the second time in eight months, American troops today headed into a foreign military operation without the special contingent of reporters and photographers that the Pentagon has pledged to summon when United States forces are sent abroad." The story explained that Secretary of Defense Cheney once again used secrecy considerations to justify the delayed deployment, while Assistant Secretary of Defense for Public Affairs Pete Williams added that the delay was the fault of the Saudi government, which was uncomfortable with the presence of a foreign press in residence (a fairly unconvincing claim given the press could deploy on ships as they had done in the region four years earlier). Wines quoted the AP's Washington bureau chief in describing this delay as "outrageous."[37]

Although a relatively minor challenge, buried as it was fairly deep in the paper, Wines's story was enough to convince Pete Williams to call for the pool to be deployed.[38] Unlike in Panama, the use of the pool made plenty of sense in this case because not only were U.S. forces deploying somewhere that lacked a resident press corps, but they were also deploying to a country without freedom of the press and with no foreign reporters.

Direct management of the pool was entrusted to Lieutenant Colonel Larry Icenogle, who, as a former member of the Defense Public Affairs Office, had previously chaperoned the pool in its early domestic deployment to the Gallant Eagle exercise. Icenogle had left the Defense Public Affairs Office for the Army War College two years earlier. When activated for the assignment in 1990, he expected it would last for a week or two. The selection of Icenogle reflects both the small number of Army officers recognized as having skills in this arena as well as the intimate and ad hoc arrangements that characterize so much of this story. Icenogle happened to be a former classmate of Williams's new deputy assistant secretary of defense for public affairs, Bob Taylor. Taylor had heard about Icenogle's experiences with Gallant Eagle and thought of him for Desert Shield. With only a day to prepare, Icenogle was brought from Carlisle, Pennsylvania, to Washington, DC, where he first took leadership of the pool and then led the pool to U.S. Central Command (CENTCOM) headquarters in Tampa, Florida.[39] There, CENTCOM commander General H. Norman Schwarzkopf Jr. met the reporters and provided an on-the-record briefing, described by one reporter later as "clear, colorful, and to the point."[40] The reporters were given a chance to file a pool report based on the briefing before being rushed onto Army aircraft to fly to Dhahran, Saudi Arabia. They arrived in the early afternoon on August 13.[41]

There were seventeen reporters in the August pool activated to deploy to Saudi Arabia.[42] Seven were journalists (referred to as "pencils"). Three had previously covered Panama, including Peter Copeland (Scripps-Howard), who had bluffed his way into Panama and broke the "women in combat" story, as well as Frank Aukofer (*Milwaukee Journal*) and Jay Peterzell (*Time*), both of whom had been in the Panama press pool, and neither of whom had managed to find much there to report.[43] The other print reporters were Jim Adams (Reuters), John King (AP), Mike Ross (*Los Angeles Times*), and John Ydstie (NPR). There were three photojournalists: J. Scott Applewhite (AP), Martin Jeong (UPI), and Dennis Branch (*Time*). Finally, there was also one television crew, a CNN team led by Carl Rochelle and including camera operators and a technical crew (chosen over ABC, NBC, and CBS only because it was CNN's turn in the rotation). These seventeen reporters would be the only foreign reporters in Saudi Arabia at the time of their initial deployment, and all the material they produced would be released as pool reports to the rest of the media. The catch was that they could not report on "critical information," which included numbers of troops, aircraft, and other equipment; names of installations and locations; security precautions; any information about plans for future operations; the names and hometowns of U.S. military personnel; and photographs that would reveal anything about the level of security at installations.

August 13 was spent unpacking and getting settled in Dhahran International Hotel. Icenogle, who had been in the position of pool manager for two days by this point, had only a four-day window of activities approved for the pool to cover but packed the schedule with as many visits to U.S. units as possible. It was "a very, very ambitious itinerary," and by the fourth day the reporters asked for a pause to catch up on their reporting and do maintenance on their equipment.[44] Hundreds of newspaper articles were published in the seven days from deployment to August 19. John King, the AP's pool member and "the one who sat at the keyboard" to pass along the pool reports early in the deployment, was credited with stories with the revealing headlines "So Far, the Enemy Is Heat" and "Culture Shock from Saudi Arabia."[45] The real story—*"Americans at War"*—had not yet broke, so the big news was coming from Washington and other capitals, where policymakers and military planners were crafting the operation to come, rather than from camps scattered around northern Saudi Arabia. Furthermore, now that the Saudi royals had accepted the pool reporters, they quickly reconciled themselves to accepting others as well. "By sundown on the 18th," Icenogle recalled, "there were around 50 or so international news media organizations" in addition to the pool.[46]

This first attempt at a Desert Shield press pool was quickly overcome by events. Much like how Copeland and other reporters had found their own creative ways into Panama, nonpool reporters from the United States and around the world found their way into Saudi Arabia. Icenogle described the intensity of media interest from the public-affairs level: "We were simply overwhelmed, outmanned, undermanned, outgunned." From the reporters' perspective, the Desert Shield pool system, despite the delay in deploying along with the initial U.S. deployment, ultimately did more or less what it was supposed to do: provide privileged and otherwise impossible access to units and commanders to create a level playing field for competing news organizations in covering highly secure and diplomatically sensitive matters. The Saudis' decision to open their country to other reporters quickly made the pool irrelevant, and by August 24 the pool was dissolved, with all news agencies granted equal access through an open-access model.[47] Most of the pool reporters were recalled home shortly after that, although several returned on multiple occasions.

Notably, two of the most prolific pool reporters would come to regret how the ground rules in the first pool compromised their reporting without them even being aware of it at the time. Both Peter Copeland and Carl Rochelle note separately that by being forced to speak in such general terms about the U.S. units they encountered, they inadvertently greatly exaggerated the perceived size of the force, thereby aiding the mission's strategic communication goals.[48]

TRANSITIONING TO OPERATION DESERT STORM

Icenogle's participation in the first Desert Shield pool was expected to last a week or two but ended up extending to September 8, almost a month. His boss at the Army War College recalled him (he was replaced by Lieutenant Colonel Arnold Laidig), but in December he was allowed to return to Saudi Arabia to help set up the combat press pools. The 50 or so nonpool reporters had now swelled to somewhere between 800 and 1,500 reporters in theater, in addition to new Pentagon-managed combat pools. In the meantime, reporting rules had repeatedly been updated and refined as the small public-affairs staff found ways to work with the ever-increasing number of reporters. During the deployment of the first pool in August, Vuono had directed Army PAOs to stress the message of the Army's professionalism: "Our success in this critical endeavor depends on the skill and courage of the soldiers who are on the move to Saudi Arabia and on the unrelenting professionalism of the entire Army."[49] Even before the pool was disbanded, the Army public-affairs office in Washington recognized that reporters were swarming installations and directed that all Army personnel be briefed on five principles: emphasize the Army's professionalism; maintain operational security; do not discuss critical information; do not respond to hypothetical questions; and treat all discussions with the press as "on the record."[50]

When the first pool was disbanded on August 24, the initial strict guidelines were relaxed slightly to allow PAOs to confirm names of service members and unit designations. Reporters were required to be constantly escorted by PAOs and to travel only on military transport.[51] The rules on releasing names were tightened again in mid-September as the Iraqis demonstrated their resolve to remain in Kuwait, making kinetic operations more likely. They were again modified in October to encourage the naming of service members in "hometown coverage" stories, a decades-long Army media-management strategy intended to generate political support for troops among their families spread throughout the country.[52] At this point, there were more than 250 reporters in the theater, and the Army had major practical problems with ensuring there were enough PAOs to shepherd them all. In a sort of triage move, to minimize critical reporting the public-affairs policy was changed yet again to attempt to keep reporters away from newly arriving units: "Until a unit receives its equipment and moves to its operational area, there is little for the media to cover except the conditions surrounding the soldiers; some of which are less than desirable."[53]

In the months after the initial press pool deployed, the hundreds of journalists in Saudi Arabia found the military's strict control efforts to be increasingly claustrophobic. A major report on ABC's *Nightline* on October 10 provided a typical perspective. The report cut between reporters in the field interviewing soldiers who refused to be filmed and PAOs carefully directing combat photographers where to shoot and when. Peter Copeland was one of the reporters on the scene when the footage was taken and described his experiences. A PAO greeted the pool reporters, which included an ABC camera operator, with a clear attempt at controlling the story: "I don't want you to ask anything negative. I want you to accentuate the positive."[54] The PAO might have taken more care with his words had the light indicating that the camera was recording not been covered with tape. Instead, the TV crew captured the PAO's attempt to shape the story. Forrest Sawyer, host of the *Nightline* segment, described the dilemma facing reporters such as Copeland: "Military commanders have announced a policy of complete cooperation with the press and assigned dozens of information officers to handle requests for information. It is simply unprecedented. But for all of that, are you really getting an accurate picture of what's going on? Many reporters say no. The U.S. military, they claim, is waging a public relations campaign, keeping real problems and mistakes out of sight and the public in the dark."[55]

Later in the segment, the *Newsday* reporter Patrick Sloyan and the AP reporter Richard Pyle were interviewed, along with the Navy captain Michael Sherman, director of the Joint Information Bureau (JIB). The discussion was heated. Sloyan accused Sherman's JIB of refusing to help, called it "a waste of time" to deal with the JIB, and accused the JIB of being directed by Cheney and Pete Williams at the DOD to "spin" the narrative in the military's favor. Sherman dismissed this accusation as "absolutely ridiculous. . . . I haven't received one iota of guidance in terms of blockage from anybody in Washington."[56] JIB staff were likely emboldened by the fact that the public was sympathetic to the Army's position. In Copeland's words, "People back home were rallying behind the troops. . . . ABC took a lot of calls, all saying the whining reporters should shut the hell up."[57] A survey conducted by the *New York Times* in January 1991 and published on January 31 had provided a similar perspective on the public's attitudes: 57 percent of respondents believed "the military should increase its control over reporting of the war."[58]

The public-affairs policy documents we can now access confirm the suspicion that PAOs received guidance to push the positive and direct away from the negative. For Sherman, the decision to deny reporters access to units that were not fully stood-up may not have seemed like "blockage" but rather a sensible precaution. Reporters evidently felt differently. However, the deeper conspiracy hinted at by Sloyan—that civilian principals were actively intervening to limit access—is not supported. No such intervention was necessary: the assistant secretary of defense for public affairs (Williams) and the Army public-affairs agencies knew well enough how to guide press interest toward the good stories and away from the bad.

Things came to a head in early January 1991 when Sloyan was again featured on TV, this time on CNN's *Crossfire*, debating with Assistant Secretary Williams. Sloyan and fellow journalist Ike Pappas of CBS took particular aim at the escort system, with Sloyan arguing that PAO escorts "would interrupt your interviews . . . Big Brother stuff. It's really bush-league censorship," and Pappas comparing Desert Shield to Vietnam: "They're trying to get away with it again."[59]

Also featured on the program was the conservative commentator and politician Pat Buchanan, who argued that tactical successes in Grenada and Panama had occurred alongside tight restrictions, thus entitling the military to continue this approach. Williams dismissed Buchanan's position and accepted the criticisms leveled against media-management policies in Grenada and Panama, stating emphatically, "The Pentagon would be the first to tell you that the way Grenada and Panama were handled were [sic] not good at all." However, in defense of the pool system, Williams claimed that most reporters (if not Sloyan and Pappas or, indeed, Pyle) were happy with how the pool was deployed in Desert Shield, citing Jay Peterzell and Frank Aukofer, two of the original seventeen deployed pool members, as strong supporters.[60]

It is telling that Williams could cite only those two reporters as supporters. Stanley W. Cloud, *Time*'s Washington bureau chief and hence Peterzell's boss, was one among many journalists uncomfortable with how Williams used Peterzell's words to suggest broad media support. Describing Peterzell as "normally the most sane of journalists," Cloud noted that Peterzell somehow "found himself a complete apologist for the pool system[;] . . . he even sent a memo, to his undying discredit, which Pete Williams goes around quoting all the time." Peterzell reportedly changed his opinion later in the war, although his perspective is not otherwise preserved for the historical record. Frank Aukofer, by contrast, was a trenchant critic of the military's management of the press from Grenada through to the end of Desert Storm, so it is unclear how Williams came to believe Aukofer was also a supporter of the military's management of the press.[61]

Major General Bill McClain, the same Army leader who had attacked Copeland's "women in combat" story two years earlier, was now serving as the Army's chief of public affairs. He was tracking the growing tension between reporters and PAOs and reached out to a familiar source for comfort and advice, the long-retired Winant Sidle. Sidle's letter to McClain, coincidentally dated the day the *Crossfire* episode aired, focused on figuring out the total number of journalists who could be effectively managed by Army PAOs; Sidle's advice was that McClain should determine this number "generously." Sidle further told McClain that once the highest capacity was identified, the Army should put in place a pool system that would provide guaranteed spaces for major news agencies and rotating positions assigned fairly to smaller news agencies. This system should include foreign journalists as well, based roughly on the share of the operation taken by each nation.[62]

If we reflect on the implications of Sidle's advice, it seems that Sidle was effectively advising a two-tier system. First, and most presciently, accredited journalists should be embedded (but without using that word) in units. Second, and equally important in Sidle's view, all other legitimate journalists (those who missed out on pool accreditation) should be provided extensive rear-area press centers, sufficiently resourced with communications equipment and knowledgeable subject-matter experts that the journalists can produce stories without having to resort to finding their own outside Army management. Sidle concluded his guidance to McClain by stressing four principles he felt Army leaders and PAOs should abide by at all times: help reporters, admit your mistakes, stress your accomplishments, and get to know the reporters personally.[63]

As Desert Shield wore on, the fundamental issues touched on in Sidle's guidance, both in his letter to McClain and in the Sidle Panel recommendations, continued to gain in importance in the eyes of lawmakers. The catalyst was a series of legal cases brought by news agencies against the DOD, culminating in a hearing before the Senate Governmental Affairs Committee on February 20, 1991, on the very precipice of major combat operations. The named parties in the lawsuits were *The Nation* magazine, Agence France-Presse, and

J. B. Pictures, Inc. The first two cases were combined because both addressed the DOD's right to impose restrictions on newsgathering in military operations, based on concerns about the First and Fifth Amendments. The third was brought by a professional photographers' association (with other parties) and concerned the closing of Dover Air Force Base to photographers seeking to photograph the arrival of the bodies of American service members killed in the Persian Gulf. The issues at stake here were strictly First Amendment concerns.[64] While these cases were being filed, tensions between journalists in the theater and PAO officers were worse than ever, with new, tighter restrictions imposed on PAOs on January 12, 1991, intended to prevent service members from speculating about the imminent war.[65]

The ground rules for transitioning from the buildup of Desert Shield to the war reporting of Desert Storm were set during the first two weeks of January. On New Year's Day, Larry Icenogle (having returned to the theater and now serving as deputy director of the JIB) assembled the reporters now in the Persian Gulf for a long meeting in the ballroom of the Dhahran International Hotel. There, "we went line by line, paragraph by paragraph, through the proposed ground rules. Very tough, very acrimonious, often bitter disputes, debates. We tried to work everything out."[66] It is unclear what matters were debated, but there is evidence to suggest that the original draft included much more severe restrictions than had been in place in August 1990. For example, there was an attempt to ban "ambush interviews" of senior officers, an item that disappeared entirely from the agenda after harsh criticism by reporters.[67] The meeting stretched to the following day, at which point the PAOs took their notes and went to work developing guidelines that would be more acceptable. It took the Public Affairs Office all the way to January 16 to set down two pages of ground rules and guidelines that the reporters accepted.

The twelve ground rules closely resembled the rules governing the August Desert Shield pool: reporters still could not report on "critical information," which included numbers of troops, aircraft, and other equipment; names of installations and locations; security precautions; information about future operations; the names and hometowns of U.S. military personnel; and photographs that would reveal the level of security at installations. The first few restrictions were loosened somewhat so that reporters could use general terms to convey the number of things. Additional restrictions were created to cover the shift to combat: rules of engagement could not be discussed, nor could troop movements, Iraqi capabilities, downed aircraft or missing ships, special-operations methods, and any vulnerabilities in U.S. forces. Damage and casualty, notably, could only be described as "light," "moderate," or "heavy."

In addition to these restrictive ground rules, all media personnel had to follow general guidelines for comportment. Participating in night operations required strict "light discipline" (i.e., caution in the use of flashlights and other forms of lighting equipment), which was at the discretion of the on-scene commander. Media personnel still had to be escorted by a PAO and were strictly limited in what they could reveal of casualties and deaths, and access was to be approved through the CENTCOM combat pool, which would also review all material for sensitive information.

At the same time as PAOs in theater were working with reporters to get those restrictions accepted, the major DOD public-affairs offices were meeting to figure out the logistics of the combat news pool. Sidle had cautioned that such logistics was the most important decision and in his opinion should be organized to include as many reporters as possible, with the most support possible in the rear theater for those not deployed. The decision was taken on January 30, 1991, to have two 18-member pools covering the Army and Marine Corps, one 5-member pool on Navy battleships, one 7-member pool covering Navy aviation, and one 7-member pool covering the Air Force. In addition, there was a "quick-reaction" 7-member pool and, added at the last minute, a 7-member pool dedicated to covering the Seventh Corps (bringing the Army's pool total to 25). This meant only 69 reporters would be responsible for covering the entire operation, which by the end of January had swelled to include nearly 600,000 coalition forces.[68] Furthermore, the reporters left behind were effectively ignored by PAOs.

OPERATION DESERT STORM: THE COMBAT POOL

When Peter Copeland returned to Saudi Arabia for another round of reporting on Desert Shield in January 1991, he found that the pool had been reactivated as a combat pool. He also found that he was no longer on the roster. He tried to join up with units he met in the field but was chased away by Military Police. He eventually turned to his fellow reporters for guidance in the hope that he could figure out a way to join an activated pool, only to discover that the frustrations and professional jealousies among the hundreds of sidelined reporters had made the community exceptionally unwelcoming. Icenogle told Copeland, "These guys [the reporters] are cutthroat. I wouldn't want to be in a trench with any of them." Rather than find together ways to break the military's tight control over the field, the reporters endlessly fought over the handful of slots that would periodically open up and worked to prevent each other from finding alternative solutions. "The military could not have planned it any better," in Copeland's view.[69]

The ratio of 69 reporters to 600,000 troops was clearly a problem to Larry Icenogle. He recalled, "Where we did things right in August [1990], things started to go wrong in January [1991], if only because there were so many forces, so many units, so few reporters actually involved in covering those units." In contrast to what Sidle had advised McClain earlier in January, little was done to help the hundreds of reporters not selected for the pools: Icenogle remembered that they "remained in the Dhahran/Riyadh area, were left with virtually no help from guys like me whose charter was to run the combat pool." Thus, in the minds of the PAOs the larger pool was separated from the activated pools, with everything geared around the reporters in the field rather than including the larger community of reporters waiting passively for the pool reports to come to them. The solution to the problem was to deploy more pools. Icenogle recalled, "We right away knew there was no way 69 people could possibly cover all the combat units that were going into combat, and combat service units, of all the services that were going to be involved[;] . . . we, Central Command, should have made sure that as many pools that could be formed were equipped and sent out to link up with all the units. That did not happen."[70]

The problem was compounded by the fact that some commands in the theater resisted accepting press pool members in the units and would find ways to sideline them. Icenogle described the conflict between Major General Ronald H. Griffith, commander of the First Armored Division, and Doug Jehl of the *Los Angeles Times*. Jehl covered the division's arrival during Desert Shield, noting in a report that there were shortfalls in supplying the unit. Griffith took offense at this suggestion of poor management and placed Jehl under the direct supervision of the unit's chief of staff to strictly monitor and limit his access—a poor use of the chief of staff's time and a poor reward for Jehl's honest reporting.[71]

Many commanders discovered a simple means of buffering themselves from close oversight by journalists: they had their PAOs talk them to death. The famed AP correspondent George Esper criticized PAOs as delivering "death by briefing," long and uninformative slideshows intended to sideline reporters. Esper also noted the punishment doled out to reporters who ignored the requirement to be accompanied by a PAO escort, noting how the AP reporters Fred Bayles and John King (a member of the original Desert Shield pool) were detained by Military Police when discovered in theater without a PAO escort, and their credentials were sent to the Saudi government in the hope of having them ejected from the theater.[72]

At the DOD level, this sort of bad-faith engagement with the press was enough of a concern that on the day the air campaign began, January 18, Secretary Cheney issued guidance that stressed the need for honesty: "Information will not be classified or otherwise withheld for the purpose of protecting military organizations, units or individuals from criticism or embarrassment. All news will be reported as forthrightly, as accurately, and as expeditiously as possible."[73]

Not all relationships soured, however, and the JIB began to notice that the best relationships emerged with the reporters who had deployed the earliest and stayed the longest. There, reporters and soldiers bonded over shared dangers. Icenogle recognized in this relationship a potent alchemy: "They [the reporters] weren't co-opted[;] don't get me wrong, they were not part of the team, but they were living and working right alongside the people that were going to undertake this operation. They were at risk."[74] The JIB viewed this embryonic form of embedding reporters as producing the most positive stories.

Copeland, who had missed out on snagging any of the sixty-nine deployed pool positions, covered the start of the war (a massive air campaign) from his hotel room, watching it live on CNN. He was, however, one of the lucky few to pick up a slot when CENTCOM opened an additional seven-member Air Force pool on February 17. His pool was placed at an air base in the Saudi city of Taif, close to Mecca. The air campaign was in full swing, and Copeland and the other reporters gathered stories told to them by returning pilots. They filed their stories with the PAOs, who faxed them over the military's fax line to the JIB, which took two days to process them. Copeland noted, "When our pool reports eventually appeared on the TV and radio, it was fifty hours after we had filed. By then they sounded stale and not interesting."[75]

Frustrated, Copeland caught a military flight back to Riyadh, where he ran into a source he had used on a story years earlier. This unnamed source "risked his job and his high-level security clearance" to tell Copeland exactly where to go to be ready when the land campaign began. Working outside the pool system, Copeland used that insider knowledge to find supportive people within an artillery unit who accepted his presence and assigned him a PAO. Thus, he was already deeply embedded with a small company, eating and sleeping with them, even sitting in a howitzer as the soldiers he was covering first fired on Iraqi forces. Since he had arrived on his own rather than through the pool system, he enjoyed the benefit of unlimited access to soldiers but was denied regular access to the leadership of the unit, located in the Tactical Operations Center. Oddly, his public-affairs escort decided to return to the rear shortly after hostilities began, which should have ended Copeland's coverage, but he was again fortunate in finding a protector: once Copeland explained the situation, the commander, Colonel Morris J. Boyd, told him to stay even without the PAO. Copeland was then presented with a golden opportunity: he could remain embedded with the troops and be briefed by Boyd daily on the operation or could be "read in" to the battle plan and effectively embed in the Tactical Operations Center itself. To do the latter, Copeland had to commit to staying for the duration of the operation, an offer he eagerly accepted. Under this new arrangement, Copeland filed his story with an intelligence officer, who approved it and allowed him to send the handwritten report to the pool via returning soldiers. Copeland continued to file this way throughout the "100 hours" of the ground war, without any further review by the intelligence officer or anyone else.[76]

Others had the opposite experience. Carl Rochelle recalled that reporters on the USS *Missouri* were largely confined to their quarters simply because the commanding officer was intolerant of the press.[77] Lynne Walker, who had pooled with the Third Armored Division, found herself at the end of the land campaign about to cover the cease-fire negotiations between Schwarzkopf and his counterparts in the Iraqi military when a PAO she had previously disagreed with excluded her from the pool at the last minute. As she instead changed plans to leave the theater, yet another PAO with whom she had previously disagreed tried various ways to bump her from her flight. In her words, "Up until the very end they were thwarting our lives."[78]

LESSONS FROM EARNEST WILL TO DESERT STORM

Desert Storm was covered by hundreds of reporters, maybe up to 1,500, depending on sources.[79] As with the invasion of Grenada, coverage of both Desert Shield and Desert Storm was far greater in quantity than in comparable periods of the Vietnam War. This was a reflection of the expanding and fracturing mediascape, which now included twenty-four-hour news channels. There was an insatiable market for Desert Storm reporting—especially reporting that came straight from a combat zone and especially live-television reporting. CNN, ABC, CBS, and NBC, among dozens of other networks globally, produced live-to-air content, revealing an intimate portrait of war that captured the American public.

The hero was not the war correspondent but the soldier, emblem once again of a trusted and often beloved institution. By the beginning of the 1990s, the Army was already well on its way to repairing the damage of the Vietnam era, moving toward its transition to most-trusted institution in American public life. Undergirding reporters' efforts to present the war to the American public was a system of control, sometimes graceful, sometimes awkward, managed on the front line by PAOs.

Although live footage was not subject to review, it was inevitably framed and contextualized by PAOs and frequently by commanders, who briefed reporters directly. Unlike television reporters, the other journalists (photo, radio, pencil) were subject to security review, which sometimes went smoothly but often enough led to heavy-handed censorship—or merely took too long, wasting the material's news value. Furthermore, most of reporting was done under conditions of pooling material, which allowed the trickle of reporting made by the dozens of pool-deployed reporters available to the hundreds left behind. Far more so than during Desert Shield, only a very small fraction of reporting on Desert Storm came from those intrepid reporters who made their own way onto the battlefield and found stories outside the framing and contextualizing done by PAO briefers and escorts.

The lessons of this situation were ambiguous. Army commanders who were intolerant of the press and eager to prevent effective reporting found themselves sufficiently empowered to do so. These media-averse officers appear to have been relatively rare in command positions, however. The lessons of Vietnam had trickled down, and many commanders welcomed reporting pools. As we see in Copeland's case, some commanders even provided privileged access to reporters they felt they could trust, fully abiding by Sidle's highest principles for good relations with the press. Reporters, for their part, found the public less willing to hear criticism of the military than they expected. In addition, as much as they disliked the pool system, the competitive realities of the media industry meant that there were always plenty of reporters willing to fight for the rare spots in the pool, affirming the legitimacy of the pool system. Lacking a clear mandate yet motivated by the looming threat of legal cases brought by unhappy news agencies against the DOD, the DOD's public-affairs community was faced with defining the lessons from the five-year-long test of press pooling. At the close of the war, it was impossible to say which elements of the new public-affairs architecture would be brought forward into the new millennium.

8

LESSONS LEARNED AND NOT LEARNED, 1991–2000

THE GULF War, as it was then called, provided complementary lessons for lawmakers, media professionals, and military officers. Each of these three groups arrived at its conclusions largely independently from one another, and each is explored in turn in this chapter. A series of hearings and a major report helped convince members of Congress that the military had its media relations well in hand. Journalists were not so easily assuaged. Key actors in the media industry worked collectively to push forward recommendations that aligned in spirit with the Sidle Panel recommendations (which had been so poorly implemented during the war). Although some in uniform continued to view the media as an annoyance, doctrine writers and many forward-thinking officers came to a quite different conclusion, and by the end of the 1990s a new set of policies had been created that finally placed media management at the center of military operations.

The media-management developments within the Army were echoed at the joint level, and in the subsequent decades the story of Army public affairs has given way to a new story of joint, Allied, interagency, and comprehensive public affairs, but that story lies beyond the purview of the present volume.[1] As such, this chapter concludes the six-decade story of Army media management.

MAKING SENSE OF DESERT STORM: THE VIEW FROM THE HILL

Media management by the Army (and, more broadly, by the Department of Defense) was a topic of fundamental interest to lawmakers throughout the duration of Desert Shield and Desert Storm but of rapidly diminishing interest thereafter. Two Senate committees, the Senate Governmental Affairs Committee (SGAC) and the Senate Armed Services Committee (SASC), held detailed hearings on the conduct of the war, the first with special focus on the role of media access to the battlefield. In addition, the Pentagon's final report on the war, required by Title V of the Persian Gulf Supplemental Authorization and Personnel Benefits Act of 1991, included an appendix (albeit a short one) on media-management policy. These three collections of documents (the two hearings and appendix S of the final report) provide important clues into how the military was internalizing the lessons of the war with respect to media management—what was being learned and what was being suppressed. More directly, the reviews appear to have ended congressional interest in the topic, allowing military leaders to craft internal DOD policy without close oversight from Congress.

THE SGAC'S PENTAGON RULES ON MEDIA ACCESS TO THE PERSIAN GULF WAR, FEBRUARY 20, 1991

Attempts to come to an agreement about the restrictions placed on reporters covering Desert Storm were ongoing throughout the operation, as indicated in chapter 7. Amid the air campaign and on the eve of the land campaign (February 20, 1991), the SGAC held a day-long session to debate the Pentagon's rules for media access to the battlefield. Three matters formed the crux of the debate: the escort system, the pool system, and the security review (or censoring) by the JIB. The committee heard from eleven of the most central figures in the recent history of the Army's public affairs. The witnesses representing the media's perspective(s) were prominent journalists: Walter Cronkite (1972's "most trusted man in America"), Malcolm W. Browne (famed Vietnam War photographer), Frank Aukofer (from the Panama and

August Saudi pools), Cragg Hines (*Houston Chronicle*), Sydney Schanberg (*Newsday*), and Paul McMasters (*USA Today*).[2] The military perspective was represented by Assistant Secretary of Defense for Public Affairs Pete Williams, architect of the current system, as well as the familiar figures Winant Sidle, Barry Zorthian, and Fred Hoffman. They were joined by the retired Army colonel Harry G. Summers Jr., a frequent guest on *NBC News*, where he commented on military matters, including Desert Shield. The committee came to no conclusion, but the hearings provided a template for thinkers in the military public-affairs community to make sense of the de facto "tests" of the pool system from Gallant Eagle to then ongoing Desert Storm.[3]

The issue of the escort system was the least contentious of the three debated topics. Of the eleven witnesses, Browne, Hines, McMasters, and Summers ignored the question, preferring to speak more generally about media access through the pool system. Both Cronkite and Schanberg opposed the use of escorts on the grounds that reporters should be free to access U.S. forces on their own. In Cronkite's words, "With a rational censorship system in place, the press should be free to go where it wants when it wants, to see, hear and photograph what it believes is in the public's interest." Only Browne, who, like Cronkite, had become a living legend among reporters, described positive experiences with "some" escorts. Sidle and Zorthian stressed their concerns that in practice escorts tended to overstep their responsibility. Zorthian thought escorts should simply escort, not monitor. Sidle went further, though, to say escorts should not simply escort but rather actively guide reporters to the stories that interest the reporters (and certainly not monitor them). Williams, defending the system he built, agreed that some escorts were either too controlling (*monitoring*) or insufficiently helpful (*not guiding*) and said, "The idea of an escort is not to have a hovering presence" but rather an officer who can help.[4]

The use of the security-review process received sharply differing perspectives. Aukofer, Hines, and Cronkite dismissed it as a source of concern. Cronkite argued, "There should be censorship on all dispatches, film and tape leaving the battle area" in order to protect soldiers. This argument evoked World War II–era policies and seems strangely out of place in an era of live TV reporting. Cronkite likely meant something more along the lines of McMasters's observation that "everyone agrees there must be some information withheld from general dissemination during wartime." Williams himself noted that the security-review system could not be applied to live broadcasts, which instead relied on reporters voluntarily following the rules (and being allowed to set up in places deemed appropriate by the military).[5]

The issue, then, was whether reporters should censor themselves or should submit their work to the military for security review. The committee heard many damning examples arguing against the latter option. Browne talked about the experience of his colleague John Fialka, who had several stories about Seventh Corps held up in the security-review process for seventy hours, only to get the revised reports back with a single change, the addition of the word *perhaps*. The delay was "long enough to destroy their use." Schanberg described how profanities attributed to soldiers were being censored. McMasters likewise described "petty editing, such as changing 'giddy' to 'proud.'"[6]

Colonel Summers, the witness with the least experience on the topic, warned the committee that "reporters are giving aid and comfort to the enemy[;] . . . legislation may serve a useful purpose"—which, like Cronkite's statement on censorship, sounded strangely out of place. Fred Hoffman, who had written the report on the use of press pools in Panama, held quite the opposite position. He told the Senate that the military should "abandon any requirement for security review of news products." Sidle also doubted whether a security-review process would be practical during the combat phase of the war and criticized the use of the security review of reporting more broadly, arguing it should be replaced by reporters choosing to abide by the ground rules and being disaccredited if found in violation. The Vietnam-era information czar Barry Zorthian stated simply that the military should "provide as much official information as possible—accurate, candid, timely, complete—as part of its accountability to the public" and that the media should "provide an independent accounting of these same activities as a check on the military's accuracy and validity."[7]

The pool system was the centerpiece of discussions, and on this point only Williams spoke in its favor. Williams quoted two journalists who had participated in the August 1990 press pool as evidence that the wider community of journalists was supportive. He loosely quoted the CNN correspondent Carl Rochelle as saying, "I am more satisfied with the pool shoot I just came off than any of the others I have been on."[8] On its own, this statement sounds like rather tepid praise from a single reporter regarding a single positive experience. Williams added Jay Peterzell's glowing comments from a letter Peterzell had sent Williams directly. Williams, however, was the only witness prepared to support the pool, and it seems likely neither Peterzell nor Rochelle was eager to be associated with supporting it by this point in the campaign.[9]

Rather than critique the pool system, Mal Browne stressed the accomplishments of those who circumvented the system, noting that "some of the most interesting and, by the way, positive reporting coming out of this prelude to war, if I may call it that, is coming from these loners, these mavericks, who are, in fact, going out on their own." Others were even more direct. Paul McMasters described the combat pools as a "mess," and Sydney Schanberg argued that "the caging of the press in the Gulf has nothing to do with military security, it is an act of political security done out of fear that a free flow of information about the war could change public opinion." Cragg Hines of the *Houston Chronicle* provided the committee with likely the most memorable metaphor to describe the pool system: "Covering a war by pools must be something like phone sex, judging by the middle-of-the-night television ads. It sounds safe and easy, and with enough imagination you could get the job done, but you instinctively know there is a better way."[10] Both Hines and Aukofer based their complaints on the unintended (or perhaps intended) effects the pool system had on the dynamics among journalists in the theater, contributing to an extremely competitive environment where reporters fought each other for places in the pool rather than worked toward finding original sources and stories.

Among the witnesses speaking from a public-affairs perspective, it was Summers, the most conservative voice, who spoke most critically: "Pool restrictions on the press [in the Gulf] are dumb. They create the erroneous impression that the military has something to hide." Hoffman, reflecting on the problems previously identified in Panama, told the committee that there was "no justification now for limiting coverage to officially-sponsored pools." Not surprisingly, Sidle offered the most nuanced position, defending the continued use of the pool system in part based on the impossibility of transitioning to a full coverage system when there are so many reporters present. Sidle calculated that to be equivalent to the Vietnam-era ratio of fielded reporter to size of force, CENTCOM should increase its number of deployed pool reporters to 150, up from the 69 that had been the original target. However, Sidle believed that CENTCOM was fundamentally mismanaging the pools that had been deployed. Reporters were kept in pools throughout their deployments. Sidle felt that the pooled reporters should instead be transported to the theater and briefed together by the local commander, but then dispersed or at least encouraged to spread among the subordinate units to find their own stories independently.[11] This understanding of how the pool system should work was almost completely the opposite of how Williams managed it in practice.

SASC'S REPORT ON OPERATIONS DESERT STORM AND DESERT SHIELD, APRIL–JUNE 1991

The SASC's eight days of hearings focused on the kinetic aspects of the war, with testimony primarily from tactical commanders from each service. The committee's perspective on the war was evident throughout, with Chairman Sam Nunn assuring star witness General H. Norman Schwarzkopf Jr. that the committee had been "extremely impressed with all of the officer and enlisted personnel who carried out your operations plan, and we understand why you are proud of them. So are we." Addressing Schwarzkopf, Nunn praised him personally and stated unequivocally that in the SASC's view the operation was a job well done: "General, you have our heartfelt gratitude for your foresight, your planning, and your inspired leadership in executing your plans to fight the war, and for achieving your objectives with a minimum loss of lives on the part of the United States and coalition forces." For his part, Schwarzkopf's testimony reaffirmed the Army and DOD view that the war was a near-total success. He attributed this success in large part to "the unwavering support of the American people."[12]

Despite this generally glowing assessment, Schwarzkopf did take pains to stress his problems with the media, particularly with what he referred to as "Friday morning quarterbacks." By this, he meant essentially civilians who second-guess the military's planning. As he explained to Senator John McCain, since the Vietnam War "there have been many, many people . . . who have said, where have all the leaders gone . . . people who, prior to the time we ever launched the battle plan, were already critiquing it." Although Schwarzkopf here had in mind some private citizens who wrote directly to him with criticisms of his performance, it becomes clear later in the testimony that his main concern was no less with public figures—journalists and pundits—questioning the military: "The Friday morning quarterbacks do not bother me much except for the fact that it does tend to erode the Nation's confidence in their military leadership, and I do not think that is warranted."[13]

Like Colonel Harry G. Summers Jr., who had testified in the February SGAC hearings, but unlike the more knowledgeable experts who had also testified at that time, Schwarzkopf viewed the press as a potential security risk—not because journalists were inclined to publicize classified information but simply because punditry debating military policy risked tipping the coalition's hand to its enemy. Schwarzkopf took serval minutes to complain bitterly about "people that feel free to go ahead and make a detailed analysis and publish it during a time of war which could eventually endanger the forces."[14]

These fears are strangely out of place when set against the actual use of the media described by tactical commanders in the SASC hearings. None of the other witnesses indicated concern with classified information being released to the public or with sensitive plans being debated openly by pundits. Senators instead heard from several marine officers about how the Marine Corps relied on their semi-embedded reporters to report on events that they wanted Iraqi forces to know about in order to gain various sorts of advantages. Senator

William S. Cohen, seeking clarity on this point, participated in a revealing exchange with Major General Harry Jenkins of the Marine Corps:

> SENATOR COHEN: It was part of our plan and part of our strategy to let them [i.e. Iraqi forces] know by telling the media that we were doing it, right?
> GENERAL JENKINS: Yes, sir.[15]

The contrast is illuminating: the Vietnam-era anger toward the media plainly lingered among some Army officers, coloring Schwarzkopf and Summers's views of the press; no such anger is evident among these marines, who had found a use for journalists in advancing the goals of their mission. Meanwhile, the journalists' and public-affairs experts' grievances voiced during the earlier hearings in February, never resolved, were entirely forgotten in the senators' rush to praise the military for its operational successes.

CONDUCT OF THE PERSIAN GULF WAR: FINAL REPORT TO CONGRESS, APRIL 1992

The United States Congress received a final report on the war in April 1992. The 1,360 pages of the report include only a single seven-page appendix on media policy. This appendix reduced the question of media management to four accomplishments (rapid establishment of the pool system; enablement of access to the front line; enablement of access to troops; and frequent briefings with commanders), three shortcomings (uneven command support; poorly trained PAOs; too many "overzealous" PAOs), and one so-called issue: "media sources have voiced dissatisfaction with some press arrangements, especially with the media pools, the need for military escorts for the news media, and security review of media pool products." The lawmakers who were the main audience for the report were reassured that this issue was being addressed: "DOD is working with news media representatives on ways to improve news coverage of future US military combat operations."[16]

WHAT THE MEDIA LEARNED FROM DESERT STORM

THE SEARCH FOR PRINCIPLES

Although the *Final Report to Congress* suggests that the military was slowly internalizing the importance of media management for commanders, this subject was not of particular interest to journalists. Rather, media agencies had repeatedly petitioned the Pentagon to adopt specific reforms intended to improve access and restrict direct military oversight. The concerns voiced by public-affairs experts before Congress in February 1991 were taken up again after the cease of hostilities when on April 15, 1991, a group of fifteen editors and bureau chiefs from the leading news outlets met to discuss their complaints regarding the military's media-management offices during Desert Storm and Desert Shield.[17] Two weeks later, these elite members of the press wrote an open letter to Secretary of Defense Dick Cheney alerting him to the frustration they felt and on June 24 followed up with a list of ten principles they felt the DOD should abide by in future conflicts.[18] They argued for the end of the clumsy security-review process and the limiting of the pool system to the first thirty-six hours of an engagement, after which reporters should be free to travel with any military unit on military transportation with assistance from well-resourced PAOs.

Cheney was personally dismissive of the concerns, noting in a response published in *USA Today* on June 27, 1991, that the public, far from feeling outraged at the mistreatment of the press, was supportive of the military and happy with the coverage. Nevertheless, Cheney met with the group in September and directed Assistant Secretary of Defense for Public Affairs Pete Williams to work with the group to negotiate the proposed principles. Following a difficult and lengthy series of meetings stretching from January to May 1992, the media group and DOD reached an agreement on nine of the ten principles proposed. The outlier was the use of a security review: the DOD insisted a review system be instituted, while the media representatives stated they would not comply.[19] The final result of these meetings are discussed later in this chapter when the DOD's media policy after Desert Storm is examined.

While the DOD worked on creating policies to manage the press in future operations, a new wrinkle emerged complicating the lessons of Desert Storm. On August 12, 1991, Patrick Sloyan, the *Newsday* reporter who had been so critical of the JIB and of PAOs back in January, broke a story about a friendly-fire incident that had occurred on February 26. Through investigating this one incident, the *Newsday* reporting team discovered that "more than half the US army deaths and injuries during the four-day Desert Storm ground war were the result of friendly fire. . . . [S]enior officers described the level of such incidents as 'staggering' and 'a disaster.' "[20] This information had been gathered by Army investigators but was suppressed within the DOD, and families were misled about causes of death. Despite the frequency of such incidents, reporters had failed to observe or report on friendly fire.[21] These statistics provided critics of the military's media management with evidence that the DOD's glowing self-assessment (accepted by Congress for the most part) was misleading in fundamental respects.

THE WOUNDED PRESS

Following Sloyan's revelations of a cover-up and the difficult process of negotiating principles for media management in future operations, a survey by Captain Jay C. Steuck, U.S. Air Force, was distributed among the editors of the country's highest-circulation newspapers. Steuck's goal was to extract lessons on what did and did not work during the war. He sent the survey to 200 editors between February and April 1992 and received 58 responses. Unsurprisingly, the editors expressed mostly negative attitudes toward the use of press pools (only three respondents felt there were "No Problems" with the system, and the rest indicated negative opinions) and the JIB (receiving only a 9 percent approval rate), which was viewed as less cooperative and less capable than press escorts. Most notably, Steuck found that only half of the respondents felt that Gulf War coverage was accurate and credible (52 percent "Agree," 14 percent "Neutral," 28 percent "Disagree").[22]

In the period immediately following Desert Storm, there was widespread condemnation by reporters from across the news media (including television, radio, newspapers, and wire services) concerning the use of press pools, PAO escorts, and security-review processes. Some journalists, such as Frank Aukofer, felt much of the blame lay with his colleagues. From Aukofer's perspective as the bureau chief for the *Milwaukee Journal*, major news agencies had supported the pool system because it provided their reporters with an advantage over reporters from smaller outlets who were less likely to be included in the pool.[23] As described in chapter 7, such dynamics contributed to an extremely competitive and antagonistic atmosphere within the media. Even these major agencies, however, ultimately came to view the arrangement as a negative. Thus, the period after the war resembled, in certain respects, the period after Vietnam, with evidence slowly emerging of dirty tricks played by the military and a broad sense of outrage and dissatisfaction among reporters concerning the military's media policies. Unlike the period after Vietnam, however, after Desert Storm unhappy members of the media found little in the way of public support for their concerns, nor did they enjoy any political support from Congress. Reduced perhaps by the reasonable belief that the DOD was indeed listening and learning from the media group's complaints, the tensions on the ground between the press (in particular correspondents covering national security and the Pentagon) and their immediate military counterparts largely evaporated, replaced by unexpected attacks on the press by intellectuals and academics concerned with the mediation of war as such.

CRITICAL FRAMES

The immediate post–Desert Storm framing of the war, advanced by critical members of the press, was that the military, despite its noteworthy accomplishments on the battlefield, acted in bad faith toward the press and toward the public's interest in transparency. Alternative framings soon emerged, however, that stressed the corrupting (or corrupted) role played by the mass media in presenting the serious matter of war to the public in ways that struck some observers as cynical, manipulative, or, indeed, exploitative.

The broadest critique came from the famed French sociologist Jean Baudrillard, who on January 4, 1991, published an influential essay in a French newspaper arguing, per its title, that "the Gulf War will not take place," despite the fact that the United Nations Security Council had approved the use of force a month earlier.[24] Following the ground war in February, Baudrillard's critics, taking his title literally, observed his apparent failure of prediction. As a result, he published two more essays, "The Gulf War: Is It Really Taking Place?" and "The Gulf War Did Not Take Place," which soon appeared as a book under the title of the third essay. The book was translated and published in English in 1995, triggering vast discussion and debate.[25]

Baudrillard's memorable and dramatic title referred not to the facticity of the conflict—whether the things reported by journalists really happened—but rather to the conflict's supposed virtuality. Baudrillard's discussion of the virtual aspect of the war blended two forms of mediation: by a wide range of novel military technologies, which created simulations of reality to achieve kinetic effects, and by journalists, PAOs, commentators, and others who framed and represented this reality (already mediated by military technology) to a global audience. For Baudrillard, these twin and doubled forms of mediation affected the world more fundamentally than did the events of the war because the virtual war demonstrated and enacted U.S. preeminence on the world's stage regardless of the facts on the ground. In Baudrillard's understanding, Desert Storm was a U.S. Tet Offensive, where the political reality created by the public perception of the event overtook the event itself in shaping subsequent events.

This fundamental reframing of the role of the media in affecting reality had a dramatic impact on the fields of media studies and communication and was prescient of many of the debates that still concern media scholars.[26] Baudrillard's institutional-level criticism was matched by finer-grained analyses that raised questions about the complicity of individual journalists and news agencies in spreading misinformation. Responding to the "schizophrenic stance" of a prominent volume that simultaneously criticized media coverage of the Gulf War while applauding the good work of the journalists involved, Marie Gottschalk, editor of the influential trade magazine *Editor & Publisher*, took a hard stance against her own industry, noting that "the failure of the media in the Gulf War was not an aberration . . . but rather the product of disturbing trends that have affected both the media and American society." Gottschalk's lengthy critique of the press applied the name "Operation Desert Cloud" to the reporting, which, she argued, willfully obscured the truth: "The problem was not simply that the Pentagon and the president misled the media, but that the media generally swallowed without question whatever the military and the administration dished out." This problem included four of the favored talking points used by the administration in its press conferences, widely reported as facts yet soon revealed to be falsehoods: that "smart bombs won the war," that "the Iraqi army was a formidable military machine," that "Iraq posed a major nuclear and chemical weapons threat," that "allied forces targeted only military targets, keeping civilian casualties to a minimum." Gottshalk came to the same conclusion regarding the lessons not learned by Congress: "The media have shown little concerted interest in exposing why they were sent in the first place, what they saw, what they did, and what the consequences have been. . . . Congress, the Democrats [the opposition party], and the American public have hardly demonstrated any greater interest."[27]

These criticisms, though by no means a comprehensive survey, suffice to convey the irony of how the media interpreted the lessons of the Gulf War.[28] At first glance, the media companies benefited from telling the story the way that PAOs wanted it told. The public accepted those stories and demonstrated little interest in rethinking the facts of the war when subsequent efforts were made to challenge the legends. However, the professional concerns raised by the practices of Desert Storm are self-evident: since the "golden age" of World War II, journalists have consistently pushed back against censorship, stage management, and the military's obsessive need for control (not to mention its dysfunctional bureaucracy). The media position remained more or less the same as ever—seeking more access and less oversight—but two things had changed. First, having gone through decades of debating media-management policies, the media group was in a position to request policy arrangements (the ten principles) that were not exceptionally far from what the military was prepared to offer. Second, the military's own learning consistently pointed toward the need for better relations with the media.

WHAT THE MILITARY LEARNED FROM DESERT STORM

As noted earlier, from January to May 1992 a media group and the DOD's top PAOs reached an agreement on nine of ten principles proposed by media representatives for media management during conflict. The tenth (contested) principle concerned the DOD's continued use of a review system, which the DOD insisted would happen and which the media representatives stated they would simply ignore.[29] Despite this anticipated tension, the other principles effectively downgraded the role of PAOs to facilitators rather than supervisors, assured the media deep and sustained access to the battlefield, and limited the use of pools to the beginning of operations and special events only. Following this agreement, the assistant secretary of defense for public affairs developed two documents: a DOD directive setting the policy and a DOD instruction providing detailed guidelines on how to apply the policy.[30] Both documents were intended for use in future joint and interagency environments. The lessons learned and not learned by the military can be traced primarily through the successor documents to that directive, which at the department level can be found in Joint Publication (JP) 3-61, *Doctrine for Public Affairs in Operations* (1997), and at the service level within the U.S. Army in *Field Manual 46-1: Public Affairs Operations* (1997).[31]

JP 3-61: THE DOD'S LESSONS LEARNED

At the department level, the new directive on public affairs was being designed under the cloud of George H. W. Bush's second presidential run. High approval ratings for Bush during and immediately following Desert Storm began to decline as the economy became the focus of election punditry.[32] Assistant Secretary of Defense for Public Affairs Williams reassigned Lieutenant Colonel Charles W. Ricks, U.S. Army, from managing public-affairs development at North Atlantic Treaty Organization (NATO) headquarters to the Pentagon to draft the initial DOD directive responsive to the media group's nine (or ten) principles.[33] Williams would not remain to see the directive to fruition. In

January 1993, the new Clinton administration replaced Dick Cheney with Les Aspin as secretary of defense, and Aspin brought with him his own team, which included replacing the long-serving Pete Williams with Vernon A. Guidry Jr., one of Aspin's policy advisers.[34] Curiously, despite Cheney's widely noted antipathy to the press, his trust in Williams ensured that public affairs remained bureaucratically central (even if routinely ignored).[35] Aspin, by contrast, quickly downgraded the public-affairs position, changing it from assistant secretary of defense for public affairs to assistant *to* the secretary of defense for public affairs. Guidry was succeeded by three others within the first Clinton administration.[36] Indeed, the DOD public-affairs policy was developed in response to the lessons from Desert Storm in a period of sudden and dramatic decline in interest by virtually all stakeholders.

The mature JP 3-61 would take five years to make it through the crucible of joint doctrine development, but in the meantime Ricks published a report with the Army's Strategic Studies Institute in December 1993. Responding to the malaise setting in (once again) concerning the question of media–military relations, the report makes an impassioned case for why commanders need to take public affairs and media management seriously. Ricks argues, "The commander's operational task is to develop a well resourced and responsive infrastructure to conduct news media relations. Failure to do so will not affect the scale of news media coverage; it will, however, limit the command's ability to communicate effectively and risk distorting the public's perception of the military's effectiveness. In the face of such challenges, efforts at control are meaningless."[37]

Central to the report is Ricks's gospel of inevitability—there is, in his view, no hiding from the press, no avoiding the media saturation of future operating environments. On the inevitability of media presence, he notes, "The instinctive military need for control is irrelevant in the face of an institution [i.e., the media] which can field . . . thousands of reporters." Throughout the report, Ricks stresses the importance of command interest and attention, which he describes as his central motif of "thinking forward," or "tak[ing] the initiative by seeking confident engagement with the news media rather than uncertain avoidance or defensive conflict."[38]

With the publication of JP 3-61, the U.S. Department of Defense finally established the principles and doctrine for how military personnel should support the media. The doctrine is not especially emphatic about the importance of the media to joint operations—that would come in time and lies beyond the scope of this book. Indeed, its first page hedges in a typical style, stating in bold text (here italicized) that its mission is *"to expedite the flow of accurate and timely information about the activities of US joint forces to the public and internal audience,"* but noting in the very next sentence that all such information must be "consistent with national and operations security."[39]

Despite its grudging tone, the doctrine conforms closely with what the media group had proposed in its consultations with Williams and staff and reflects an important step in formalizing the media–military relationship. Notably, the joint doctrine firmly establishes the media group's third principle ("reporters should be granted access to all major units").[40] Combatant commanders "shall ensure that news media representatives and military journalists *are granted all possible access to all unclassified activities* on a not-to-interfere basis" and shall "assist news media representatives and military journalists in *gaining access to military units and personnel.*" Journalists "will be provided access to all major military units. . . . To ensure complete coverage of joint operations, *commanders should plan to assist journalists in gaining access.*"[41]

Read on its own, the sixty pages of JP 3-61 (1997) make clear that public affairs is an important command responsibility, with many tasks, many authorities, and many personnel involved in its smooth operation. Most critically, it makes clear that commanders not only should plan to have journalists present throughout the deployed force but also should actively plan to assist them in getting there. The doctrine also establishes a joint perspective that trumps parochial service approaches, demanding that subordinate units abide by joint norms.

Read in context, though, the document is more ambiguous. The doctrine emphasizes public affairs yet insistently diminishes it, placing its potential to benefit an operation below the risk it poses of breaching operational security. JP 3-61 is perhaps reflective of a DOD that was supremely confident, acknowledging that media concerns are real but not doubting that its own interests must be prioritized and secure in its ability to mitigate any risk from such quarters. Nevertheless, a combatant commander managing a joint operation was now required to plan for embedded journalists throughout the force—a major development building on the key lessons from Panama to Kuwait.

FIELD MANUAL 46-1: THE DOD'S LESSONS LEARNED (AND SUPPRESSED)

As public-affairs doctrine worked its way through the DOD, the Army's formal lessons identified/lessons learned process was hard at work making sense of the entire Gulf War campaign. The official document available for reference—by officers, by historians, or anyone else—is titled *Certain Victory: The US Army in the Gulf War*, attributed to General Robert H. Scales, director of the Desert Storm Study Project. Originally published in 1993 by the Office of the Chief of Staff of the Army, the report is more than 400 pages and covers a broad range of topics—from the Army's posture heading into the war to the transition back to peace. Its assessment of media issues is perfunctory at best. The only reference to the media listed in the index occurs in chapter 2, where the secrecy over the operation is acknowledged as having "created friction with the media," although this secrecy is immediately justified on the grounds that "perhaps at no time since the Inchon Landing during the Korean War had it become so essential to cloak from the enemy such a major operational maneuver."[42] The issue of friendly fire, later discovered by the press, is glossed over, with no indication that it was a serious concern for commanders. Public affairs, public information, PAOs, and the JIB also go without mention.

Based on this official history of Desert Storm/Desert Shield, it would seem that officers charged with learning lessons from the campaign simply found no lessons relevant with respect to the press. The truth of this has become unknowable through an obvious act of suppression. *Certain Victory*, as is made plain in its preface, was based on the multivolume *Desert Storm After-Action Report* by a study group under the command of Major General (ret.) Thomas H. Tait. Army chief of staff Gordon R. Sullivan personally asked Tait to oversee the production of the report.⁴³ After six months, the team had produced roughly 1,000 pages spread over multiple volumes. In a review of *Certain Victory* in *Foreign Affairs* in March 1995, Eliot Cohen revealed the truth of the relationship between the two documents: "The book [*Certain Victory*] is not nearly as good as it should have been given the talents of its principal author, a serious military intellectual. The study was a replacement for a vastly more critical internal army report by Major General (Ret.) Thomas Tait, who receives scant mention."⁴⁴

What was in the critical Tait Report, and did any of it concern media-management issues? The longtime Leavenworth instructor Roger Spiller appears to have had access to it and described it in 1995 as "elaborate" and "forthright."⁴⁵ At the time, the report was classified, and Spiller provided no further insights into its content. Subsequent attempts to find a copy have been unsuccessful.⁴⁶ Nearly a dozen Freedom of Information Act requests have failed to unearth any part of the report. Whatever lessons it sought to impart about the media and Army command have been effectively suppressed.

It may seem an inevitable conclusion, then, that the Army failed to evolve its thinking about the media in the wake of the Gulf War. Once again, though, the truth is more complicated. Let us return briefly to Jean Baudrillard, mentioned earlier in this chapter. Baudrillard and likeminded thinkers had a tremendous impact on the rise of new interdisciplinary studies, in particular cultural studies, in the United States in the 1990s.⁴⁷ The influence of the new fields, especially of Baudrillard's thought, was felt within military educational institutions as well. Plenty of Army officers had progressive views on how to respond to the media dilemmas posed by the conflict. For example, Lieutenant Colonel James R. Callard submitted a thesis titled "The Changing Nature of American Democracy: Consequences for the Military" to the Advanced Research Department of the Naval War College in 1996. There, he argued that "the impact on the military" of Baudrillard's claims about the role of the media in affecting political life "could be profound." Taking Baudrillard's arguments more seriously than many critics, Callard noted that "efforts to shape public opinion have increased public cynicism toward government, leading to less real participation. . . . Baudrillard argues that uncertainty results not only from lack of information, but from an excess of information." Callard expanded on the implications for the military by predicting frustration and the need to change commanders' expectations: "As an institution with high standards, the military should continue to expect frustration caused by the media's ability to put and keep it on the stage and in the spotlight. Military leaders also should expect to be frustrated over the superficial nature of that exposure, and the lack of real understanding of what the military's mission involves."[48]

Callard's perspective was suggestive of a new approach within the Army. Compared with joint doctrine, Army doctrine was unapologetically committed to foregrounding media concerns, refusing—at long last—to fall back into its customary positions of hypersensitivity to criticism and excessive need for control. The Army's public-affairs community seems to have internalized Lieutenant Colonel Ricks's "thinking forward" notion, and the first Army public-affairs doctrine produced after the war, *Field Manual 46-1* (1997), provides a strong and consistent case for the importance of public affairs to any future campaign. The logic used to justify the importance of public affairs is inevitability: media oversight is simply a fact of the future operating environment, and thus effective relations with the media are critical to success. Following this logic, it becomes especially important to combine media-management policy across the width and breadth of a force because inconsistencies can quickly erode trust: "Public affairs must be integrated with other battlefield functions to achieve the desired effect of an accurate, balanced, credible presentation of information that leads to confidence in the force and the operation," states the field manual. "Synchronization requires that public affairs be considered throughout the decision-making process since everything that occurs in an operation has public affairs implications."[49]

This theme gained in importance in the minds of Army doctrine writers, and the next version of the doctrine, *Field Manual 3-61* (2000), states on its second page, "[Public affairs] must be integrated into the planning and decision-making process from receipt of the mission."[50] In other words, public affairs is always important and must be a central part of planning operations (and subsequently of the execution and assessment of that plan). Like joint doctrine, Army doctrine demanded that commanders view the future operating environment as populated with journalists spread among—embedded within and reporting across—the entire deployed force.

LESSONS LEARNED, LESSONS NOT LEARNED

The *Final Report to Congress* on the conduct of the Gulf War is in effect the end of a debate between the Department of Defense and lawmakers over the military's degree of control over the media. Two aspects of this debate are noteworthy. First, the DOD appears to have placated Congress in the face of sustained media criticisms. Media complaints about the military's restrictions on the press were not reflected, though, in public-opinion polling about the military's handling of the operation: journalists were unhappy, but their concerns do not appear to have been broadly shared by the public and so could be brushed aside by members of Congress. Second, despite lingering resentments and suspicions by many in uniform, including such prominent figures as Schwarzkopf, the DOD's final report had finally captured the most fundamental of Sidle's insights: media management is a command concern. The calculus is fairly simple: there are risks associated with offloading media management to junior or undertrained PAOs, and there are opportunities associated with commanders prioritizing relations with the press.

The media's response to Desert Storm is most directly felt in the brief alignment of interests among media companies that allowed for the ten principles to be drafted by media representatives and debated with DOD public-affairs offices. These principles, consolidating all that had been learned by the press since the Sidle Panel, argued for more and deeper access as well as more consistency and less heavy-handed and arbitrary control by those in uniform. Beyond these lessons, a deepening cynicism began to take hold not only among media insiders such as Marie Gottschalk but more broadly among the educated members of the public. The messiness of the media–military relationship was coming into focus, but it was a relationship that was less adversarial and more collaborative, for better or worse. No longer viewed as either cheerleader (as during World War II) or scold (as during the Vietnam War), the press was understood as another complex part of the machinery of war.

At the joint military level, public affairs underwent a shift from charismatic to bureaucratic authority, moving from the empowered personal direction of Pete Williams to a less powerful system under the assistant to the secretary of defense for public affairs, but based on a much broader foundation of engagement from the joint leadership (mandated by and described in the joint doctrine). Among those Army officers writing and reading doctrine, the joint commitment to public affairs was echoed powerfully in the Army's own commitment to a future warfighting environment, which would include journalists across the width and breadth of the deployed force—or at least nearly across them. Journalistic access would remain at the discretion of commanders, after all, and sensitive areas or units could easily be buffered.

Lieutenant Colonel Lawrence S. Epstein interviewed Air Force colonel Ryan Sconyers for a study project at the U.S. Army War College in 1992.[51] Sconyers will be recalled from chapter 7, where his ill-fated role as chief of public affairs for the task force deployed to Panama in 1989 was described. Reflecting on his own lessons learned since Panama, he articulated a perspective that was likely representative of the public-affairs community across the services:

> We have known for a long time that we can't enact a war without some level of public support. . . . We learned in Desert Shield and Desert Storm that public support can be there if we provide the right level of information. I'm not saying censored information or targeted information, I'm just saying information. . . . So we need to understand that the media can't be the adversary, we need to use the media, the media needs us as much as we need them. . . . Public Affairs, if practiced correctly, needs to be aggressive, needs to be assertive, needs to be proactive, and [I] think a lot was learned from that . . . a lot was learned[,] and I think we are going more in the right direction.[52]

Returning to the Sidle Panel recommendations, we see clear evidence that the doctrine that followed from Desert Storm agreed in spirit with those eight points. The new doctrine, as explained in *Field Manual 46-1* and updated in *Field Manual 36-1*, requires public-affairs planning to be concurrent with operations planning, effectively injecting media sensitivity into the conception of an operation and requiring commanders to look upon the logistical support and personal safety of journalists as critical elements of the operation (addressing Sidle Panel recommendations 1, 5, 6, and 7; see table 7.1). The use of news pools is heavily curtailed in the joint and Army doctrine, agreeing with recommendations 2 and 3. The Sidle Panel recommendation for ground rules (recommendation 4) held that they be few in number, tailored to each operation, and voluntary. A simple template, intended to be adapted for given operations, is provided in appendix E of *Field Manual 36-1*. The voluntary principle is upheld in Army doctrine: "Some reporters will choose not to cooperate [with the ground rules], and in those cases, commanders have no responsibility for such individuals and should focus attention on the reporters who desire to abide by the procedures."[53] The joint doctrine laid out in *JP 3-61* takes a less conciliatory stance: "*Violation of the ground rules can result in suspension of credentials and expulsion* from the combat zone of the journalists involved."[54] The word *can* is, however, critical: again, the commander's discretion is paramount. This in turn aligns with the eighth and final recommendation, that media–military understanding and cooperation should be improved, a point argued again and again in both doctrine documents.

The development of U.S. joint doctrine gave rise to NATO Allied doctrine, which differs from but is generally closely inspired by the former. Higher-level doctrine in turn spurs reform processes at lower levels, intended to align policies and procedures to ever greater degrees. The story of public affairs following the creation of joint and Allied doctrine must therefore be told from a perspective that encompasses the joint and Allied operating experiences. From 2000 on, the Army's experience of media management becomes inextricable from these other layers. As such, this chapter truly brings the six-decade story of Army media management to a close.

We end far from where we began. The U.S. Army at the end of the millennium was a force poised to embrace media management as a warfighting function, furthermore a function that inextricably linked the Army's way of war with the joint level and ultimately—in years to come—with partner organizations across other branches of government, other nations, and even nongovernmental actors.[55] This version of the Army was the product of decades of debate about public oversight among factions of officers who competed to define warfighting and media-management policies. Its professional understanding of warfighting was fundamentally committed to enabling democratic oversight and actively aligning Army efforts with the broader political campaign (taking an active role in shaping the campaign). It had become America's political army, buffered from criticism, deeply embedded in shaping the flow of information that constitutes the nation's democratic oversight of armed conflict.

CONCLUSION

The Birth, Fall, and Rise of the Political Army

THAT THE U.S. Army views itself as an apolitical institution, standing apart from the messy and polluting world of politics, is widely noted and frequently asserted.[1] This book adopts a different perspective, one that will likely irritate some readers, outrage others, and reaffirm what yet others have long asserted.[2] I hope readers have discovered in these pages a wealth of evidence to support this reframing.

Each of the three parts of this book has told a different piece of the story of how and why the U.S. Army at the end of the twentieth century found itself with a profoundly political warfighting approach, one that (finally) took seriously the intrinsically political character of warfare and the complex, mass-mediated politics of anticipated future battlefields. In the introduction, I delimit what I mean by "the political" to an exceptionally narrow slice of what militaries do—namely, the field of military professional activity called "public information." This narrow slice is metonymic of military politics broadly conceived: it is one critical form of military political behavior, representing but also enacting a broader set of sensibilities. The first part of the book therefore describes the sudden birth of the "political army"—that is, of an Army wielding a powerful political tool in its public-information competencies. The second part describes the fall of this same political army, explaining why its ability to shape its environment through those competencies declined so dramatically. The third part describes the rise of a mature political army that, despite some lingering opposition, had finally internalized its hard-won lessons on the centrality of media management to senior officership.

This concluding chapter briefly summarizes the "story so far," taking the reader once more step by step through the arguments of the preceding chapters, and then considers where future research might profitably focus.

THE STORY SO FAR

Although this book has focused on the U.S. Army, we began by looking over the shoulder of the Irish reporter William Howard Russell as he wrote his legendary dispatches from Crimea in 1853–1856 that galvanized the British public and created modern war correspondence. At first barely noticed by British forces in theater, his impact back home was immense, and soon a policy was established for Russell and his followers that provided access and protection in exchange for their self-censorship of any dispatches about British battlefield performance. Journalists and their counterparts struck various arrangements to balance the journalists' desire for access against the military's desire to censor content. In the U.S. Civil War and throughout World War I, war correspondents began to view their role as cheerleader rather than as an independent check. In World War II, the American press became complicit in supporting the government's propaganda campaigns, abandoning entirely its role as a critical voice.

From Crimea to Pearl Harbor, the U.S. military had ample opportunity to learn not only that the press could be a risk factor if ignored but also that a compliant press could be a useful tool. The close study of General George C. Marshall in chapter 1 revealed the active role he took in managing the U.S. news media. This was a routine part of his job. Humble, diffident, the archetype of the professional officer, Marshall nevertheless had no illusions that senior officers could focus solely on battlefield concerns and ignore how the Army's efforts were mediated to the American public. Marshall understood that the press was a critical resource, but he managed it cautiously, using the subtle strategies of anticipation, alignment, and (more rarely) intentional misdirection to ensure that the Army was perceived in a positive light.

Chapter 2 explored an irony. Victims of their own success, Marshall and his fellow senior officers exited the war with an exaggerated conception of how the Army fit into the broader American political landscape. The Army's senior leaders as well as its junior public-information experts typically overreached in their vision of what the Army should mean to Americans, a reflection of what I term "Army utopianism."

Chapter 3 provided the first piece of the explanation of why the Army mismanaged its media relations during the Vietnam War. Those same unrealistic expectations of Army authority and competence led to disastrous media-management policies, and the Army lagged behind a sophisticated press corps that had deeply embedded in the theater. Chapter 4 demonstrated how the unhappy media–military relationship came to a head with the paradox of the Tet Offensive: the adversary's operational failure led to its strategic success. Chapter 5 explored how this paradox was recognized but suppressed in the period of doctrinal innovation that followed the Vietnam War. Chapter 6 described the organizational renewal that culminated in the Sidle Panel Report. Chapter 7 analyzed the Army's partly successful attempts to resist key elements of the report. Chapter 8 explains why the Army, despite lack of congressional pressure, ultimately accepted the logic of the Sidle Panel and began to take seriously media management as a command concern at both the individual-service and joint levels.

LOOKING AHEAD

The story comes to an abrupt end in 2000 with the publication of the Army's *Field Manual 3-61: Public Affairs Operations*. There, public-information activities are enshrined as central elements of the planning and conduct of military operations at all scales, a fundamental concern of commanders and an essential element of what makes operations successful.

There is, of course, an artificiality in ending our story on the eve of September 11, 2001. In certain respects, however, the year 2000 really did mark the end of the story of the Army coming to terms with the important role played by media management in affecting military operations. The previous decades had taught Army leaders to finally take media management seriously, and this approach was reflected in the doctrine development. However, the Army had also learned a great deal about the need for better and closer relations with both its sister services and allied militaries. These lessons were not entirely separate from the lessons the Army had learned about the media, and together they were reflected in an Army that was organizationally and doctrinally prepared for work in joint and Allied settings moving forward. Thus, once the initial shock of the terrorist attacks of September 11, 2001, gave way to military preparations for the invasion of Afghanistan and ultimately the invasion of Iraq, the Army that responded was the political Army forged by the story told in these pages. What followed was a new story, one we are still observing: the slow transformation of the political Army into a political military, one mastering the political character of modern conflict. That story has yet to be told.

Although the book argues that the U.S. Army became the political Army, this argument should not be read as implying that the Army flawlessly executes on its political vision or that it is a rapacious, insatiable, or rogue political agent undermining democracy. The theoretical position informing the present argument is that militaries are intrinsically political and that doing political work (such as press work and media management) does not automatically threaten democratic principles. Everything depends on how officers use the political competencies of their organizations. America's political Army did not rise to conquer. Its domestic strategy is much more complicated than that and deserves many more volumes of dedicated research to fully untangle.

As a starting point, Sharon K. Weiner's book *Managing the Military: The Joint Chiefs of Staff and Civil-Military Relations* (2022) has masterfully unraveled the first layer of the Army's domestic political strategy, situating Army interests in relation to its sister services.[3] Thus, for now, we pass in silence over such critical questions as the wisdom of the Army's uniformed leaders, their political efficacy, the consequences of the Army's political posture, the link between its doctrine and its ultimate manifestation on the battlefields of Afghanistan, Iraq, and beyond, and so many other questions. My hope for this volume is not simply to tell this one story of the Army's sixty years of learning lessons in democracy from the press but rather to raise new questions about the often obscure but profoundly consequential democracies of war.

NOTES

INTRODUCTION: THE DEMOCRACY OF WAR

1. My reading of the democratic state's inclusionary and exclusionary dynamics comes especially from John Dryzek. These dynamics are well known and have given rise to large literatures emphasizing one side or the other. The present work attempts to navigate between Jeffrey Alexander's democratic idealism and Theda Skocpol's more pessimistic account. See John S. Dryzek, "Political Inclusion and the Dynamics of Democratization," *American Political Science Review* 90, no. 3 (September 1996): 475–87, https://doi.org/10.2307/2082603; Jeffrey C. Alexander, *The Civil Sphere* (New York: Oxford University Press, 2006); and Theda Skocpol, *States and Social Revolutions: A Comparative Analysis of France, Russia, and China* (Cambridge: Cambridge University Press, 1979).
2. Samuel P. Huntington, *The Soldier and the State: The Theory and Politics of Civil-Military Relations* (Cambridge, MA: Harvard University Press, 1957), 13.
3. Max Weber, "Politics as a Vocation," in *From Max Weber: Essays in Sociology*, ed. and trans. H. H. Gerth and C. Wright Mills (New York: Routledge, 2009), 78, emphasis in original.
4. Reinhard Bendix, *Max Weber: An Intellectual Portrait* (Berkeley: University of California Press, 1977), 1–11. For Weber's political attitudes in relation to the Weimar Republic, see Fritz Ringer, *Max Weber: An Intellectual Biography* (Chicago: University of Chicago Press, 2010).
5. George Washington, "First State of the Union Address," January 8, 1790, https://en.wikisource.org/wiki/George_Washington%27s_First_State_of_the_Union_Address.

6. "SIPRI Military Expenditure Database," n.d., accessed July 8, 2024, https://www.sipri.org/databases/milex. SIPRI estimated the total global defense expenditures as of June 2024 to be U.S.$2,387,628,600 and U.S. expenditures at $916,014,700, or approximately 38 percent of the global total. Detailed comparisons of U.S. defense spending with that of other militaries can also be found at the GlobalFirepower website at https://www.globalfirepower.com.
7. Chief among these dangers are the erosion of the democratic process caused by militarism and securitization as well as an unduly powerful and resource-draining defense industry. On militarism, see Alfred Vagts, *A History of Militarism* (Fort Worth, TX: Perpetua, 1986); and Alexis de Tocqueville, *Democracy in America*, trans. Henry Reeve (Clark, NJ: Lawbook Exchange, 2003). For securitization, see Barry Buzan, Ole Wæver, and Jaap de Wilde, *Security: A New Framework for Analysis* (Boulder, CO: Lynne Rienner, 1998). The dangers of a wasteful military-industrial complex were brought to the public's attention by Dwight Eisenhower. See Dwight D. Eisenhower, "Farewell Address," January 17, 1961, https://www.archives.gov/milestone-documents/president-dwight-d-eisenhowers-farewell-address.
8. See, e.g., Huntington, *The Soldier and the State*; and Morris Janowitz, *The Professional Soldier: A Social and Political Portrait* (New York: Free Press, 1960).
9. Steffen Böhm, Ana C. Dinerstein, and André Spicer, "(Im)Possibilities of Autonomy: Social Movements in and Beyond Capital, the State, and Development," *Social Movement Studies* 9, no. 1 (January 2010): 17–32, quote on 19, https://doi.org/10.1080/14742830903442485.
10. Eisenhower, "Farewell Address"; Gregory Hooks, "The Rise of the Pentagon and U.S. State Building: The Defense Program as Industrial Policy," *American Journal of Sociology* 96, no. 2 (September 1990): 358–404, https://doi.org/10.1086/229533; Gregory Hooks and Brian McQueen, "American Exceptionalism Revisited: The Military-Industrial Complex, Racial Tension, and the Underdeveloped Welfare State," *American Sociological Review* 75, no. 2 (2010): 185–204.
11. Huntington, *The Soldier and the State*; Peter Feaver, *Armed Servants: Agency, Oversight, and Civil-Military Relations* (Cambridge, MA: Harvard University Press, 2003).
12. Meyer Kestnbaum, "Citizenship and Compulsory Military Service: The Revolutionary Origins of Conscription in the United States," *Armed Forces & Society* 27, no. 1 (October 2000): 7–36, https://doi.org/10.1177/0095327X0002700103; Pablo La Porte, "Civil-Military Relations in the Spanish Protectorate in Morocco: The Road to the Spanish Civil War, 1912–1936," *Armed Forces & Society* 30, no. 2 (Winter 2004): 203–26.
13. Peter B. Evans, Dietrich Rueschemeyer, and Theda Skocpol, eds., *Bringing the State Back In* (Cambridge: Cambridge University Press, 1985); Kenneth Finegold and Theda Skocpol, *State and Party in America's New Deal* (Madison: University of Wisconsin Press, 1995); Hooks, "The Rise of the Pentagon and U.S. State Building."

14. Charles Tilly, *Coercion, Capital, and European States: AD 990–1992* (New York: Wiley, 1993).
15. Examples include Vivek Chibber, "Bureaucratic Rationality and the Developmental State," *American Journal of Sociology* 107, no. 4 (2002): 951–89, https://doi.org/10.1086/341010; and Kimberly J. Morgan and Monica Prasad, "The Origins of Tax Systems: A French–American Comparison," *American Journal of Sociology* 114, no. 5 (March 2009): 1350–94, https://doi.org/10.1086/595948. Those finding fault include Miguel Angel Centeno, "Blood and Debt: War and Taxation in Nineteenth-Century Latin America," *American Journal of Sociology* 102, no. 6 (May 1997): 1565–605, https://doi.org/10.1086/231127; and Philip S. Gorski, *The Protestant Ethic Revisited* (2011; reprint, Philadelphia: Temple University Press, 2013). For an overview, see Ann Shola Orloff, "Social Provision and Regulation: Theories of States, Social Policy, and Modernity," in *Remaking Modernity: Politics, History, and Sociology*, ed. Julia Adams, Elisabeth S. Clemens, and Ann Shola Orloff (Chapel Hill, NC: Duke University Press, 2005), 190–224.
16. Greg McLaughlin, *The War Correspondent* (Ann Arbor, MI: Pluto Press, 2002), 67.
17. Samuel Johnson, *The Idler*, vol. 30 (London: J. Newbery, 1761). The convoluted history of how Johnson's saying, given in this chapter's epigraph, has been (mis)attributed and reimagined is explored in detail in "Truth Is the First Casualty in War," *Quote Investigator* (blog), April 11, 2020, https://quoteinvestigator.com/2020/04/11/casualty/.
18. See, e.g., Lewis A. Coser, *Functions of Social Conflict* (New York: Simon and Schuster, 1964); Michael Schudson, "The Ideal of Conversation in the Study of Mass Media," *Communication Research* 5, no. 3 (1978): 320–29; Jürgen Habermas, *The Structural Transformation of the Public Sphere: An Inquiry Into a Category of Bourgeois Society*, trans. Thomas Berger with the assistance of Frederick Lawrence (Cambridge, MA: MIT Press, 1991); Alexander, *The Civil Sphere*; and Monika Krause, "Reporting and the Transformations of the Journalistic Field: US News Media, 1890–2000," *Media, Culture, & Society* 33, no. 1 (2011): 89–104.
19. I capitalize "Army" throughout when referring to the United States Army (or U.S. Army). The Army was formed by the Continental Congress's authorization to muster troops on June 14, 1775, and since the National Security Act of 1947, it is one of the four armed services of the U.S. Department of Defense. See Russell F. Weigley, *History of the United States Army* (Bloomington: Indiana University Press, 1984). I use the term *military* to refer to all the U.S. Department of Defense's combatant services (Army, Navy, Marine Corps, and Air Force). The lowercase word *army* is a technical term applied to the largest organizational unit within the U.S. Army: armies are normally subdivided into (from the largest group to the smallest) corps, divisions, brigades, regiments, companies, platoons, and squads.
20. Bruce Carruthers makes this point explicitly, but many others have offered compelling lessons on the state's multiple, relatively autonomous structures.

Bruce G. Carruthers, "When Is the State Autonomous? Culture, Organization Theory, and the Political Sociology of the State," *Sociological Theory* 12, no. 1 (1994): 19–44, https://doi.org/10.2307/202033. See also Hooks, "The Rise of the Pentagon and U.S. State Building"; Centeno, "Blood and Debt"; Chibber, "Bureaucratic Rationality and the Developmental State"; Simone Polillo and Mauro F. Guillén, "Globalization Pressures and the State: The Worldwide Spread of Central Bank Independence," *American Journal of Sociology* 110, no. 6 (May 2005): 1764–802, https://doi.org/10.1086/428685.

21. See, for example, Schudson, "The Ideal of Conversation in the Study of Mass Media"; Bruce Bimber, *Information and American Democracy: Technology in the Evolution of Political Power* (Cambridge: Cambridge University Press, 2003); Krause, "Reporting and the Transformations of the Journalistic Field"; Michael Hameleers and Toni G. L. A. van der Meer, "Misinformation and Polarization in a High-Choice Media Environment: How Effective Are Political Fact-Checkers?," *Communication Research* 47, no. 2 (March 2020): 227–50, https://doi.org/10.1177/0093650218819671.

22. Gregory Daddis, "Eating Soup with a Spoon: The U.S. Army as a 'Learning Organization' in the Vietnam War," *Journal of Military History* 77, no. 2 (2013): 229–54.

23. Michael Mann, *The Sources of Social Power*, vol. 1: *A History of Power from the Beginning to AD 1760* (New York: Cambridge University Press, 1986); Stephen D. Biddle, *Military Power: Explaining Victory and Defeat in Modern Battle* (Princeton, NJ: Princeton University Press, 2004).

24. Anthony King, *The Combat Soldier: Infantry Tactics and Cohesion in the Twentieth and Twenty-First Centuries* (Oxford: Oxford University Press, 2013); Edward A. Shils and Morris Janowitz, "Cohesion and Disintegration in the Wehrmacht in World War II," *Public Opinion Quarterly* 12, no. 2 (1948): 280–315, https://doi.org/10.1086/265951; Paul L. Savage and Richard A. Gabriel, "Cohesion and Disintegration in the American Army," *Armed Forces & Society* 2, no. 2 (1976): 340–76; Morris Janowitz and Charles C. Moskos Jr., "Five Years of the All-Volunteer Force: 1973–1978," *Armed Forces & Society* 5, no. 2 (1979): 171–218; Anthony King, "The Existence of Group Cohesion in the Armed Forces: A Response to Guy Siebold," *Armed Forces & Society* 33, no. 4 (2007): 638–45; Anthony King, "Cohesion, Combat Performance, and Civil–Military Relations: Contextualizing 'the Word of Command,'" *Armed Forces & Society* 32, no. 1 (2024): 493–512, https://doi.org/10.1177/0095327X231181611.

25. Max Weber, *Economy and Society: An Outline of Interpretive Sociology*, ed. Guenther Roth and Claus Wittich, trans. Ephraim Fischoff et al. (Berkeley: University of California Press, 1978), 1152. Charles Tilly's thesis that the bureaucratic organization of militaries is a key mechanism in the development of modern states descends from this line of thought, but note, too, Philip Gorski's objection to this thesis. Tilly, *Coercion, Capital, and European States*; Gorski, *The Protestant Ethic Revisited*.

26. These are Weber's own examples. To this list we might add the Ottoman Janissary class.
27. Weber, "Bureaucracy," in *From Max Weber*, 232.
28. Weber, "Bureaucracy," in *From Max Weber*, 225.
29. Weber, "Bureaucracy," in *From Max Weber*, 231. Among German-speaking scholars, Karl Demeter reinforced this link between military professionalism and the ascendency of bureaucracy, and Talcott Parsons would import it to the United States in his influential theories of structural functionalism. See Karl Demeter, *The German Officer-Corps in Society and State, 1650–1945* (London: Weidenfeld and Nicolson, 1965); Bernard Boëne, "Social Science Research: War and the Military in the United States," in *Military Sociology: The Richness of a Discipline*, ed. Gerhard Kümmel and Astrid Albrecht-Heide (Baden-Baden, Germany: Nomos, 2000), 149–210. Although Edgar Kiser and Justin Baer argue that bureaucracy fell out of the equation for many American sociologists during the ascendency of Parson's theories, in particular following the translation of Weber's *Economy and Society* and new work on microlevel interactions from the 1970s to the 1990s, bureaucracy has come to occupy a central role in the disciplinary conception of the state, especially among the so-called analytical Weberians. See Edgar Kiser and Justin Baer, "The Bureaucratization of States: Toward an Analytical Weberianism," in *Remaking Modernity*, ed. Adams, Clemens, and Orloff, 225–46.
30. Jonathan Simon, "Rise of the Carceral State," *Social Research: An International Quarterly* 74, no. 2 (2007): 471–508; Stuart Schrader, "Global Counterinsurgency and the Police–Military Continuum: Introduction to the Special Issue," in "From Condottieri to Cyber-mercenaries: The Past, Present, and Future of Private Security Forces," ed. Stuart Schrader, special issue, *Small Wars & Insurgencies* 33, nos. 4–5 (2022): 553–80, https://doi.org/10.1080/09592318.2022.2054113; Brett Story, *Prison Land: Mapping Carceral Power Across Neoliberal America* (Minneapolis: University of Minnesota Press, 2019).
31. See, e.g., Andrew Hoskins and Ben O'Loughlin, *War and Media* (Cambridge: Polity, 2010); and Sarah Maltby, *Military Media Management: Negotiating the "Front" Line in Mediatized War* (London: Routledge, 2013).
32. Frederic A. Bergerson, *The Army Gets an Air Force: Tactics of Insurgent Bureaucratic Politics* (Baltimore, MD: Johns Hopkins University Press, 1980).
33. Dana Priest and William M. Arkin, " 'Top Secret America': A Look at the Military's Joint Special Operations Command," *Washington Post*, September 3, 2011. My work with Ori Swed provides an overview of the sociology of privatized security and how it pertains to military concerns. Ori Swed and Thomas Crosbie, "Private Security and Military Contractors: A Troubling Oversight," *Sociology Compass* 11, no. 11 (2017): art. e12512, https://doi.org/10.1111/soc4.12512; Ori Swed and Thomas Crosbie, eds., *The Sociology of Privatized Security* (New York: Palgrave Macmillan, 2018).

34. Andreas Wimmer and Brian Min note that "sociologists have discussed war as a cause for other phenomena of interest to them, but rarely as an explanandum in its own right." Andreas Wimmer and Brian Min, "From Empire to Nation-State: Explaining Wars in the Modern World, 1816–2001," *American Sociological Review* 71, no. 6 (2006): 868. Jennifer Hickes Lundquist describes the military as an "underutilized" setting for sociological research, and Gregory Hooks and Brian McQueen explicitly call for war making to be brought into the mainstream of the discipline. Jennifer Hickes Lundquist, "Ethnic and Gender Satisfaction in the Military: The Effect of a Meritocratic Institution," *American Sociological Review* 73, no. 3 (2008): 477; Hooks and McQueen, "American Exceptionalism Revisited."
35. Kiser and Baer, "The Bureaucratization of States"; Ezra W. Zuckerman, "Towards the Social Reconstruction of an Interdisciplinary Turf War," *American Sociological Review* 69, no. 3 (2004): 458–65; Lauren A. Rivera, "Managing 'Spoiled' National Identity: War, Tourism, and Memory in Croatia," *American Sociological Review* 73, no. 4 (August 2008): 613–34, https://doi.org/10.1177/000312240807300405; Henning Hillmann, "Mediation in Multiple Networks: Elite Mobilization Before the English Civil War," *American Sociological Review* 73, no. 3 (June 2008): 426–54, https://doi.org/10.1177/000312240807300304; Gary Marks, Heather A. D. Mbaye, and Hyung Min Kim, "Radicalism or Reformism? Socialist Parties Before World War I," *American Sociological Review* 74, no. 4 (August 2009): 615–35, https://doi.org/10.1177/000312240907400406; Barış Büyükokutan, "Toward a Theory of Cultural Appropriation: Buddhism, the Vietnam War, and the Field of U.S. Poetry," *American Sociological Review* 76, no. 4 (August 2011): 620–39, https://doi.org/10.1177/0003122411414820; Miloš Broćić and Andrew Miles, "College and the 'Culture War': Assessing Higher Education's Influence on Moral Attitudes," *American Sociological Review* 86, no. 5 (October 2021): 856–95, https://doi.org/10.1177/00031224211041094.
36. "Federal Agency Spending Profiles," USAspending, accessed April 17, 2024, https://www.usaspending.gov/agency.
37. GDP data come from "Report for Selected Countries and Subjects," International Monetary Fund, accessed April 17, 2024, https://www.imf.org/external/datamapper/NGDPD@WEO/OEMDC/ADVEC/WEOWORLD.
38. See Sharon K. Weiner, *Managing the Military: The Joint Chiefs of Staff and Civil-Military Relations* (New York: Columbia University Press, 2022).
39. Clausewitz was primarily concerned with creating objective knowledge of a state of social interaction (war) that is often powerfully infused with nonrationality and irrationality. Although writing before the development of a robust public sphere, Clausewitz (like Machiavelli) did perceive the relationship between military command and the polity as a trinitarian relationship, involving the military, political authorities, and a public that could act upon those political authorities in often chaotic ways. See Carl von Clausewitz, *On War*,

indexed ed., ed. and trans. Michael Howard and Peter Paret (Princeton, NJ: Princeton University Press, 1984).
40. Game theorists have long modeled this effect; see, e.g., Thomas C. Schelling, *Micromotives and Macrobehavior* (New York: Norton, 2006).
41. Michael Howard, "The Forgotten Dimensions of Strategy," *Foreign Affairs* 57, no. 5 (1979): 975-86, https://doi.org/10.2307/20040266.
42. Barry Buzan and Lene Hansen, *The Evolution of International Security Studies* (Cambridge: Cambridge University Press, 2009); for a critical perspective, see Ole Wæver, "Towards a Political Sociology of Security Studies," *Security Dialogue* 41, no. 6 (2010): 649-58.
43. Barry D. Baysinger, "Domain Maintenance as an Objective of Business Political Activity: An Expanded Typology," *Academy of Management Review* 9, no. 2 (April 1984): 248-58, https://doi.org/10.5465/amr.1984.4277642.
44. Douglas A. Schuler, Kathleen Rehbein, and Roxy D. Cramer, "Pursuing Strategic Advantage Through Political Means: A Multivariate Approach," *Academy of Management Journal* 45, no. 4 (2002): 659-72; Amy Hillman and Gerald Keim, "International Variation in the Business–Government Interface," *Academy of Management Review* 20, no. 1 (January 1995): 193-214.
45. Baysinger, "Domain Maintenance as an Objective of Business Political Activity"; Ivar Berg and Mayer N. Zald, "Business and Society," *Annual Review of Sociology* 4, no. 4 (August 1978): 115-43, https://doi.org/10.1146/annurev.so.04.080178.000555.
46. Allen W. Palmer and Edward L. Carter, "The Smith-Mundt Act's Ban on Domestic Propaganda: An Analysis of the Cold War Statute Limiting Access to Public Diplomacy," *Communication Law and Policy* 11, no. 1 (January 2006): 1-34, https://doi.org/10.1207/s15326926clp1101_1.
47. Baysinger, "Domain Maintenance as an Objective of Business Political Activity"; Martin B. Meznar and Douglas Nigh, "Buffer or Bridge? Environmental and Organizational Determinants of Public Affairs Activities in American Firms," *Academy of Management Journal* 38, no. 4 (1995): 975-96.
48. Amy J. Hillman and William P. Wan, "The Determinants of MNE Subsidiaries' Political Strategies: Evidence of Institutional Duality," *Journal of International Business Studies* 36, no. 3 (May 2005): 322-40, https://doi.org/10.1057/palgrave.jibs.8400137.
49. Scott Boorman is a rare exception, singling out the accomplishments of Rear Admiral Henry C. Eccles in developing creative solutions to logistics problems. Scott A. Boorman, "Fundamentals of Strategy—the Legacy of Henry Eccles," *Naval War College Review* 62, no. 2 (2009): 91-115.
50. Gil Eyal, "Dangerous Liaisons Between Military Intelligence and Middle Eastern Studies in Israel," *Theory and Society* 31, no. 5 (2002): 653-93; Meyer Kestnbaum, "Mars Revealed: The Entry of Ordinary People Into War Among States," in *Remaking Modernity*, ed. Adams, Clemens, and Orloff, 250-90; Yoram Peri,

Generals in the Cabinet Room: How the Military Shapes Israeli Policy (Washington, DC: United States Institute of Peace, 2006).

51. Palmer and Carter, "The Smith-Mundt Act's Ban on Domestic Propaganda."
52. Sean J. Kealy, "Reexamining the Posse Comitatus Act: Toward a Right to Civil Law Enforcement," *Yale Law & Policy Review* 21, no. 2 (2003): 383–442.
53. Mordecai Lee, "Too Much Bureaucracy or Too Little? Congressional Treatment of Defense Department Legislative Liaison, 1950s–1990s," *Public Administration and Management* 14, no. 2 (2009): 327.
54. Stephen K. Scroggs, *Army Relations with Congress: Thick Armor, Dull Sword, Slow Horse* (New York: Praeger, 2000), 7.
55. Like legislative affairs, public affairs is split between an Army chief of public affairs and an assistant secretary of defense for public affairs. Notably, both the chief of legislative liaison and chief of public affairs occupy unique organizational positions that require them to report directly to the civilian secretary of the army (rather than to the Army chief of staff, a uniformed position). This is indicative of the importance of these positions. Public affairs is split into three fields of activity: community relations, command information, and public information.
56. Major General Anthony Cucolo, interviewed by the author, Carlisle, PA, April 12, 2013.
57. Christoph S. DeRosa, *Political Indoctrination in the U.S. Army: From World War II to Vietnam* (Lincoln: University of Nebraska Press, 2006).
58. Sarah Maltby, "The Mediatization of the Military," *Media, War, & Conflict* 5, no. 3 (December 2012): 255–68, https://doi.org/10.1177/1750635212447908; Maltby, *Military Media Management*.
59. Todd C. Helmus, Christopher Paul, and Russell W. Glenn, *Enlisting Madison Avenue: The Marketing Approach to Earning Popular Support in Theaters of Operation* (Santa Monica, CA: RAND, June 30, 2007), https://www.rand.org/pubs/monographs/MG607.html.
60. James N. Dertouzos and Steven Garber, *Is Military Advertising Effective? An Estimation Methodology and Applications to Recruiting in the 1980s and 90s* (Santa Monica, CA: RAND, January 1, 2003), https://www.rand.org/pubs/monograph_reports/MR1591.html.
61. Karen S. Miller, *The Voice of Business: Hill & Knowlton and Postwar Public Relations* (Chapel Hill: University of North Carolina Press, 1999), 180.
62. Risa A. Brooks, "Militaries and Political Activity in Democracies," in *American Civil-Military Relations: The Soldier and the State in a New Era*, ed. Suzanne C. Nielsen and Don M. Snider (Baltimore, MD: Johns Hopkins University Press, 2009), 213–38.
63. Even politically savvy civil-military relations scholars miss this important insight. For example, in reporting on a high-level meeting of Army leaders convened to discuss civil-military relations, Eliot A. Cohen notes that they found definite evidence of the politicization of the force and argued for corrective

action but left unexplored the consequences of this development. In a later work, Cohen argues that U.S. military personnel tend to stay out of politics. See Eliot A. Cohen, "Civil–Military Relations," *Orbis* 41, no. 2 (March 1997): 177–86, https://doi.org/10.1016/S0030-4387(97)90061-2; and Cohen, "The Historical Mind and Military Strategy," *Orbis* 49, no. 4 (September 2005): 575–88, https://doi.org/10.1016/j.orbis.2005.07.002.

64. See, e.g., Thomas Crosbie, "What Is Military Politics?," in *Military Politics: New Perspectives*, ed. Thomas Crosbie (London: Berghahn, 2023), 19–48; Crosbie, "Michael Howard and Military Politics, in Roundtable: Remembering Sir Michael Howard (1922–2019)," *Texas National Security Review*, February 24, 2020, https://tnsr.org/roundtable/roundtable-remembering-sir-michael-howard-1922-2019/; Crosbie, "Clausewitz and Military Politics: Theoretical Reflections on a Strong Program Approach to War and the Military," in *Militarization and the Global Rise of Paramilitary Culture: Post-heroic Reimaginings of the Warrior*, ed. Brad West and Thomas Crosbie (Singapore: Springer, 2021), 17–36; Damon Coletta and Thomas Crosbie, "The Virtues of Military Politics," *Armed Forces & Society* 47, no. 1 (January 2021): 3–24, https://doi.org/10.1177/0095327X19871605.

65. William M. Hammond, *Public Affairs: The Military and the Media, 1962–1968* (Washington, DC: Center of Military History, United States Army, 1990); William M. Hammond, *Public Affairs: The Military and the Media, 1968–1973* (Washington, DC: Center of Military History, United States Army, 1996).

66. Jeffrey Haydu, "Making Use of the Past: Time Periods as Cases to Compare and as Sequences of Problem Solving," *American Journal of Sociology* 104, no. 2 (1998): 339–71, https://doi.org/10.1086/210041; Daddis, "Eating Soup with a Spoon."

1. THE ARMY ASCENDANT: MARSHALL'S MEDIA MANAGEMENT, 1939–1945

1. See, e.g., Morris Janowitz, *The Professional Soldier: A Social and Political Portrait* (New York: Free Press, 1960), 395–414. For contemporary discussions, see the journal *Media, War, & Conflict*; Dennis McQuail, "On the Mediatization of War: A Review Article," *Communication Gazette* 68, no. 2 (2006): 107–18; Lloyd J. Matthews, *Newsmen and National Defense: Is Conflict Inevitable?* (Washington, DC: Brassey's, 1991); Cantigny Conference Series, *The Military and the Media: Facing the Future* (Wheaton, IL: Robert R. McCormick Tribute Foundation, 1998); Major General Tony Cucolo, "The Military and the Media: Shotgun Wedding, Rocky Marriage, Committed Relationship," *Media, War, & Conflict* 1, no. 1 (2008): 84–89.

2. Russell F. Weigley, *History of the United States Army* (Bloomington: Indiana University Press, 1984), 421.

3. Michael MacDonagh, "Can We Rely on Our War News?," *Fortnightly Review* 63, no. 374 (1898): 612–26; Philip Knightley, *The First Casualty: From the Crimea to Vietnam* (New York: Harcourt Brace Jovanovich, 1975), 4; Miles Hudson and John

Stanier, *War and the Media: A Random Searchlight* (Phoenix Mill, U.K.: Sutton, 1997).

4. In *The First Casualty*, Philip Knightley offers a few possibilities for the first war correspondent, including Thucydides, Willem van de Velde, Henry Crabb Robinson, and G. L. Gruneisen. Most scholars name William Howard Russell, however; see, e.g., MacDonagh, "Can We Rely on Our War News?"; and Hudson and Stanier, *War and the Media*.
5. According to Michael MacDonagh, "[Russell's] movements were not in the slightest degree restricted; he had perfect freedom of action; he could go where he pleased; and what he wrote was subject to no censorship; but he was unable to procure rations for himself" ("Can We Rely on Our War News?," 613).
6. When pointed critiques of strategy and tactics occurred in Russell's writing, they were muted by his editors and sent secretly to members of the War Cabinet (Hudson and Stanier, *War and the Media*, 7).
7. J. Cutler Andrews, *The North Reports the War* (Pittsburgh: University of Pittsburgh Press, 1955), 60. Andrews places the number of correspondents at more than 300 (p. 60), with 50,000 miles of telegraph lines in place (p. 6).
8. J. Cutler Andrews noted, "From time to time, certain bold spirits criticized the abuses in army administration, abuses such as vandalism, unsanitary camps, shocking neglect of the wounded by incompetent surgeons, waste in the commissariat, clothing Union troops in Confederate gray uniforms, and many others. The unpopularity of such correspondents at army headquarters readily can be understood." Andrews, *The North Reports the War*, 74.
9. Knightley, *The First Casualty*, 90–91; Matthew Farish, "Modern Witnesses: Foreign Correspondents, Geopolitical Vision, and the First World War," *Transactions of the Institute of British Geographers* 26, no. 3 (2001): 273-87.
10. Knightley, *The First Casualty*, 80–81.
11. Clarence R. Wyatt, *Paper Soldiers: The American Press and the Vietnam War* (New York: Norton, 1993), 15.
12. Knightley, *The First Casualty*, 276.
13. William M. Hammond, *Public Affairs: The Military and the Media, 1962–1968* (Washington, DC: Center of Military History, United States Army, 1990), 6; Mary S. Mander, *Pen and Sword: American War Correspondents, 1898–1975* (Urbana: University of Illinois Press, 2010), 114.
14. Alan Fern, foreword to Frederick S. Voss, *Reporting the War: The Journalistic Coverage of World War II*, exhibit catalog (Washington, DC: Smithsonian Institution Press for the National Portrait Gallery, 1994), x.
15. Wyatt, *Paper Soldiers*, 15. See also James L. Baughman, *The Republic of Mass Culture: Journalism, Filmmaking, and Broadcasting in America since 1941* (Baltimore, MD: Johns Hopkins University Press, 1992), 6.
16. Kendrick Oliver, *The My Lai Massacre in American History and Memory* (Manchester, U.K.: Manchester University Press, 2006), 14; Garth S. Jowett and Victoria O'Donnell, *Propaganda and Persuasion* (Newberry Park, CA: Sage, 1986), 143.

17. Knightley, *The First Casualty*, 276; Dale Minor, *The Information War* (New York: Hawthorn, 1970), 7; Voss, *Reporting the War*, 19.
18. Philip M. Taylor, *Munitions of the Mind: War Propaganda from the Ancient World to the Nuclear Age* (Glasgow, Scotland: Patrick Stephens, 1990), 188; Greg McLaughlin, *The War Correspondent* (London: Pluto Press, 2002), 68; Lynch quoted in Knightley, *The First Casualty*, 333.
19. Glora Goodman, "'Palestine's Best': The Jewish Agency's Press Relations, 1946–1946," *Israel Studies* 16, no. 3 (2011): 1–27.
20. *Field Manual 46-1: Public Affairs Operations* (Washington, DC: Headquarters, U.S. Department of the Army, 1997).
21. General George C. Marshall to General Thomas T. Handy, memorandum, October 29, 1942, in *The Papers of George Catlett Marshall*, vol. 3: *"The Right Man for the Job," December 7, 1941–May 31, 1943*, ed. Larry I. Bland (Baltimore, MD: Johns Hopkins University Press, 1996), 415.
22. Hammond, *Public Affairs, 1962–1968*; William M. Hammond, *Public Affairs: The Military and the Media, 1968–1972* (Washington, DC: Center of Military History, United States Army, 1996); William M. Hammond, "The Army and Public Affairs: Enduring Principles," *Parameters* 19 (1989): 57–74; Sarah Maltby, "The Mediatization of the Military," *Media, War, & Conflict* 5, no. 3 (2012): 255–68; Sarah Maltby, *Military Media Management: Negotiating the "Front" Line in Mediatized War* (New York: Routledge, 2012).
23. Taylor, *Munitions of the Mind*, 202.
24. John W. Henderson, *The United States Information Agency* (New York: Praeger, 1969), 31–32.
25. Sidney Alvin Knutson, "History of the Public Relations Program in the United States Army," master's thesis, University of Wisconsin, 1953, 186.
26. James R. Mock and Cedric Larson, "Public Relations of the U.S. Army," *Public Opinion Quarterly* 5, no. 2 (1941): 275.
27. Forrest C. Pogue, *George C. Marshall: Organizer of Victory, 1943–1945* (New York: Penguin, 1973), 127–28.
28. Knutson, "History of the Public Relations Program in the United States Army," 177–78.
29. Knutson, "History of the Public Relations Program in the United States Army," 179.
30. Hammond, "The Army and Public Affairs," 66; Knutson, "History of the Public Relations Program in the United States Army," 187.
31. Paul Herbert, "The Battle of Cantigny and the Dawn of the Modern American Army," *On Point: The Journal of Army History* 13, no. 4 (2008): 11.
32. Forrest C. Pogue, *George C. Marshall: Education of a General, 1880–1939* (New York: Penguin, 1963), 326–27, 328, 330.
33. The four volumes of Marshall's collected papers that cover this period are: George C. Marshall, *The Papers of George Catlett Marshall*, vol. 2: *"We Cannot Delay," July 1, 1939–December 6, 1941*, ed. Larry I. Bland (Baltimore, MD: Johns

Hopkins University Press, 1986); Marshall, *The Papers of George Catlett Marshall*, vol. 3: *"The Right Man for the Job," December 7, 1941–May 31, 1943*; Marshall, *The Papers of George Catlett Marshall*, vol. 4: *"Aggressive and Determined Leadership," June 1, 1943–December 31, 1944*, ed. Larry I. Bland (Baltimore, MD: Johns Hopkins University Press, 1996); and Marshall, *The Papers of George Catlett Marshall*, vol. 5: *"The Finest Soldier," January 1, 1945–January 7, 1947*, ed. Larry I. Bland (Baltimore, MD: Johns Hopkins University Press, 2003). The four volumes of Marshall's biography are: Pogue, *Education of a General*; Forrest C. Pogue, *George C. Marshall: Ordeal and Hope, 1939–42* (New York: Penguin, 1966); Pogue, *Organizer of Victory*; and Pogue, *George C. Marshall: Statesman, 1945–1959* (New York: Penguin, 1987). Although firsthand cross-checking was somewhat redundant, it proved necessary because of an oversight in the third volume of *Papers of George Catlett Marshall*, which omits Surles's name in the index. Significantly, six of the items listed in the case studies (and referenced in later notes) were found in the George C. Marshall Papers held by the George C. Marshall Foundation but not in the published papers.

34. Pogue, *Ordeal and Hope*, 11, 12.
35. Pogue, *Organizer of Victory*, 128.
36. Colonel Luther L. Hill to General George C. Marshall, memorandum, May 18, 1945, copy in Marshall Foundation National Archives Project, Xerox 2103, George C. Marshall Foundation Research Library, Lexington, VA. (The archives provide incomplete documentation on the location of the original.)
37. Wyatt, *Paper Soldiers*, 15; Larry I. Bland, editorial commentary, in Marshall, *Papers*, 4:527.
38. Marshall to General Wade Haislip, August 18, 1941, in Marshall, *Papers*, 2:590.
39. Pogue, *Ordeal and Hope*, 27.
40. Marshall to Bernard M. Baruch, August 19, 1941, in Marshall, *Papers* 2:591.
41. Pogue, *Ordeal and Hope*, 156.
42. Marshall to Franklin D. Roosevelt, September 9, 1941, in Marshall, *Papers*, 2:602.
43. Marshall to General Alexander Surles, memorandum, October 13, 1941, box 65: Correspondence, Pentagon Office, 1938–1951, folder 23, George C. Marshall Foundation Research Library.
44. Marshall to Ben Lear, October 25, 1941, in Marshall, *Papers*, 2:651, 652.
45. Press release, November 13, 1941, in Marshall, *Papers*, 2:671, 672. The Sherrod quotation comes from his memorandum to David W. Hulburd Jr. of *Time* magazine, in Members of the Overseas Press Club, *I Can Tell It Now*, ed. David Brown and W. Richard Bruner (New York: Dutton, 1964), 39–43.
46. Pogue, *Ordeal and Hope*, 201–2, 203.
47. Marshall/Sherrod meeting, December 21, 1941, in Marshall, *Papers*, 2:234.
48. Members of the Overseas Press Club, *I Can Tell It Now*, 39–43.
49. Marshall to F. Warren Pershing, December 13, 1941, in Marshall, *Papers*, 3:19.
50. Marshall to Surles, memorandum, November 25, 1942, in Marshall, *Papers*, 3:451.

1. THE ARMY ASCENDANT   229

51. Marshall to Surles, memorandum, December 1, 1942, box 65: Correspondence, Pentagon Office, 1938–1951, folder 23, George C. Marshall Foundation Research Library; Marshall to Surles, memorandum, December 7, 1942, in Marshall, *Papers*, 3:474.
52. Marshall to Surles, memorandum, February 7, 1943, box 65: Correspondence, Pentagon Office, 1938–1951, folder 24, George C. Marshall Foundation Research Library.
53. Marshall to Surles, memoranda, February 22 and 24, 1943, and Surles to Marshall, February 24, 1943, in Marshall, *Papers*, 3:561, 562.
54. Marshall to Roosevelt, draft letter, November 7, 1942, in Marshall, *Papers*, 3:13.
55. Marshall to Dwight D. Eisenhower, November 20, 1942, in Marshall, *Papers*, 3:445.
56. Quoted in Pogue, *Ordeal and Hope*, 418, 483.
57. Eisenhower to Marshall, November 20, 1942, in Marshall, *Papers*, 3:446 n. 3; the note quotes Eisenhower to Marshall, Radio No. 837, November 18, 1942.
58. Marshall to Elmer Davis, December 12, 1942, and Marshall to Walter Lippmann, January 7, 1943, in Marshall, *Papers*, 3:480–81, 508.
59. Marshall to American Society of Newspaper Editors, talk, February 13, 1943, in Marshall, *Papers*, 3:543.
60. Marshall to Colonel McCarthy, March 15, 1943, in Marshall, *Papers*, 3:584.
61. Marshall to Lowell Mallett, September 10, 1940, in Marshall, *Papers*, 2:303.
62. Marshall to Surles, memorandum, April 4, 1943, in Marshall, *Papers*, 3:632.
63. Marshall to the BPR, memorandum, February 2, 1944, box 65: Correspondence, Pentagon Office, 1938–1951, folder 26, George C. Marshall Foundation Research Library.
64. Marshall to editor of the *Kansas City Star*, April 6, 1944, in Marshall, *Papers*, 4:391, emphasis in original.
65. Marshall to Eisenhower, April 13, 1943, quoted in Pogue, *Organizer of Victory*, 189.
66. Marshall to Surles, memorandum, November 22, 1944, box 65: Correspondence, Pentagon Office, 1938–1951, folder 26, George C. Marshall Foundation Research Library.
67. Marshall to the BPR, memorandum, February 7, 1943, box 65: Correspondence, Pentagon Office, 1938–1951, folder 24, George C. Marshall Foundation Research Library.
68. Marshall to staff member, May 15, 1940, in Marshall, *Papers*, 2:213.
69. Pogue, *Organizer of Victory*, 129.
70. Quoted in Ed Cray, *General of the Army: George C. Marshall, Soldier and Statesman* (New York: Norton, 1990), 210.

2. ARMY OVERREACH: DOMESTIC POLITICS AND COMMAND CULTURE, 1945–1963

1. Samuel P. Huntington, *The Soldier and the State: The Theory and Politics of Civil-Military Relations* (Cambridge, MA: Harvard University Press, 1957), 74.
2. George C. Marshall, commencement address, Trinity College, June 5, 1941, in *The Papers of George Catlett Marshall*, vol. 2: *"We Cannot Delay," July 1, 1939–December 6, 1941*, ed. Larry I. Bland (Baltimore, MD: Johns Hopkins University Press, 1986), 534.
3. Adam J. Berinsky, *In Time of War: Understanding American Public Opinion from World War II to Iraq* (Chicago: University of Chicago Press, 2009).
4. In fiscal year 1946, total Department of War expenses came to $5,703,989, of which $3,809,000 was for recruiting and $1,894,989 was for all other costs. In fiscal year 1945, by contrast, the Department of War spent $3,423,126 on nonrecruiting tasks alone. See box 3, folder 6.1.45–12.31.45, Army AG, Decimal File 1940–45, Record Group 407, National Archives II, College Park, MD.
5. John Sager, "Universal Military Training and the Struggle to Define American Identity During the Cold War," *Federal History* 5 (2013): 57–74.
6. Charles H. Lyttle, "Review of *Universal Military Training and National Security*, ed. Paul Russell Anderson," *Social Service Review* 20, no. 1 (1946): 111–12.
7. Alfred Vagts, *A History of Militarism* (Fort Worth, TX: Perpetua, 1986), 13.
8. August B. Hollingshead, "Adjustment to Military Life," *American Journal of Sociology* 51, no. 5 (1946): 439–47.
9. Kennon H. Nakamura and Matthew C. Weed, *US Public Diplomacy: Background and Current Issues* (Washington, DC: Congressional Research Service, 2009), 14.
10. Both departments would move through a quick succession of name changes for its top position but would eventually settle on "assistant secretary of defense for public affairs" (Collins's job) and "Army chief of public affairs" (Parks's job).
11. Sidney Alvin Knutson, "History of the Public Relations Program in the United States Army," master's thesis, University of Wisconsin, Madison, 1953, 322.
12. Major General Floyd L. Parks, "A Creed for Army Public Relations," *Army Information Digest*, August 1946, 7.
13. Their ranks are not listed, nor is Notestein's first name. "Sidle" was Winant Sidle, who will appear repeatedly throughout these chapters.
14. Winant Sidle and Notestein [*sic*], "Suggested Public Informational Activities for PMS&Ts, Sixth Army Area," April 3, 1951, box 2, folder 4, Miscellaneous Correspondence re. PA, Winant Sidle Papers, 1950–1999, United States Army Heritage and Education Center, Carlisle, PA.
15. Edwin P. Hoyt, *Japan's War: The Great Pacific Conflict* (New York: Cooper Square Press, 2001), 401–4.
16. Hanson W. Baldwin, "Atom Bomb Is Proved Most Terrible Weapon," *New York Times*, July 7, 1946.

17. Hadley Cantril at Cornell University headed the survey. See "Public Reaction to the Atomic Bomb: A Nationwide Survey of Attitudes and Information," Subcommittee on Public Relations, Social Science Research Council, Cornell University, 1947; and Patricia Woodward, "How Do the American People Feel About the Atomic Bomb?," *Journal of Social Issues* 4, no. 1 (1948): 7–14.
18. Russell F. Weigley, *History of the United States Army* (Bloomington: Indiana University Press, 1984), 596–97; "Public Reaction to the Atomic Bomb," appendix B.
19. "Public Reaction to the Atomic Bomb," 26–28.
20. Walter E. Kretchik, *U.S. Army Doctrine: From the American Revolution to the War on Terror* (Lawrence: University Press of Kansas, 2014), 160.
21. Michael Timonin, "Demobilization and Its Discontents: Soldiers, Wives, and the Contested Demobilization at World War II's Close," PhD diss., State University of New York, Binghamton, 2015.
22. William A. Taylor, *The Advent of the All-Volunteer Force: Protecting Free Society* (New York: Routledge, 2023), 1–17.
23. James F. Schnabel, *United States Army in the Korean War*, vol. 1: *Policy and Direction: The First Year* (Washington, DC: Center of Military History, United States Army, 1972), 1–40. For a wider perspective on the Korean War, see also Clay Blair, *The Forgotten War: America in Korea, 1950–1953* (New York: Times, 1987).
24. Schnabel, *United States Army in the Korean War*, 1:71–73.
25. Robert T. Davis II, *The US Army and the Media in the 20th Century* (Fort Leavenworth, KS: Combat Studies Institute Press, 2009), 54.
26. Douglas MacArthur, quoted in Jeffery A. Smith, *War and Press Freedom: The Problem of Prerogative Power* (New York: Oxford University Press, 1999), 169.
27. Clark Lee and Richard Henschel, *Douglas MacArthur* (New York: Holt, 1952), 188–90.
28. Daniel Fazio, "Censorship in the Korean War: Press-Military Relations, June 1950–January 1951," *Australasian Journal of American Studies* 26, no. 2 (2007): 5; Davis, *The US Army and the Media in the 20th Century*, 55.
29. Fazio, "Censorship in the Korean War," 13.
30. Melvin B. Voorhees, *Korean Tales* (New York: Simon and Schuster, 1952), 111; Paul L. Aswell, "Wartime Press Censorship by the U.S. Armed Forces: A Historical Perspective," master's thesis, U.S. Army Command and General Staff College, 1978, 155–62.
31. Circular No. 234 re. Army Regulation (AR) 600-700, *Public Relations*, August 6, 1946, box 3, folder 6, Record Group 407, Decimal Files from the Office of the Adjutant General, 1940–1945, National Archives II.
32. Although the terms are at times confusing, *public relations*, *public information*, and *public affairs* must be distinguished from one another. Army public relations in the 1940s and 1950s was broadly concerned with domestic messaging. With AR 360-5 (1950), those elements of domestic messaging other than marketing and advertising were retitled "public affairs." Public affairs is subdivided into three parts: public information (liaising with the press), community

relations (liaising with local civilians), and command information (liaising with the troops). It briefly included troop education as a fourth component.
33. The complete text of AR 360-5, *Public Information*, can be found in appendix D in Knutson, "History of the Public Relations Program in the United States Army."
34. AR 360-5, appendix D in Knutson, "History of the Public Relations Program in the United States Army," 430.
35. Davis, *The US Army and the Media in the 20th Century*, 57.
36. General Matthew B. Ridgway to all commanders in the U.S. Army, June 4, 1954, preserved with *An Army Public Relations Plan*, March 7, 1956, p. 216, Chief of Information, Programs Branch, Correspondence, Information Officers' Conference (1959–60), box 5, Army Staff—Record Group 319, National Archives II.
37. Saki Dockrill, *Eisenhower's New-Look National Security Policy, 1953–61* (New York: Macmillan, 1996), 57.
38. *An Army Public Relations Plan*, 7.
39. Sen. Lyndon B. Johnson, TX, "State, Justice, and Judiciary Appropriations, 1958," *Congressional Record* 103 (May 1957): 6968.
40. *An Army Public Relations Plan*, 66.
41. Eisenhower made the following campaign pledge in 1952: "I shall go to Korea." Dwight D. Eisenhower, speech, October 24, 1952, box 2: October 23, 1952, to November 3, 1952, and December 1952 (1), Speech Series, Papers of Dwight D. Eisenhower, NAID #12012607.
42. "Public Opinion on the Korean War, 1953," memorandum on recent polls, June 2, 1953, box 4: Korea (3), C. D. Jackson Records, Dwight D. Eisenhower Library, Abilene, KS.
43. W. S. Parsons, "Capabilities of the Atomic Bomb, Including Naval Thinking on Its Employment," *Naval War College Review* 3, no. 4 (1950): 24.
44. Donald B. Beary, "Strategic Employment of the Navy: Past, Present, and Future," *Naval War College Review* 3, no. 4 (1950): 5.
45. Maxwell D. Taylor, *The Uncertain Trumpet* (Westport, CT: Greenwood Press, 1974), 6.
46. Dockrill, *Eisenhower's New-Look National Security Policy*, 259, 262, 271. As it turned out, strategic deterrence was not a cheaper option because the arms race quickly drove the cost of deterrence to unexpected heights.
47. Donald Alan Carter, "Eisenhower Versus the Generals," *Journal of Military History* 71, no. 4 (2007): 1181.
48. General Lyman L. Lemnitzer, "Address to the National Association of State and Territorial Civil Defense Directors," April 6, 1960, box 1, folder 1, Lyman L. Lemnitzer Papers, 1960–1990, United States Army Heritage and Education Center.
49. General Lyman L. Lemnitzer, "Address to Association of the United States Army," August 9, 1960, box 1, folder 1, Lyman L. Lemnitzer Papers, 1960–1990.

50. General George H. Decker, "The Army Today—Address to the Calvin Bullock Forum," March 23, 1961, box 6, folder 2, George H. Decker Papers, 1959–1962, United States Army Heritage and Education Center.
51. General Lyman L. Lemnitzer, quoted in Fred Kaplan, *The Wizards of Armageddon* (Stanford, CA: Stanford University Press, 1983), 273.
52. Maxwell D. Taylor, "Report on General Taylor's Mission to South Vietnam," November 3, 1961, General CIA Records, CREST (CIA Records Search Tool), https://www.cia.gov/readingroom/docs/CIA-RDP86B00269R000200030001-5.pdf.
53. Graham A. Cosmas, *MACV: The Joint Command in the Years of Escalation, 1962–1967* (Washington, DC: Center of Military History, United States Army, 2006), 43.
54. Weigley, *History of the United States Army*, 556.

3. OUTPACED: THE PRESS AND PUBLIC AFFAIRS IN VIETNAM, 1963–1968

1. Daniel C. Hallin, *The Uncensored War: The Media and Vietnam* (New York: Oxford University Press, 1986), 29.
2. David Halberstam, *The Making of a Quagmire: America and Vietnam During the Kennedy Era* (Lanham, MD: Rowman & Littlefield, 2008); Marguerite Higgins, *Our Vietnam Nightmare* (New York: Harper & Row, 1965).
3. J. Fred MacDonald, *Television and the Red Menace: The Video Road to Vietnam* (New York: Praeger, 1985), 169, 171, emphasis in original.
4. Hallin, *The Uncensored War*.
5. William M. Hammond, *Public Affairs: The Military and the Media, 1962–1968* (Washington, DC: Center of Military History, United States Army, 1990), 12.
6. Graham A. Cosmas, *MACV: The Joint Command in the Years of Escalation, 1962–1967* (Washington, DC: Center of Military History, United States Army, 2006), 27, 24.
7. William S. Turley, *The Second Indochina War: A Concise Political and Military History* (Lanham, MD: Rowman & Littlefield, 2008), 62.
8. See, e.g., Hammond, *Public Affairs, 1962–1968*, 15; and David C. Snow, "Creating the Credibility Gap: Military Advisory Command, Vietnam, and the Media," master's thesis, U.S. Army Command and General Staff College, 2006, https://apps.dtic.mil/sti/citations/ADA452044.
9. Peter Arnett, *Live from the Battlefield: From Vietnam to Baghdad, 35 Years in the World's War Zones* (New York: Simon and Schuster, 1995), 89.
10. Hammond, *Public Affairs, 1962–1968*, 24–25.
11. Homer Bigart, "Vietnam Victory Remote Despite U.S. Aid to Diem; Victory in South Vietnam Considered Remote Despite U.S. Aid to Diem's Regime," *New York Times*, July 15, 1962, https://www.nytimes.com/1962/07/25/archives/vietnam-victory-remote-despite-us-aid-to-diem-victory-in-south.html.

12. Malcolm Browne, quoted in Arnett, *Live from the Battlefield*, 76–77. The correspondents I spoke to in researching this book remembered Browne's pamphlet, and one mailed me a photocopy of the well-worn copy Browne had given him on arrival in Saigon.
13. They were only one of the breeds of journalists producing copy for the U.S. market. Another breed entirely were the columnists and celebrated public intellectuals, such as Joseph Alsop, Marguerite Higgins, James Reston, and Walter Lippmann, who would cycle through for much shorter periods, had very different interactions with their official sponsors, and were viewed as outsiders by the Saigon-based correspondents. A third category might include the late-arriving strand of reporters who traveled briefly through Vietnam to "get their ticket punched."
14. John Mecklin, *Mission in Torment: An Intimate Account of the U.S. Role in Vietnam* (New York: Doubleday, 1965), 134; Hammond, *Public Affairs, 1962–1968*, 27.
15. Hammond, *Public Affairs, 1962–1968*, 28.
16. Arnett, *Live from the Battlefield*, 90.
17. William Prochnau, *Once Upon a Distant War: Reporting from Vietnam* (New York: Mainstream, 1996), 215, 216.
18. Compare, for example, Turley, *The Second Indochina War*, and Hammond, *Public Affairs, 1962–1968*.
19. Turley, *The Second Indochina War*, 72–73; Hammond, *Public Affairs, 1962–1968*, 3.
20. Turley, *The Second Indochina War*, 81.
21. David Halberstam, quoted in Prochnau, *Once Upon a Distant War*, 220.
22. David Halberstam, *The Making of a Quagmire*, 77.
23. Hammond, *Public Affairs, 1962–1968*, 33.
24. Michael Maclear, *The Ten Thousand Day War: Vietnam, 1945–1975* (New York: Avon, 1982), 183.
25. Hammond, *Public Affairs, 1962–1968*, 76, 75.
26. Westmoreland wore two hats. He was both the head of the Army component in the MACV mission and the head of MACV under the title "commanding general." As a component commander, he advocated the Army cause against competing claims by Navy and Marine component commanders; and as commanding general, he adjudicated the competing claims. See Dr. Donald J. Mrozek, *Air Power and the Ground War in Vietnam: Ideas and Actions* (Maxwell Air Force Base, AL: Air University Press, 1988), 37. As Ian Horwood notes, this combined role continued a practice observed by Dwight D. Eisenhower in North Africa and Douglas MacArthur in Korea; regardless, it is a clear indication of the Army's dominant role in the theater. See Ian Horwood, *Interservice Rivalry and Airpower in the Vietnam War* (Fort Leavenworth, KS: DIANE, 2010), 9. A further degree of complexity emerged from the independent command role called "commander in chief, Pacific" (CINCPAC), a maritime command that included a significant Air Force component. This position was occupied by Admirals H. D. Felt until 1964, U. S. G. Sharp until 1968, J. S.

McCain until 1972, and N. Gayler until 1976. Lewis Sorley notes, CINCPAC "had some responsibility for the bombing campaign outside South Vietnam, but little else to do with the war." Lewis Sorley, *Thunderbolt: General Creighton Abrams and the Army of His Times* (New York: Simon and Schuster, 1992), 327. Interservice rivalry existed throughout the U.S. mission to Vietnam, but for our purposes the most significant point is simply that Westmoreland "did not have overall control of all the air assets committed to Southeast Asia, or even to South Vietnam.... Westmoreland could not, therefore, use all these air assets exactly as he saw fit" (Horwood, *Interservice Rivalry and Airpower in the Vietnam War*, 175). In the absence of complete command over the Air Force in the region, Westmoreland tacitly gave priority to Army aviation. See Lieutenant General John J. Tolson, *Airmobility, 1961–1971* (Washington, DC: U.S. Department of the Army, 1973), 193.

27. Hammond, *Public Affairs, 1962–1968*, 79, 80.
28. Hammond, *Public Affairs, 1962–1968*, 81.
29. William C. Westmoreland, *A Soldier Reports* (1976; reprint, New York: Hachette, 1989), 49; see also Hammond, *Public Affairs, 1962–1968*, 82.
30. Quoted in Hammond, *Public Affairs, 1962–1968*, 82.
31. The North Vietnamese certainly fired their weapons. Consistent speculation about the affair has ultimately unearthed official confirmation that the "attack" consisted entirely of the U.S. vessels firing at the ghost images they saw on their radar. Some believe Johnson acted in bad faith.
32. Turley, *The Second Indochina War*, 84.
33. Maclear, *The Ten Thousand Day War*, 121.
34. Hallin, *The Uncensored War*.
35. Maclear, *The Ten Thousand Day War*, 122.
36. Turley, *The Second Indochina War*, 124.
37. Hammond, *Public Affairs, 1962–1968*, 136.
38. Maclear, *The Ten Thousand Day War*, 135–36.
39. Hammond, *Public Affairs, 1962–1968*, 146–48.
40. Tolson, *Airmobility, 1961–1971*, 61–62.
41. Marvin Wolf, phone interview by the author, April 19, 2013.
42. Wolf interview, April 19, 2013.
43. Wolf interview, April 19, 2013.
44. John Laurence, *The Cat from Hue: A Vietnam War Story* (London: Hachette UK, 2002), 99–121.
45. Turley, *The Second Indochina War*, 108.
46. Hammond, *Public Affairs, 1962–1968*, 212.
47. Hammond, *Public Affairs, 1962–1968*, 195.
48. Maclear, *The Ten Thousand Day War*, 155–56.
49. Hammond, *Public Affairs, 1962–1968*, 290.
50. Snow, "Creating the Credibility Gap," 60.

4. THE TET PARADOX: MEDIA-MANAGEMENT REGIMES IN VIETNAM, 1968–1975

1. William S. Turley, *The Second Indochina War: A Concise Political and Military History* (Lanham, MD: Rowman & Littlefield, 2008), 145–46.
2. Michael Maclear, *The Ten Thousand Day War: Vietnam, 1945–1975* (New York: Avon, 1982), 205.
3. William C. Westmoreland, *A Soldier Reports* (1976; reprint, New York: Hachette, 1989), 324.
4. Westmoreland, *A Soldier Reports*, 325.
5. Charles Mohr, "Hue Is Embattled: Other Cities Besieged—Allies Bomb Foe in Cholon Area," *New York Times*, February 1, 1968.
6. Don North, interviewed by the author by phone, April 13, 2013.
7. Aide quoted in Lewis Sorley, *Thunderbolt: General Creighton Abrams and the Army of His Times* (New York: Simon and Schuster, 1992), 212.
8. General Creighton Abrams, quoted in Sorley, *Thunderbolt*, 212–13.
9. Don Oberdorfer, *Tet! The Turning Point in the Vietnam War* (Baltimore, MD: Johns Hopkins University Press, 2001), 203.
10. "Johnson, H.K. (1968, February 24)" (backchannel message to Sharp, Nazzaro, and Westmoreland), box 77, folder 3: "Backchannel Messages," Harold K. Johnson Collection, 1931–1978, United States Army Military History Institute, Carlisle, PA.
11. William M. Hammond, *Public Affairs: The Military and the Media, 1962–1968* (Washington, DC: Center of Military History, United States Army, 1990), 366, 367.
12. Maclear, *The Ten Thousand Day War*, 210, 274.
13. Maclear, *The Ten Thousand Day War*, 221.
14. Sorley, *Thunderbolt*, 200, 232, 233.
15. Charles Hirschman, Samuel Preston, and Vu Manh Loi, "Vietnamese Casualties During the American War: A New Estimate," *Population and Development Review* 21, no. 4 (1995): 792, https://doi.org/10.2307/2137774.
16. Sorley, *Thunderbolt*, 245, 229.
17. General C. W. Abrams, "Public Affairs Guidance," memorandum to senior commanders and PAOs, July 1968, box 2, folder 4: "Miscellaneous Correspondence re. PA," Winant Sidle Papers, 1950–1999, United States Army Military History Institute.
18. William Thomas Allison, *My Lai: An American Atrocity in the Vietnam War* (Baltimore, MD: Johns Hopkins University Press, 2012), 75.
19. Westmoreland, *A Soldier Reports*, 375.
20. Allison, *My Lai*, 84–85.
21. One strategic lesson was certainly clear: reduce U.S. involvement. But at this stage of the war, reduction was a given. See Graham A. Cosmas, *MACV: The Joint Command in the Years of Escalation, 1962–1967* (Washington, DC: Center of Military History, United States Army, 2006). What was not obvious was whether the

public would be satisfied with fewer casualties or indeed with Americans acting in strictly support roles, on the one hand, or the Army had well and truly lost the American public's support, on the other.
22. Maclear, *The Ten Thousand Day War*, 296.
23. The repercussions of this event at Kent State in particular would stay with the Army. Charles D. Allen, a retired Army colonel who now teaches at the Army War College, recalls the formative effect of the day: "[Before Kent State] I viewed the Army as protecting my family from the civil unrest that was rampant across the United States and which found its way to my town. . . . The protectors were thrust off the pedestal upon which I had placed them and that positive image was shattered." Charles D. Allen, "Four Dead in Ohio," *Washington Post*, November 9, 2009. He introduces new Army War College with his story of that day.
24. Richard Milhous Nixon, *RN: The Memoirs of Richard Nixon* (New York: Grosset & Dunlap, 1978), 460.
25. John Erlichman, quoted in Maclear, *The Ten Thousand Day War*, 298.
26. William M. Hammond, *Public Affairs: The Military and the Media, 1968–1973* (Washington, DC: Center of Military History, United States Army, 1996), 288.
27. David C. Snow, "Creating the Credibility Gap: Military Advisory Command, Vietnam, and the Media," master's thesis, U.S. Army Command and General Staff College, 2006, 73, https://apps.dtic.mil/sti/citations/ADA452044.
28. Don North, phone interview by the author, April 17, 2014.
29. North interview, April 17, 2014.
30. North interview, April 17, 2014.
31. Hammond, *Public Affairs, 1968–1973*, 369.
32. Hammond, *Public Affairs, 1968–1973*, 378.
33. John Laurence later described his embedding experience with the First Team and his CBS report in *The Cat from Hue: A Vietnam War Story* (London: Hachette UK, 2002), quotes on 728.
34. Laurence, *The Cat from Hue*, 730, 731, 740.
35. The requirement that members of the press fly on South Vietnamese helicopters was also enforced because of a DOD regulation preventing government aircraft from competing with commercial airlines. In Cambodia, as Craig Whitney pointed out at the time, the regulation was not invoked, and following a series of deaths of reporters (including the legendary figures François Sully, Larry Burrows, and Henri Huet as well as the younger reporters Kent Potter and Keisaburo Shimamoto), "quietly, without announcement, the American policy was changed." Craig Whitney, "War Coverage," *New York Times*, February 21, 1971.
36. Hammond, *Public Affairs, 1968–1973*, 9–10.
37. Hammond, *Public Affairs, 1968–1973*, 414.
38. Maclear, *The Ten Thousand Day War*, 299.
39. Turley, *The Second Indochina War*, 183.
40. Snow, "Creating the Credibility Gap," 77.

41. Sorley, *Thunderbolt*, 309.
42. Hammond, *Public Affairs, 1968–1973*, 525.
43. Sorley, *Thunderbolt*, 257.
44. Office of the Chief of Information, *Annual Historical Summary*, June 30, 1969, p. 7, Annual Historical Reviews, Unclassified Documents, Center of Military History, United States Army, Fort McNair, Washington, DC.
45. Sorley, *Thunderbolt*, 273.
46. Maclear, *The Ten Thousand Day War*, 270.
47. Turley, *The Second Indochina War*, 169. See also Jeffrey P. Kimball and William Burr, *Nixon's Nuclear Specter: The Secret Alert of 1969, Madman Diplomacy, and the Vietnam War* (Lawrence: University of Kansas Press, 2015).
48. Richard M. Nixon, "Address to the Nation on the War in Vietnam," November 3, 1969, American Presidency Project, ed. Gerhard Peters and John T. Woolley, https://www.presidency.ucsb.edu/documents/address-the-nation-the-war-vietnam.
49. Turley, *The Second Indochina War*, 170.
50. Frederick C. Weyand, "George Catlett Marshall Memorial Reception and Dinner Speech," October 18, 2000, Association of the United States Army Convention, http://www.i-served.com/Reference/GeneralFredWeyand_speech.htm.
51. Howard H. Callaway to Frederick C. Weyand, "Secretary of the Army's Top 5," memorandum, January 21, 1975, box 7, folder 5: "Correspondence: Army Secretariat," Frederick C. Weyand Papers, 1972–1999, United States Army Military History Institute.
52. Sorley, *Thunderbolt*, 363.
53. Fox Butterfield, "Reporter's Notebook," *New York Times*, May 5, 1975.
54. Peter Arnett, *Live from the Battlefield: From Vietnam to Baghdad, 35 Years in the World's War Zones* (New York: Simon and Schuster, 1995), 291.
55. Arnett, *Live from the Battlefield*, 298.
56. Ben Stocking, Thomas Maresca, and Associated Press Writers, "Vietnam War Journalists Reunite for Anniversary," *San Diego Union-Tribune*, April 30, 2010, https://www.sandiegouniontribune.com/sdut-vietnam-war-journalists-reunite-for-anniversary-2010apr30-story.html.
57. Don North, "Requiem for a Vietnam War Reporter—George Esper, 1932–2012," May 9, 2012, Historynet, https://www.historynet.com/requiem-for-a-vietnam-war-reporter-george-esper-1932-2012/.

5. TET SUPPRESSED: ARMY DOCTRINAL INNOVATIONS, 1976–1982

1. Lewis Sorley describes Westmoreland as a Taylor protégé. Westmoreland is less forthcoming in his autobiography, saying only that he admired and was close to Taylor, but it was Taylor who had the final say in naming Westmoreland to

command MACV. Lewis Sorley, *Honorable Warrior: General Harold K. Johnson and the Ethics of Command*, Modern War Studies (Lawrence: University Press of Kansas, 1998), 156–57; William C. Westmoreland, *A Soldier Reports* (1976; reprint, New York: Hachette, 1989), 20.
2. Sorley, *Honorable Warrior*, 94.
3. Sorley describes Harold K. Johnson's complex relationship with Wheeler in his biography of Johnson, *Honorable Warrior* (182–89). There he also notes that Johnson emphatically denied responsibility for Westmoreland being given command of MACV. In his biography of Abrams, Sorley discusses how Abrams was up for the job at the same time and was certainly Johnson's choice, and, indeed, Johnson told President Lyndon Johnson that Abrams was the top soldier in the Army. Lewis Sorley, *Thunderbolt: General Creighton Abrams and the Army of His Times* (New York: Simon and Schuster, 1992), 194. When Abrams finally took command of MACV, General Johnson was delighted. He later recalled, "We had about as close a relationship as any two men can have." Quoted in Sorley, *Honorable Warrior*, 175.
4. Weyand and Abrams's relationship is not very well documented, but an emotional speech given by Weyand to the Army Association in 2000 gives a sense of the two men's friendship. In late 2000, Weyand described his long-deceased friend as "a rare amalgam of leadership, wisdom, human understanding and intellectual capacity. And all of that packed into the uniform of an American soldier. I never knew anyone like Abe." Frederick C. Weyand, "George Catlett Marshall Memorial Reception and Dinner Speech," October 18, 2000, Association of the United States Army Convention, http://www.i-served.com/Reference/GeneralFredWeyand_speech.htm. The esteem in which Abrams was held in the Army more generally is reflected in the decision to name the replacement for the M60 Patton tank the M1 Abrams tank in his honor.
5. Richard R. Lock-Pullan, "'An Inward Looking Time': The United States Army, 1973–1976," *Journal of Military History* 67, no. 2 (2003): 511.
6. Major Paul H. Herbert, *Deciding What Has to Be Done: General William E. DePuy and the 1976 Edition of* FM 100-5: Operations, Leavenworth Papers no. 16 (Fort Leavenworth, KS: Combat Studies Institute, U.S. Army Command and General Staff College, 1988), 22, https://www.armyupress.army.mil/Portals/7/combat-studies-institute/csi-books/herbert.pdf.
7. William E. DePuy, quoted in Lock-Pullan, "'An Inward Looking Time,'" 492.
8. Herbert, *Deciding What Has to Be Done*, 5.
9. Richard Winship Stewart, *Operation Urgent Fury: The Invasion of Grenada, October 1983* (Washington, DC: U.S. Department of Defense, 2008), 380.
10. Herbert, *Deciding What Has to Be Done*, 77.
11. Major Robert A. Doughty, *The Evolution of US Army Tactical Doctrine, 1946–76*, Leavenworth Papers no. 1 (Forth Leavenworth, KS: Combat Studies Institute, U.S. Army Command and General Staff College, August 1979), 40.
12. Herbert, *Deciding What Has to Be Done*, 12, 38.

13. G. W. Gawrych, *The 1973 Arab-Israeli War: The Albatross of Decisive Victory*, Leavenworth Papers no. 21 (Forth Leavenworth, KS: Combat Studies Institute, U.S. Army Command and General Staff College, 1996), 12, https://www.semanticscholar.org/paper/The-1973-Arab-Israeli-War%3A-The-Albatross-of-Victory-Gawrych/99b28e30229978fe5272ee55df01988f54be8525.
14. Gawrych, *The 1973 Arab-Israeli War*, 14.
15. Herbert, *Deciding What Has to Be Done*, 25.
16. Doughty, *The Evolution of US Army Tactical Doctrine*, 40.
17. Leonard Wong and Stephen J. Gerras, *Lying to Ourselves: Dishonesty in the Army Profession* (Carlisle, PA: U.S. Army War College Monographs, Books, and Publications, 2012), 21–22.
18. An example is Sten Rynning, *Changing Military Doctrine: Presidents and Military Power in Fifth Republic France, 1958–2000* (London: Bloomsbury Academic, 2002).
19. Barry R. Posen, *The Sources of Military Doctrine: France, Britain, and Germany Between the World Wars* (Ithaca, NY: Cornell University Press, 1984), 14.
20. Harald Hoiback, *Understanding Military Doctrine: A Multidisciplinary Approach* (London: Routledge, 2013).
21. *Joint Publication 1-02: Department of Defense Dictionary of Military and Associated Terms* (Washington, DC: Joint Chiefs of Staff, 2016), s.v. "doctrine," https://apps.dtic.mil/sti/pdfs/ADA542006.pdf.
22. It is difficult to prove just what officers have in mind when they talk about doctrine, and it is possible that common usage slips between the broad and narrow definitions. However, officers closely involved with TRADOC almost certainly have a narrow definition in mind. For example, DePuy's successor, General Donn A. Starry, described technical manuals as "real honest-to-goodness doctrine." Donn A. Starry, "Life and Career of General Donn A. Starry" (interviews), in *Press On! The Selected Works of General Donn A. Starry*, ed. Lewis Sorley, vol. 2 (Fort Leavenworth, KS: Combat Studies Institute Press, 2009), 1036.
23. Herbert, *Deciding What Has to Be Done*, 106.
24. Herbert, *Deciding What Has to Be Done*, 12.
25. William E. DePuy, "Remarks by General William E. DePuy at TRADOC Commanders' Conference, 25 May 1977," in *Selected Papers of General William E. DePuy*, comp. Richard M. Swain, ed. Donald L. Gilmore and Carolyn D. Conway, TRADOC Twentieth Anniversary Commemoration (Fort Leavenworth, KS: Combat Studies Institute Press, 1995), 256.
26. Herbert, *Deciding What Has to Be Done*, 39.
27. *Field Manual (FM) 100-5: Operations* (The Pentagon, Arlington County, VA: Headquarters, U.S. Department of the Army, July 1, 1976), 1-1.
28. William E. DePuy, "Letter to General Frederick C. Weyand from General DePuy, 8 July 1976," in *Selected Papers of General William E. DePuy*, 194.
29. Herbert, *Deciding What Has to Be Done*, 23, 41.

30. Starry, "Life and Career of General Donn A. Starry," in *Press On!*, 2:1111. In his memoir and oral history, John H. Cushman addresses Starry's claims. In his memoir, he notes that he had resisted being interviewed by Herbert for the book *Deciding What Has to Be Done* (1988) because his experience with *Field Manual 100-5: Operations* had been "very painful," but he ultimately agreed to be interviewed and considers the book to be accurate. See John H. Cushman, "Fort Leavenworth—a Memoir," n.d., folder 3, Lieutenant General John H. Cushman, U.S. Army, Retired, Library, https://www.west-point.org/publications/cushman/index.html. In his oral history, he rejects Starry's suggestion that he was insubordinate but offers no other insights on *Active Defense* or his relationship with DePuy. John H. Cushman, "Oral History, Volumes One Through Seven," vol. 5, n.d., folder 2, Lieutenant General John H. Cushman, U.S. Army, Retired, Library, https://www.west-point.org/publications/cushman/.
31. Herbert, *Deciding What Has to Be Done*, 7.
32. See, e.g., R. J. Spiller, "In the Shadow of the Dragon: Doctrine and the U.S. Army After Vietnam," *RUSI Journal* 142, no. 6 (1997): 41–54.
33. Herbert, *Deciding What Has to Be Done*, 7–9.
34. Edward N. Luttwak, "The American Style of Warfare," in *Strategy and History: Collected Essays*, vol. 2 (Oxford: Transaction, 1985), 174; William S. Lind, "Some Doctrinal Questions for the United States Army," *Military Review*, February 1997, 135–43.
35. John L. Romjue, *From Active Defense to AirLand Battle: The Development of Army Doctrine, 1973–1982* (Newport News, VA: Historical Office, U.S. Army Training and Doctrine Command, 1984), 65.
36. Romjue, *From Active Defense to AirLand Battle*, 73.
37. Romjue, *From Active Defense to AirLand Battle*, 72.
38. *Field Manual (FM) 100-5: Operations* (The Pentagon, Arlington County, VA: Headquarters, U.S. Department of the Army, August 20, 1982), 1, 7, 22–25.
39. *FM 100-5* (1982), appendix B-4, emphasis in original.
40. Donn A. Starry, "Desert Storm Lessons Learned" (interview), in *Press On!*, 2:1246.
41. Jack E. Pulwers, "A Quest for Excellence, Chapter 22: An Aftermath of War and an Organization in Transition (1973–1980)," n.d., 3, box 3, folder 7, United States Heritage and Education Center, Carlisle, PA.
42. Major General L. Gordon Hill, quoted in Pulwers, "A Quest for Excellence, Chapter 22," 28–29.
43. Charles A. Stevenson, *Warriors and Politicians: US Civil–Military Relations Under Stress* (London: Taylor & Francis, 2006), 121.
44. Pulwers, "A Quest for Excellence, Chapter 22," 16.
45. Pulwers, "A Quest for Excellence, Chapter 22," 13–16, 15.
46. Robert A. Sullivan, quoted in Pulwers, "A Quest for Excellence, Chapter 22," 32–33, emphasis in original.
47. Pulwers, "A Quest for Excellence, Chapter 22," 33, 35. An even more intense schedule was kept by Major General Anthony Cucolo during his time as chief

of public affairs in 2006–2008. Cucolo would meet every morning with the secretary of the Army, the head of legislative affairs, and other top officers and then again at night with the secretary of the Army and the Army chief of staff.

6. RECOVERY: SMALL WARS AND ORGANIZATIONAL RENEWAL, 1983–1989

1. *Field Manual (FM) 100-5: Operations* (The Pentagon, Arlington County, VA: Headquarters, U.S. Department of the Army, July 1, 1976); *Field Manual (FM) 100-5: Operations* (The Pentagon, Arlington County, VA: Headquarters, U.S. Department of the Army, August 20, 1982).
2. *FM 100-5* (1982), 1-5.
3. Lawrence Freedman, *The Official History of the Falklands Campaign*, vol. 1: *The Origins of the Falklands War* (London: Routledge, 2005), 27–28.
4. "Britons Given Only 2 Official Reports During Day," *New York Times*, May 20, 1982; William Borders, "British Journalists Voice Complaints Over Being 'Used' by the Government," *New York Times*, May 24, 1982.
5. Greg McLaughlin, *The War Correspondent* (Ann Arbor, MI: Pluto Press, 2002), 32, 78.
6. Arthur A. Humphries, "Two Routes to the Wrong Destination: Public Affairs in the South Atlantic War," *Naval War College Review* 36, no. 3 (1983): 62.
7. Humphries, "Two Routes to the Wrong Destination," 57.
8. For the interpretation of the mantra as the rediscovery of censorship, see, e.g., Jacqueline E. Sharkey, *Under Fire: U.S. Military Restrictions on the Media from Grenada to the Persian Gulf* (Washington, DC: Center for Public Integrity, 1991), 4.
9. Humphries, "Two Routes to the Wrong Destination," 58.
10. Ronald H. Cole, *Operation Urgent Fury: The Planning and Execution of Joint Operations in Grenada, 12 October–2 November 1983* (Washington, DC: Joint History Office, Office of the Chairman of the Joint Chiefs of Staff, 1997).
11. Sharkey, *Under Fire*, 68.
12. David R. Kiernan, *Headlines from the Frontline: The Military and Media Relationship . . . an Uneasy Truce* (Bloomington, IN: AuthorHouse, 2005).
13. Sharkey, *Under Fire*, 69.
14. Richard W. Stewart, *Operation Urgent Fury: The Invasion of Grenada, October 1983* (Washington, DC: U.S. Department of Defense, 2008), 9–10.
15. Sharkey, *Under Fire*, 68; Stewart, *Operation Urgent Fury*, 9; Ronald H. Cole, *Operation Just Cause: The Planning and Execution of Joint Operations in Panama* (Washington, DC: Joint History Office, Office of the Chairman of the Joint Chiefs of Staff, 1995), 9.
16. Kiernan, *Headlines from the Frontline*, 106.

17. Christopher Paul and James J. Kim, *Reporters on the Battlefield: The Embedded Press System in Historical Context* (Santa Monica, CA: RAND, 2005), 39.
18. Kiernan, *Headlines from the Frontline*, 106.
19. Paul and Kim, *Reporters on the Battlefield*, 39.
20. Kiernan, *Headlines from the Frontline*, 106.
21. Paul and Kim, *Reporters on the Battlefield*, 39.
22. Sharkey, *Under Fire*, 69–70, citing Lou Cannon and David Hoffman, "Invasion Secrecy Creating a Furor—Speakes Complained in Memo," *Washington Post*, October 27, 1982.
23. McLaughlin, *The War Correspondent*, 83.
24. Cole, *Operation Urgent Fury*, 2, 6.
25. Cole, *Operation Urgent Fury*, 5–6, 64, quoting Vessey on *Meet the Press*, NBC, November 6, 1983.
26. Stewart, *Operation Urgent Fury*, 32.
27. Paul and Kim, *Reporters on the Battlefield*, 40.
28. Sharkey, *Under Fire*, 86–87.
29. Jonathan Friendly, "Reporting the News in a Communiqué War," *New York Times*, October 26, 1983.
30. W. E. Farrell, "U.S. Allows 15 Reporters to Go to Grenada for Day," *New York Times*, October 28, 1983.
31. AP, "*Newsweek* Is Dropped from Grenada Visits," *New York Times*, October 30, 1983.
32. AP, "Editors Protest to Pentagon Over Press Curbs in Grenada," *New York Times*, November 1, 1983.
33. Bernard Weintraub, "Reporter's Notebook: Darkness and Light on the Isle of Spice," *New York Times*, November 4, 1983.
34. McLaughlin, *The War Correspondent*, 126, citing Peter Braestrup, *Battle Lines: Report of the Twentieth Century Fund Task Force on the Military and the Media* (New Haven, CT: Yale University Press, 1985), and Mark Hertsgaard, *On Bended Knee: The Press and the Reagan Presidency* (New York: Schocken, 1988).
35. G. H. Quester, "Grenada and the News Media," in *American Intervention in Grenada: Implications of Operation "Urgent Fury,"* ed. Peter M. Dunn and Bruce W. Watson (Boulder, CO: Westview Press, 1985), 109.
36. Kiernan, *Headlines from the Frontline*, 104.
37. *Meet the Press*, NBC, November 6, 1983.
38. Kiernan, *Headlines from the Frontline*, 117.
39. "The Sidle Panel Report," appendix 14 in Kiernan, *Headlines from the Frontline*, 260. Kiernan's book reproduces the entire Sidle Panel Report, 257–80.
40. "The Sidle Panel Report," appendix 14 in Kiernan, *Headlines from the Frontline*, 261.
41. "The Sidle Panel Report," appendix 14 in Kiernan, *Headlines from the Frontline*, 265–67.

244 6. RECOVERY

42. Major General Winant Sidle, "Public Affairs: Open Lines Important," in *Vietnam 10 Years Later: What Have We Learned?* (Fort Benjamin Harrison, Lawrence Township, KS: Defense Information School, 1983), 89.
43. Sidle, quoted in "The Issues: The Military Versus the Press," in *Vietnam 10 Years Later*, 18.
44. E. C. Meyer, speech to the Association of the United States Army, October 21, 1981, in *E. C. Meyer: General, United States Army, Chief of Staff, June 1979–June 1983* (Washington, DC: U.S. Department of the Army, 1983), 237, 239.
45. E. C. Meyer, speech at the AirLand Battle 2000 Symposium, May 10, 1982, in *E. C. Meyer: General*, 294.
46. Colonel Michael Sullivan, quoted in Richard F. Machamer, "An Incident in Korea: A Case Study of U.S. Army Public Affairs Activities in Response to the Ingman Range Murders in 1981," master's thesis, Kansas State University, 1991, 75, https://apps.dtic.mil/sti/citations/tr/ADA244556.
47. John A. Wickham Jr., "Oral History," 1991, 42–43, 50, box 4, folder 1, J. A. Wickham Jr. Papers, 1946–1991, United States Army Heritage and Education Center, Carlisle, PA.
48. Wickham, "Oral History," 89.
49. Office of the Chief of Public Affairs, United States Army, *Annual Historical Review* (Washington, DC: Center of Military History, United States Army, 1987), 14–16, 6.
50. Carl E. Vuono, speech, Worldwide Public Affairs Conference, October 23, 1987, box 2, folder 12, Carl E. Vuono Papers, United States Army Heritage and Education Center.
51. Vuono, speech, October 23, 1987.

7. THE TEST: MEDIA-MANAGEMENT REGIMES IN THE GULF WAR, 1990–1991

1. Kenneth S. Plato, "Military–Media Relations: First Impressions of Operation Desert Shield," paper submitted to the Naval War College, 1991, 2, https://apps.dtic.mil/sti/tr/pdf/ADA236365.pdf.
2. "The Sidle Panel Report," appendix 14 in David R. Kiernan, *Headlines from the Frontline: The Military and Media Relationship . . . an Uneasy Truce* (Bloomington, IN: AuthorHouse, 2005), 265, 264.
3. Plato, "Military–Media Relations," 5.
4. "The Sidle Panel Report," appendix 14 in Kiernan, *Headlines from the Frontline*, 270.
5. This was also true for the other services, of course.
6. Lawrence S. Epstein, "Interview with LTC Larry Icenogle," February 16, 1992, Persian Gulf War—the Military, the Press, and the Gulf War, 1990–1992 (B1F2), United States Army Heritage and Education Center, Carlisle, PA. Readers may

remember Icenogle as the media-savvy colleague mentioned by Donn Starry in his oral history, noted in chapter 5.
7. H. L. Timboe, "Mass Casualty Situation: Gallant Eagle 82 Airborne Operations: A Case Study," *Military Medicine* 153, no. 4 (1988): 199.
8. Unfortunately, the Army's OCI temporarily stopped archiving the *Annual Historical Summaries* from 1979 to 1986, so the Army's view of the Gallant Eagle risks is not known.
9. AP, "Massive Joint-Service 'Gallant Eagle' Exercise Concluding," August 2, 1986; UPI, "Soldier Killed in War Games," July 31, 1986.
10. See, e.g., S. E. Martin, "US Media Pools and Military Intervention in the 1980s and 1990s," *Journal of Peace Research* 43, no. 5 (2006): 601–16.
11. Epstein, "Interview with LTC Larry Icenogle."
12. Pascale Combelles-Siegel, *The Troubled Path to the Pentagon's Rules on Media Access to the Battlefield: Grenada to Today* (Carlisle, PA: Strategic Studies Institute, 1996), 12–13.
13. Combelles-Siegel, *The Troubled Path*, 12.
14. Ronald H. Cole, *Operation Just Cause: The Planning and Execution of Joint Operations in Panama* (Washington, DC: Joint History Office, Office of the Chairman of the Joint Chiefs of Staff, 1995).
15. Cole, *Operation Just Cause*.
16. R. H. Scales, *Certain Victory: The US Army in the Gulf War. A Select Report* (Fort Leavenworth, KS: Office of the Chief of Staff, U.S. Army, 1994), 35.
17. F. S. Hoffman, "Review of Panama Pool Deployment," appendix C in Jacqueline E. Sharkey, *Under Fire: U.S. Military Restrictions on the Media from Grenada to the Persian Gulf* (Washington, DC: Center for Public Integrity, 1990), 5 (paginated separately).
18. Hoffman, "Review of Panama Pool Deployment," 1.
19. Hoffman, "Review of Panama Pool Deployment," 2. See also Lawrence Epstein's long interview with Ron Sconyers, where Sconyers shares his later views on media management. Lawrence S. Epstein, "Interview with COL Ron Sconyers," March 25, 1992, Persian Gulf War—the Military, the Press, and the Gulf War, 1990–1992 (B1F5), United States Army Heritage and Education Center.
20. Peter Copeland, *Finding the News: Adventures of a Young Reporter* (Baton Rouge: Louisiana State University Press, 2019), 194.
21. Hoffman, "Review of Panama Pool Deployment," 9.
22. Copeland, *Finding the News*, 209.
23. Valerie Richardson, "Why Women Make Better Warriors," *Washington Times*, January 10, 1990.
24. John M. Broder, "Female's War Exploits Overblown, Army Says," *Los Angeles Times*, January 6, 1990; Philip Shabecoff, "The U.S. and Panama: Combat; Report of Woman's Role Is Called Into Question," *New York Times*, January 8, 1990.
25. Copeland, *Finding the News*, 196–237; Colleen L. McGuire, "Military–Media Relations and the Gulf War: A Compromise Between Vietnam and Grenada?,"

master's thesis, U.S. Army Command and General Staff Course, 1992, 24–26, https://apps.dtic.mil/sti/tr/pdf/ADA257146.pdf.
26. Hoffman, "Review of Panama Pool Deployment."
27. Hoffman, "Review of Panama Pool Deployment," 1.
28. McGuire, "Military–Media Relations and the Gulf War," 5–6.
29. Carl E. Vuono, "Address to the Command and General Staff College. Gen. Vuono Speeches and Remarks," September 24, 1987, box 1, folder 41, Carl E. Vuono Papers, 1987–1991, United States Heritage and Education Center, Carlisle, PA.
30. Jeffrey Record, "The Army's Clouded Future," *Washington Post*, November 15, 1988, https://www.washingtonpost.com/archive/opinions/1988/11/15/the-armys-clouded-future/36fa4e37-2e84-4957-bf3c-308991e4146f/.
31. Carl E. Vuono, "Today's Army, Powerful and Prepared," *Washington Post*, December 7, 1988.
32. Carl E. Vuono to Army general officers, December 8, 1988, in Carl E. Vuono, *A Trained and Ready Army: The Collected Works of the Thirty-First Chief of Staff of the Army* (Washington, DC: Carl E. Vuono, 1994), 126.
33. Carl E. Vuono, address to the Army's public-affairs community, October 1989, in *A Trained and Ready Army*, 209.
34. Carl E. Vuono, White Paper, January 1990, in *A Trained and Ready Army*, 411.
35. Richard W. Stewart, *War in the Persian Gulf: Operations Desert Shield and Desert Storm, August 1990–March 1991* (Washington, DC: Center of Military History, United States Army, 2010).
36. Carl E. Vuono, quoted in Scales, *Certain Victory*, 51.
37. Michael Wines, "Confrontation in the Gulf: Press Left Out of Gulf Alert," *New York Times*, August 9, 1990.
38. Williams, a journalist by trade, took a personal interest in supporting the pool reporters. Peter Copeland writes about how he was almost denied a place in the pool because his passport had no space left for the Saudi visa, so he called Williams and explained the situation. Williams then personally drove to the State Department to obtain extra pages for Copeland's passport. Copeland, *Finding the News*, 291.
39. Icenogle had a good rapport with the pool members. Copeland remembers him as "big and gruff, loud and confident, extremely smart and even a little bit funny. We called him the Iceman." Copeland understood Icenogle's role to be "to make sure the pool didn't endanger the troops by revealing too much about their numbers and capabilities[;] . . . the Iceman checked our stories but made few changes." Copeland, *Finding the News*, 245.
40. Copeland, *Finding the News*, 242. See also Epstein, "Interview with LTC Larry Icenogle."
41. Epstein, "Interview with LTC Larry Icenogle."
42. There were 36 members of the national press pool, with 17 positions available for the first deployment to Desert Shield. These positions were filled

according to a standing rotation, but major news agencies were guaranteed a certain number of spots. By September, there were around 400 reporters in theater, and by January approximately 800 to 1,000. Epstein, "Interview with LTC Larry Icenogle."

43. Although Peterzell did contribute to a cover story for *Time* on Bush's foreign policy, the story made no use of the reporting Peterzell would have done with the pool in Panama. See George J. Church, Dan Goodgame, Chrisopher Ogden, and Jay Peterzell, "Showing Muscle with the Invasion of Panama, a Bolder—and Riskier—Bush Foreign Policy Emerges," *Time*, January 1, 1990.
44. Epstein, "Interview with LTC Larry Icenogle."
45. Copeland, *Finding the News*, 244.
46. Epstein, "Interview with LTC Larry Icenogle."
47. Epstein, "Interview with LTC Larry Icenogle."
48. Copeland, *Finding the News*, 245; Carl Rochelle, "Carl Rochelle on Persian Gulf War Pool Coverage," C-SPAN, March 20, 1991, https://www.c-span.org/video/?c4670731/carl-rochelle-persian-gulf-war-pool-coverage.
49. Carl E. Vuono, quoted in G. H. Stinnett, "OPSEC Awareness Guidance for Operation Desert Shield," 1990, F1, Gulf War Collection, Historical Resources Collection II, Center of Military History, United States Army, Washington, DC.
50. U.S. Central Command, "Official: Security Guidelines for Media Encounters," 1990, F1, Gulf War Collection, Historical Resources Collection II, Center of Military History.
51. Pete Williams, "Media Travel—Operation Desert Shield," F1, Gulf War Collection, Historical Resources Collection II, Center of Military History.
52. Secretary of the Army and Public Affairs, "Public Affairs Guidance—Desert Shield Speculation," 1991, F1, Gulf War Collection, Historical Resources Collection II, Center of Military History.
53. Commander in Chief, Forces Command (CINCFOR), "Local Media Travel," October 31, 1990, folder 1, Gulf War Collection, Historical Resources Collection II, Center of Military History.
54. Copeland, *Finding the News*, 271.
55. Forrest Sawyer, "Media and Military at Odds in Desert," *ABC News Nightline*, October 10, 1990.
56. Sawyer, "Media and Military at Odds in Desert."
57. Copeland, *Finding the News*, 273.
58. The survey is covered in *Pentagon Rules on Media Access to the Persian Gulf: Hearing Before the Committee on Governmental Affairs, United States Senate, 102nd Cong.* (Washington, DC: U.S. Government Printing Office, 1991), 1091.
59. *Crossfire*, CNN, January 4, 1991.
60. *Crossfire*, CNN, January 4, 1991. Peterzell's support of the pool system was made public when Williams quoted him at length while appearing before the Senate Committee on Governmental Affairs. See *Pentagon Rules on Media Access to the Persian Gulf*, 8.

61. John R. MacArthur, *Second Front: Censorship and Propaganda in the 1991 Gulf War* (Berkeley: University of California Press, 1995), 11, 154.
62. Winant Sidle to BG Charles W. McClain Jr., U.S. Army Chief of Public Affairs, January 4, 1991, box 2, folder 4: "Miscellaneous Correspondence re. Public Affairs," United States Army Heritage and Education Center.
63. Sidle to McClain, January 4, 1991.
64. *Nation Magazine v. U.S. Dept. of Defense* (762 F. Supp. 1558 (S.D.N.Y. 1991)) was dismissed on May 2, 1991, on the grounds that the complaint was "too abstract and conjectural" (at 3) to argue once the regulations became moot on March 4, 1991. This ruling invited future litigation if the DOD reprised the pool model and defied a press agency access to the battlefield. *J.B. Pictures, Inc. v. U.S. Dept. of Defense* (86 F.3d 236 (DC Cir. 1996)) was decided in favor of the DOD on June 18, 1996.
65. Secretary of the Army and Public Affairs, "Public Affairs Guidance—Desert Shield Speculation."
66. Epstein, "Interview with LTC Larry Icenogle."
67. John King, "Revisions Leave Most Combat Reporting Restrictions Intact," AP, January 8, 1991. See also Frank Aukofer and William P. Lawrence, *America's Team—the Odd Couple: A Report on the Relationship Between the Media and the Military* (Nashville, TN: Vanderbilt University Press, 1995), 43–47; and *Pentagon Rules on Media Access to the Persian Gulf*, 60.
68. Epstein, "Interview with LTC Larry Icenogle." These pools would draw from nine pool categories, arranged so that each deployed pool would cover most if not all of the categories: television (open to major U.S. networks), radio, wire service, news magazine, newspaper (subdivided into major papers and minor papers), "pencil" (other print journalists), "photo" (alternating among wire, news magazine, and newspaper), Saudi, and international (the latter two categories were required to file their stories in English). *Pentagon Rules on Media Access to the Persian Gulf*, vi.
69. Copeland, *Finding the News*, 261–62. In his witness statement to the Senate Committee on Governmental Affairs, Frank Aukofer described the relations between members of the press during the war in damning terms: "Instead of battling for access for all in the name of press freedom, they eagerly traded their journalistic principles for a few crumbs for themselves and starvation for many of their colleagues." *Pentagon Rules on Media Access to the Persian Gulf*, 36.
70. Epstein, "Interview with LTC Larry Icenogle."
71. Epstein, "Interview with LTC Larry Icenogle."
72. George Esper, "One Month Into War, U.S. Military Still Curbs Access," AP, February 16, 1991.
73. Office of the Secretary of Defense for Public Affairs, "Operation Desert Storm Release Authority," January 18, 1991, folder 1, Gulf War Collection, Historical Resources Collection II, Center of Military History.
74. Epstein, "Interview with LTC Larry Icenogle."

75. Copeland, *Finding the News*, 268.
76. Copeland, *Finding the News*, 290, 291, 300.
77. Rochelle, "Carl Rochelle on Persian Gulf War Pool Coverage."
78. Lawrence S. Epstein, "Interview with S. Lynne Walker," July 20, 1992, Persian Gulf War—the Military, the Press, and the Gulf War, 1990–1992 (B1F9), United States Army Heritage and Education Center.
79. Pete Williams often repeated the high count of 1,500. The most accurate count was probably kept by the JIB's Larry Icenogle, who believed there were never more than 800 reporters in the theater at a time. Epstein, "Interview with LTC Larry Icenogle." Notably, famed AP bureau chief George Esper also believed 800 to be the right number. Esper, "One Month Into War, U.S. Military Still Curbs Access."

8. LESSONS LEARNED AND NOT LEARNED, 1991–2000

1. *Allied* refers to interactions between NATO member states, either between allied militaries or linking through the NATO command structure. *Interagency* refers to military organizations coordinating with civilian agencies within the organizations' own government. See *DOD Dictionary of Military and Associated Terms* (Washington, DC: Joint Chiefs of Staff, 2017), s.v. "interagency." *Comprehensive* is a NATO term referring to the coordination of military organizations across all political, military, and civilian capabilities within a group of nations, including host nations. See NATOTerm, s.v. "comprehensive approach," accessed August 15, 2024, https://nso.nato.int/natoterm/content/nato/pages/home.html?lg=en.
2. According to W. Joseph Campbell, Cronkite's reputation had been bolstered by a flawed poll conducted in 1972 that was then widely promoted by CBS News in its advertising. W. Joseph Campbell, *Getting It Wrong: Debunking the Greatest Myths in American Journalism* (Oakland: University of California Press, 2017), 100–15. Despite revisionist critiques, though, Cronkite was by all accounts a trusted and respected journalist in the early 1990s.
3. At more than 1,500 pages, the published record of the hearings is a treasure trove of information about Army public affairs. See *Pentagon Rules on Media Access to the Persian Gulf War: Hearing Before the Committee on Governmental Affairs, United States Senate, 102nd Cong.* (Washington, DC: U.S. Government Printing Office, 1991).
4. *Pentagon Rules on Media Access to the Persian Gulf War*, 21, 32, 58–59, 52–55, 14.
5. *Pentagon Rules on Media Access to the Persian Gulf War*, 21, 44.
6. *Pentagon Rules on Media Access to the Persian Gulf War*, 54, 46.
7. *Pentagon Rules on Media Access to the Persian Gulf War*, 58, 60, 79.
8. *Pentagon Rules on Media Access to the Persian Gulf War*, 13.
9. Speaking to C-SPAN audiences on March 20, 1991, about a month after the hearings, Rochelle provided more context to his earlier support: "The press pools

that were over there did not work exactly right. It was either feast or famine. I was fortunate." Carl Rochelle, "Carl Rochelle on Persian Gulf War Pool Coverage," C-SPAN, March 20, 1991, https://www.c-span.org/video/?c4670731/carl-rochelle-persian-gulf-war-pool-coverage.
10. *Pentagon Rules on Media Access to the Persian Gulf War*, 33, 43–44, 58.
11. *Pentagon Rules on Media Access to the Persian Gulf War*, 56, 60, 52–53.
12. *"Operation Desert Storm / Desert Shield": Hearings Before the Committee on Armed Services, United States Senate, One Hundred Second Congress, First Session, April 24, May 8, 9, 16, 21, June 4, 12, 20, 1991* (Washington, DC: U.S. Government Printing Office, June 24, 1991), 312, 316. Hereafter referred to as *SASC Report*.
13. *SASC Report*, 340–41.
14. *SASC Report*, 341.
15. *SASC Report*, 206.
16. *Conduct of the Persian Gulf War: Final Report to Congress* (Washington, DC: U.S. Department of Defense, 1992), S-7.
17. Pascale Combelles-Siegel, *The Troubled Path to the Pentagon's Rules on Media Access to the Battlefield: Grenada to Today* (Carlisle, PA: Strategic Studies Institute, 1996), 19–22; Jacqueline E. Sharkey, *Under Fire: U.S. Military Restrictions on the Media from Grenada to the Persian Gulf* (Washington, DC: Center for Public Integrity, 1990), 152–54. The agencies represented in this group were: the newspapers *Chicago Tribute, Los Angeles Times, New York Times, Wall Street Journal*, and *Washington Post*; the news groups Cox Newspapers, Hearst Newspapers, and Knight-Ridder; the magazines *Newsweek* and *Time*; the television networks ABC, CBS, CNN, and NBC; and the AP.
18. Sharkey, *Under Fire*, 152.
19. Combelles-Siegel, *The Troubled Path to the Pentagon's Rules on Media Access*, 20.
20. Patrick Sloyan, "US Covers Up Deaths by 'Friendly Fire': Half Gulf Ground War Casualties Caused by Own Side, Writes Patrick Sloyan," *The Guardian*, August 12, 1991.
21. An exception is the reporting by the AP's John King, which had revealed the death of British soldiers by a U.S. A-10 Warthog plane. John King, "Kuwait All but Liberated; Tank Battle Rages," AP, February 27, 1991. American-on-American casualties, so frequent during the four days of the operation, were missed by reporters, indicating the small number of reporters able to accurately report events on the battlefield.
22. Jay C. Steuck, "Press Pools and Newspaper Coverage of the Gulf War: Attitudes of Newspaper Editors," master's thesis, Arizona State University, 1992, 52–75, 51.
23. Frank Aukofer, "The Independent Reporter: Fighting the Elitist Clique," *Nieman Reports* 45, no. 2 (1991): 24–27. The *Milwaukee Journal* was ranked 18 by size of circulation in Steuck's list of 200 newspapers. Steuck, "Press Pools and Newspaper Coverage of the Gulf War," 112. Aukofer's ire was directed toward the most elite members of the press, likely a similar list to the group of fifteen agencies

8. LESSONS LEARNED AND NOT LEARNED, 1991-2000   251

that met to debate the principles of media management for future operations, mentioned in note 17.

24. Jean Baudrillard, "La guerre du Golfe n'aura pas lieu," *Libération*, January 4, 1991. An English translation of Baudrillard's newspaper article is included in Jean Baudrillard, *The Gulf War Did Not Take Place*, trans. Paul Patton (Bloomington: Indiana University Press, 1995), 23–28.
25. Jean Baudrillard, "La guerre du Golfe a-t-elle vraiment lieu?," and "La Guerre du Golfe n'a pas eu lieu," *Libération*, February 6 and March 29, 1991, translated in Baudrillard, *The Gulf War Did Not Take Place*, 29–60 and 61–87. The third article's title has become iconic, with authors frequently asserting that events they study "did not take place." See, for example, Jonathan Beecher Field, "The Antinomian Controversy Did Not Take Place," *Early American Studies* 6, no. 2 (2008): 448–63.
26. See, e.g., James Morris, "Simulacra in the Age of Social Media: Baudrillard as the Prophet of Fake News," *Journal of Communication Inquiry* 45, no. 4 (2020): 319–36.
27. The comments appeared in an article Gottschalk published in *World Policy Journal* rather than in her own trade magazine. See Marie Gottschalk, "Operation Desert Cloud: The Media and the Gulf War," *World Policy Journal* 9, no. 3 (1992): 450, 451–52, 480. In her critique of the "schizophrenic stance" taken by one publication, Gottschalk was referring to Craig LaMay, Martha FitzSimon, and Jeanne Sahadi, eds., *The Media at War: The Press and the Persian Gulf Conflict: A Report of the Gannett Foundation* (McLean, VA: Gannett Foundation Media Center, 1991).
28. Criticism of the media was wide ranging. The Norwegian scholar Rune Ottosen's position is typical of the most critical strand, arguing explicitly that Gulf War reporting should be understood as "advertising for the arms industry." See Rune Ottosen, "The Media and the Gulf War Reporting: Advertising for the Arms Industry?," *Bulletin of Peace Proposals* 23, no. 1 (1992): 71–83.
29. Combelles-Siegel, *The Troubled Path to the Pentagon's Rules on Media Access*, 20.
30. The directive was published as Joint Chiefs of Staff Publication 5-02.2. The instruction, titled "Procedures for Joint Public Affairs Operations," then in draft form, is cited extensively in Combelles-Siegel, *The Troubled Path to the Pentagon's Rules on Media Access*. Recent versions of that instruction are in the 5400.14 series.
31. The Army's *Field Manual 46-1* was renumbered 3-61 in the 2000 edition.
32. See Cliff Goddard, "'It's the Economy, Stupid': The Everyday Semantics of a Geopolitical Key Word," *Journal of Postcolonial Linguistics* 5, no. 1 (2021): 226–38.
33. When Ricks retired, he was replaced by a civilian, Brian Kilgallen. See Combelles-Siegel, *The Troubled Path to the Pentagon's Rules on Media Access*, 21.
34. David Griffiths, "News Blues at the Pentagon," *American Journalism Review* 15, no. 7 (September 1993): 13–15.

35. John Nichols, "Cheney vs. Journalism," *The Nation*, June 13, 2005.
36. Combelles-Siegel, *The Troubled Path to the Pentagon's Rules on Media Access*, 44.
37. Charles W. Ricks, *The Military–News Media Relationship: Thinking Forward*, final report (Carlisle, PA: Strategic Studies Institute, December 1, 1993), 21.
38. Ricks, *The Military–News Media Relationship*, 2, 35.
39. *Joint Publication 3-61, Doctrine for Public Affairs in Joint Operations* (Washington, DC: Joint Chiefs of Staff, 1997), 1-1, italicized text originally in bold type.
40. Combelles-Siegel, *The Troubled Path to the Pentagon's Rules on Media Access*, 20.
41. *Joint Publication 3-61* (1997), II-4, III-3, emphasis in the original.
42. Robert H. Scales, *Certain Victory: The US Army in the Gulf War* (Fort Leavenworth, KS: US Army Command and General Staff College Press, 1993), 138.
43. Victoria Ferris, "Major General Thomas Harrison Tait '55: 'The Big Stick,'" Virginia Military Institute Alumni Agencies, March 8, 2023, https://www.vmialumni.org/major-general-thomas-harrison-tait-55-the-big-stick/.
44. Eliot A. Cohen, "*Certain Victory: The U.S. Army in the Gulf War*" (review), *Foreign Affairs*, March 1, 1995, https://www.foreignaffairs.com/reviews/capsule-review/1995-03-01/certain-victory-us-army-gulf-war.
45. Roger J. Spiller, "In the Shadow of the Dragon: Doctrine and the US Army after Vietnam," in *From Past to Future—the Australian Experience of Land / Air Operations*, Proceedings of the 1995 Australian Army History Conference, ed. Jeffrey Grey and Peter Dennis (Canberra: Australian Defence Force Academy, 1995), 2.
46. Before his death, General Tait urged me to find a copy but had no personal copy of his own to share. The suggestions he made for where to find it proved fruitless. Major General (ret.) Thomas Tait, personal communication with the author, November 24, 2010.
47. Kourtney M. Maison and Katelyn E. Brooks, "Years in Cultural Studies: 1990—Alliances from the Rubble," *Lateral* 9, no. 1 (2020), https://doi.org/10.25158/L9.1.10.
48. James R. Callard, "The Changing Nature of American Democracy: Consequences for the Military," advanced research project, Naval War College, 1996, 60, 45, 46.
49. *Field Manual (FM) 46-1: Public Affairs Operations* (Washington, DC: Headquarters, U.S. Department of the Army, 1997), 31. This point is emphasized in future versions of the *Field Manual*. The second version, for example, states emphatically on the second page that "PA [public affairs] must be integrated into the planning and decision-making process from receipt of the mission." *Field Manual (FM) 3-61: Public Affairs Operations* (Washington, DC: Headquarters, U.S. Department of the Army, 2000), 1-1.
50. *FM 3-61* (2000), 1-2.
51. The project was published and is easily available as Lawrence S. Epstein, "The Military, the Press, and the Gulf War," independent study project, U.S. Army War College, 1992. The full text of Epstein's interview with Sconyers is part of the Persian Gulf War Collection at the United States Army Heritage and

Education Center in Carlisle, Pennsylvania. See Lawrence S. Epstein, "Interview with COL Ron Sconyers," March 25, 1992, Persian Gulf War—the Military, the Press, and the Gulf War, 1990–1992 (B1F5), United States Army Heritage and Education Center, Carlisle, PA.
52. Epstein, "Interview with COL Ron Sconyers."
53. *FM 3-61* (2000), 25.
54. *Joint Publication 3-61* (1997), III-3, emphasis in original.
55. Thomas Crosbie, "Getting the Joint Functions Right," *Joint Force Quarterly* 94, no. 3 (2019): 96–100.

CONCLUSION: THE BIRTH, FALL, AND RISE OF THE POLITICAL ARMY

1. For an extended discussion of this view, see Thomas Crosbie, "What Is Military Politics?," in *Military Politics: New Perspectives*, ed. Thomas Crosbie (London: Berghahn, 2023), 19–48.
2. See, for example, Charles D. Allen and Breena E. Coates, "The Engagement of Military Voice," *Parameters* 39, no. 4 (2009): 73–87; Mackubin Thomas Owens, "Military Officers: Political Without Partisanship," *Strategic Studies Quarterly* 9, no. 3 (2015): 88–101; William E. Rapp, "Ensuring Effective Military Voice," *Parameters* 46, no. 4 (2016): 13–25; Carsten Roennfeldt, "Wider Officer Competencies: The Importance of Politics and Practical Wisdom," *Armed Forces and Society* 45, no. 1 (2019): 59–77; Hew Strachan, "The Lost Meaning of Strategy," *Survival* 47, no. 3 (2006): 33–54; Thomas Crosbie, "Six Scenarios for Military Intervention After January 20," Defense One, August 18, 2020, https://www.defenseone.com/ideas/2020/08/six-scenarios-military-intervention-after-january-20/167777/; Crosbie, "Clausewitz and Military Politics: Theoretical Reflections on a Strong Program Approach to War and the Military," in *Militarization and the Global Rise of Paramilitary Culture: Post-heroic Reimaginings of the Warrior*, ed. Brad West and Thomas Crosbie (Singapore: Springer, 2021), 17–36; Thomas Crosbie and Anders Klitmøller, "Beyond the Neutral Card: From Civil–Military Relations to Military Politics," Strategy Bridge, December 12, 2023, https://thestrategybridge.org/the-bridge/2023/12/12/beyond-the-neutral-card-from-civil-military-relations-to-military-politics.
3. Sharon K. Weiner, *Managing the Military: The Joint Chiefs of Staff and Civil–Military Relations* (New York: Columbia University Press, 2022). Further advances along these lines have been made by several of the contributors to Crosbie, ed., *Military Politics: New Perspectives*, including James D. Campbell, Steven Lee Katz, Carrie A. Lee, and Lena Trabucco.

INDEX

Page numbers in *italics* denote tables in the text.

ABC News: Grenada coverage, 148; Gulf War coverage, 178–79, 187; Vietnam War coverage, 107

Abrams, Creighton W., Jr. (Army chief of staff): Army priorities post-Vietnam, 114, 115; bombing campaigns hidden from press, 106–7, 108; investigation of double-agents' murder, 112; news embargo, 110–13; press style, 98, 101–3, 106, 108; Vietnamization policy, 100–101, 121

Abu Ghraib prisoner-abuse scandal, 104–5

Active Defense (DePuy). *See Field Manual 100-5: Operations (Active Defense) (DePuy)*

Adams, Jim (journalist), 175–77

Afghanistan War, 215

Agence France-Presse, 181–82

Air Force, 61, 70

AirLand Battle (Starry). *See Field Manual 100-5: Operations (AirLand Battle) (Starry)*

AirLand Battle 2000 Symposium, 154

Alexander, Jeffrey, 217n1

Allen, Charles D., 237n23

American public: acceptance of large standing army, 60–61; Army's reputation, 54, 73, 105, 108–9, 154, 171–73, 179, 187–88; attitude toward press, 179, 199; cynicism toward government, 206–7, 208–9; militarization of, 54–55, 58, 60; Pax Americana and, 12; public support needed for war, 209; second-guessing military decisions, 195; Vietnam War, 105, 106, 113

American Society of Newspaper Editors: Grenada coverage, 149; Marshall's talk to, 46–47, 48

Andrews, Bert (journalist), 41

Andrews, J. Cutler, 226n8

Annual Historical Reports of chief of information, 19

Applewhite, J. Scott (journalist), 175–77

Army: *Active Defense*, 128–31, 132, 141, 142, 158; *AirLand Battle*, 131–32, 141, 142, 146; AR 360-5, *Public Information*, 65; Army Regulation 600-700, *Public Relations*, 64–65; Center of Military History, 145; changes to, in 1980s, 170–73; Cold War Army, 53–55;

Army (continued)
    combat photography, 91–92, 178–79;
    combat readiness, 171; command
    (troop) information, 17, 31; commu-
    nity relations, 16; congressional
    criticism of, 112; conventional force,
    use of, 121–23; demobilization and
    drawdown, 54; domestic politics,
    153–57; embedding journalists, 181,
    185–86, 195–96, 205; First Team (First
    Air Cavalry), 90–91, 92, 93, 108–9;
    free press as operational concern,
    132, 153; Information Division (G-2),
    33; interdisciplinary studies,
    impact on, 206–7; interservice
    rivalry, 70, 234–35n26; joint and
    Allied operations, 215; Joint History
    Office, 145, 146–47; land power,
    71–73, 74, 95, 122; legislative liaising,
    16; maneuverability prioritized, 130;
    marketing and public relations, 16,
    17; media work outsourced to
    civilians, 91, 92; modern depictions
    of, 156–57; modernization, 171;
    Morale Branch, 40; nuclear power
    and, 58–61, 70–73, 74, 113; opera-
    tional hierarchies, 128; operational
    versus political success, 78, 98, 106,
    122; operations and politics
    balanced, 142; pivot to Europe,
    123–26, 128–29; political strategy,
    13–18, 22, 212; Posse Comitatus Act,
    16; post-Vietnam Army, 114–15;
    post–World War II Army, 124;
    pre–World War II Army, 21; public
    support needed for war, 209;
    reputation domestically, 54, 73, 105,
    108–9, 154, 171–73, 179, 187–88;
    Selective Training and Service Act,
    39; Sidle-Notestein report, 56–57,
    66–67; size of, 60; Table of Organi-
    zations and Elements, 92; winning
    the first battle, 126, 128, 141, 158;
    women in combat, 167–68. *See also*
    democratic oversight; Department
    of Defense (DOD); doctrine; media
    management; Pentagon; press
    relations; public affairs; public
    information; public relations;
    individual Army chiefs of staff;
    individual conflicts

Army Information Digest, 19
Army Public Relations Plan, An,
    67–68, 69
Army utopianism: author's overview, 21,
    52, 214; as cultural structure, 53–58;
    Eisenhower's disagreement with, 70;
    lessons from, 74; messaging to
    public, 55; as miscalculation, 74; in
    Pentagon versus on the frontline, 65;
    Ridgway and, 66–67; Sidle-Notestein
    report, 56–57; Vietnam War and, 73,
    78, 94, 125
Arnett, Peter (journalist), 81, 82, 83,
    117–18
Aspin, Les, 203
Associated Press (AP): Gallant Eagle
    coverage, 162; Grenada coverage, 149;
    Gulf War coverage, 175–77, 179–80,
    185, 250n21; Korean War coverage,
    62–63, 64; Marshall's relationship
    with, 41; Op. Earnest Will coverage,
    163; Vietnam War coverage, 82, 83,
    84, 117–18
atomic bombs. *See* nuclear power
Aukofer, Frank (journalist), 180, 190–94,
    199, 248n69

Baer, Justin, 221n29
Baldwin, Hanson W., 59
Bankson, Rogher, 88
Baruch, Bernard M., 39
Baudrillard, Jean, 199–200, 206–7
Bayles, Fred (journalist), 185
Baysinger, Barry, 14–15
Beary, Donald B., 70
Beech, Keyes (journalist), 151
Berg, Ivar, 15
Bernsen, Harold, 163
Bigart, Homer (journalist), 81
Bishop, Maurice, 145
Böhm, Steffen, 3
Bomar, Edward E. (journalist), 41
Boorman, Scott, 223n49
Borders, William (journalist), 143
Boyd, Morris J., 186–87
BPR. *See* Bureau of Public Relations
    (BPR)
Braestrup, Peter, 149
Branch, Dennis (journalist), 175–77
Bray, Linda, 167–68
British Ministry of Defence, 142

Broder, John M. (journalist), 168
Brooks, Risa, 17
Brown, Harold, 134
Browne, Malcolm W. (journalist), 82, 83, 84, 190–94
Buchanan, Pat, 180
Bundy, McGeorge, 89
bureaucracy, 7–10, 13
Bureau of Public Relations (BPR): propaganda and photography, 40–41, 48; purpose and function, 33–34, 44, 55; Review Board, 34
Burrows, Larry (journalist), 91
Bush, George H. W., 164–65, 202
Bussey, C. D., 155
Butterfield, Fox (journalist), 116–17, 118

Callard, James R., 206–7
Callaway, Howard H., 115
Calley, William, 99–100, 105
Cannon, Lou (journalist), 146, 147
Carter, Jimmy, 134–35
CBS News: Grenada coverage, 148; Gulf War coverage, 180, 187; Vietnam War coverage, 107, 108–9
censorship: Falklands War, 144; by JIB, 190, 191–92, 197–98; in Korean War, 64–66; logistics of, 144; under Marshall, 38, 39, 43, 44–45, 49, 51; PAO escorts as, 180; press response to, 29, 64; self-censorship by journalists, 29, 213; in Vietnam War, 93–94; voluntary press censorship model, 63–64, 66; in World War II, 30, 33. See also Office of Censorship; propaganda
CENTCOM, 175, 183, 186, 194
Cheney, Dick, 164, 165, 169, 174, 185
Christian Science Monitor, 36
Church, John H., 62
CINCPAC, 234n26
Citizens' Defense Corps, 41
civil affairs, defined, 32
Civilian Defense organization, 40
civilian oversight, 3, 6, 98. See also democratic oversight
Civil War, 29, 213
Clausewitz, Carl von, 13
Clifford, Clark, 99
Cloud, Stanley W. (journalist), 180

CNN: Grenada coverage, 148; Gulf War coverage, 176–77, 180, 187
CNN effect, 160
Cohen, Eliot, 206, 224n63
Cohen, William S., 196
Cold War, 53–55, 70–73. See also Army utopianism; Korean War; nuclear power; Universal Military Training (UMT); Vietnam War
Cole, Ronald, 147
Collins, J. Lawton (Army chief of staff), 55–56, 67
command (troop) information, 17, 31
community relations, 16, 31–32
CONARC, 123
Congress, 115. See also democratic oversight; Senate Armed Services Committee (SASC); Senate Governmental Affairs Committee (SGAC)
Constant, Maurice, 40
Continental Army Command (CONARC), 123
Copeland, Peter (journalist): embedding with troops, 186–87; in Gulf War press pools, 175–77, 178–79, 186; on Icenogle, 246n39; silenced and undermined, 169, 178–79; visa issues, 246n38; working outside pool system, 166–68, 184, 186
Corlett, Charles, 48
correspondents. See journalists
Cramer, Roxy, 14–15
Crimean War, 28, 213
Cronkite, Walter (journalist), 190–94
Crossfire (CNN), 180
Crowe, William James, Jr., 163
Cucolo, Anthony, 16, 241n47
Cushman, John H., 129, 130, 241n30
Cutlip, Scott M., 151

Davis, Elmer, 34, 46
Decker, George H. (Army chief of staff), 72
Demeter, Karl, 221n29
democracies of war, 1–3, 23
democratic oversight, 3, 4–6, 10, 118–19, 121–23, 142. See also civilian oversight; journalists; press; press relations; Senate Armed Services Committee (SASC); Senate Governmental Affairs Committee (SGAC)

Department of Defense (DOD): defense spending and scale of, 3, 11–12; *Field Manual 46-1: Public Affairs Operations*, 202, 207–8, 210; friendly-fire incidents covered-up, 198, 205, 250n21; interpretation of Sidle Panel Report, 160, 161, 165, 168; JP 3-61, *Doctrine for Public Affairs in Operations*, 202–5, 210; lawsuits against, 181–82; legislative liaising, 16; media management as command concern, 208; press pools normalized, 162–63; press relations policy revised, 99, 134–35; security-review process for news stories, 197–98, 202; ten principles of media management (1992), 197–98, 202, 208; Vietnam War information policies, 80; Vietnam War leadership and, 80, 85. *See also* Army; doctrine; Joint Information Bureau (JIB); Pentagon
Department of War, 54
DePuy, William E., 123–26, 127, 128–31, 132–33, 137, 158. *See also Field Manual 100-5: Operations (Active Defense)* (DePuy)
Desert Victory (film), 47
Dinerstein, Ana, 3
doctrine: *AirLand Battle* doctrine, 171; Army doctrine, 64, 98, 131, 157, 207–8, 209–11; centrality of media, 157, 204–5, 207–8, 209–11; combat readiness and, 171; defined, 127; DePuy's doctrinal revision, 124–26; for DOD media management, 204–5; flexible response doctrine, 71, 73; Guam Doctrine, 124; as hierarchical, 128; joint doctrine, 171, 203, 204, 207, 209, 210; meaning and purpose of, 127–29; NATO Allied doctrine, 210–11; New Look doctrine, 70, 71; press omitted from development of, 132–33; press pools curtailed, 210
DOD. *See* Department of Defense (DOD)
Donnelley, Dixon, 94
Drum, Hugh A., 35
Dryzek, John, 217n1
Duncan, Charles, 134

Egypt, 125–26, 158
Eisenhower, Dwight D., 45–46, 49, 69–70, 71

embedding journalists, 181, 185–86, 195–96, 205. *See also* PAO escorts
Epstein, Lawrence S., 209
Erlichman, John, 106
Esper, George (journalist), 117–18, 185
Evans, Peter, 4

Falklands War, 141, 142–44, 148, 158
Feder, Barnaby J. (journalist), 148
Fern, Alan, 30
Fialka, John (journalist), 192
Field Manual 3-61: Public Affairs Operations, 207, 210, 214
Field Manual 46-1: Public Affairs Operations, 202, 207–8, 210
Field Manual 100-5: Operations (Active Defense) (DePuy), 128–31, 132, 141, 142, 158
Field Manual 100-5: Operations (AirLand Battle) (Starry), 131–32, 141, 142, 146
Fifth Amendment, 182
First Amendment, 182
Franjola, Matt (journalist), 117–18
Fredendall, Lloyd, 45
Freedman, Lawrence, 142–43
Friendly, Jonathan (journalist), 148
friendly-fire incidents, 198, 205, 250n21
Frizell, Bernard (journalist), 79

Gallagher, Wes (journalist), 117
Gallant Eagle airborne exercises, 162, 175
Gottschalk, Marie (journalist), 200–201, 208
Grenada: damaging media-military relationship, 147–49; Falklands War influence on, 144, 148; goals of invasion, 145; operational secrecy, 147; press coverage, 146, 147–49; press management, 141–42, 146–50, 157; Vessey managing invasion, 146. *See also* Sidle Panel Report
Griffith, Ronald H., 185
Guidry, Vernon A., Jr., 203
Gulf War: *Certain Victory*, 205–6; combat press pools, 177, 183, 184–87, 193; criticism of media's role in, 199–201, 251n28; criticism suppressed, 205–6; *Desert Storm After-Action Report*, 205–6; *Final Report to Congress*, 196, 208; journalists second-guessing

INDEX   259

decisions, 195; lessons from, 190–96, 197–201, 202–8, 209; press ground rules, 178, 182–83; SASC's report on operations, 194–96; SGAC's Pentagon rules on media access, 190–94; as U.S. Tet Offensive, 200; as virtual war, 200. *See also* Operation Desert Shield; Operation Desert Storm; PAO escorts; security review for news stories

Haislip, Wade, 38
Halberstam, David (journalist), 82, 83, 84, 85
Hallin, Daniel, 80
Halsky, Milton B., 56
Hammond, William M., 20, 30, 84–85, 94, 108
Hangen, Welles (journalist), 107
Harkins, Paul D., 83, 84
Herbert, Paul, 129–30
Hersh, Seymour M. (journalist), 104
Hertsgaard, Mark, 149
Higgins, Marguerite (journalist), 64
Hill, L. Gordon, 133
Hill, Luther L., 37
Hill & Knowlton, 17
Hillman, Amy, 14–15
Hines, Cragg (journalist), 191–94
Hiroshima, atomic bomb on, 59
HMS *Invincible*, 144
Hodge, John R., 62
Hoffman, David (journalist), 146, 147
Hoffman, Fred S. (journalist), 169, 191–94
Hoffman Report, 169, *170*
Hollingshead, August, 55
Hooks, Gregory, 222n34
Horwood, Ian, 234n26
Houston Chronicle, 191–94
Howard, Dan, 163
Howard, Michael, 14, 15
Humphries, Arthur A., 144
Huntington, Samuel P., 52
Hurd, Charles W. B. (journalist), 41
Hussein, Saddam, 173–74. *See also* Iran-Iraq War

Icenogle, Larry: career trajectory, 175; on competition between journalists, 184; press pools and, 162, 176, 177,
246n39; relationship with press, 132, 182, 185
International News Service, 62–63
Iran, 163
Iran-Iraq War, 163, 173–74
Iraq, 163
Iraq War, 215
Israel, 125–26, 158

J. B. Pictures, Inc., 182
Jehl, Doug (journalist), 185
Jenkins, Harry, 196
Jeong, Martin (journalist), 175–77
JIB. *See* Joint Information Bureau (JIB)
Johnson, Harold K. (Army chief of staff), 90, 99, 121, 239n3
Johnson, Lyndon B., 88–89, 100
Joint Information Bureau (JIB): censorship by, 190, 191–92, 197–98; disliked by journalists, 198; positive relationships with press, 185–86; spinning the narrative, 179. *See also* security review for news stories
Joint Publication 3-61, *Doctrine for Public Affairs in Operations*, 202–5, 210
Joint United States Public Affairs Office, 90
Jones, Melvin, 109
journalists: Abu Ghraib coverage, 104–5; Army public information strategy and, 17; backchannel sources, 106; categories of, 234n13; competition between, 99, 107–8, 117, 148, 184, 199, 248n69; complicit in government propaganda, 29, 31–32, 213; dislike of JIB, 198; embedding with Army, 181, 185–86, 195–96, 205; local versus State-side reporters, 165–67, 168–69; mediating military actions, 5; as part of machinery of war, 208–9; rogue reporters, 166–69; second-guessing military decisions, 195; timidity of, 30. *See also* censorship; PAO escorts; photography; press; press pools; press relations; public affairs; *individual conflicts*; *individual journalists*

Kalischer, Peter (journalist), 64
Kansas City Star, 49

Kaufman, Michael T. (journalist), 148
Keim, Gerald, 14–15
Kennedy, John F., 72, 73, 78–80, 86
Kent State University, Ohio, 105–6
Kiernan, David, 150
Kim, James, 146, 147
Kim Il-sung, 62
King, Anthony, 7
King, John (journalist), 175–77, 185, 250n21
Kiser, Edgar, 221n29
Knightley, Philip, 30
Korean War, 62–66, 69–70, 73
Kraft, Joseph (journalist), 150
Kuwait, 17, 163, 174, 205

Lambert, Tom (journalist), 64
Langguth, A. J. (journalist), 151
Larson, Arthur V., 69
Laurence, John "Jack" (journalist), 92, 93, 108–9
Lear, Ben, 41
Lee, Mordecai, 16
legislative liaising, 32. *See also* legislative affairs
Lemnitzer, Lyman L. (Army chief of staff), 71, 72–73
Lind, William, 130
Lindley, Ernest K. (journalist), 41
Lippmann, Walter, 46
Lockhart Report (1946), 56
Lodge, Henry Cabot, Jr., 87
Los Angeles Times: Gulf War coverage, 168, 175–77, 185
Lundquist, Jennifer Hickes, 222n34
Luttwak, Edward, 130
Lynch, Charles (journalist), 31

MAAG-V, 77, 80
MacArthur, Douglas, 50, 62, 63–64, 66
MacDonagh, Michael, 226n5
MACOI, 87–89, 93
MACV. *See* Military Assistance Command, Vietnam (MACV)
Mander, Mary, 30
Mann, Michael, 7
Marine Corps, 90, 171–72, 195–96
Maris, Ward, 33
Marsh, John O., 155
Marshall, George C. (Army chief of staff): alignment with press, 48–49, 51; anticipating versus reacting to press, 40–41, 47–48, 51; Army chief of staff, tenure as, 34–35; author's overview, 18, 21, 27; censorship press work, 38, 39, 43, 44–45, 49, 51; influence on Cold War Army, 53–55; messages to Eisenhower, 45–46, 49; messages to Surles, 44–45, 48; misdirecting the press, 41–42, 44–45, 49–50, 51; North African campaign, 44, 45–46; Patton's slapping incident, 49; press as critical resource, 213–14; press as obstacle, 35; press-management strategy, 34, 38, 40–43, 44–47, 51; press work, overview, 35–38, 36, 50–51; propagandistic press work, 38, 39, 40–41, 43, 44–45, 47, 51; protecting generals from press, 45, 48, 63; support for Universal Military Training, 54–55, 57; talk to American Society of Newspaper Editors, 46–47; troop morale, 39–40, 41; types of press work, 35–36, 36, 38, 39, 43, 43–44; use of NBC Radio, 41; work habits, 36–37, 50
McCain, John S., Jr., 110, 195
McCarthy, Joseph, 30
McClain, Bill, 168, 181
McGuire, Colleen L., 169
McLaughlin, Greg, 149
McMasters, Paul (journalist), 191–94
McNamara, Robert S., 72, 80, 86–87, 99
McQueen, Brian, 222n34
media management: at center of military operations, 153, 189, 213; *CNN effect*, 160; as command concern, 22–23, 208; data for, 18–21; DOD's principles for, 197–98, 202, 208; formalization of, 204–5; lessons from Army utopianism, 74; lessons from Falklands War, 142–44; lessons from Gulf War, 190–96, 197–201, 202–8, 209; lessons from Korean War, 66; lessons from Kuwait, 205; lessons from Panama, 205, 209; lessons from Vietnam War, 95, 118–19, 121–23, 132, 141, 153; lessons from World War II, 50–51; lessons in media sensitivity, 157–59; necessity of, 142; Ricks's "thinking forward"

notion and, 203. *See also* doctrine; Gulf War; Marshall, George C.; press pools; press relations; public information; Vietnam War; war correspondence
media management, British, 142, 158
Medina, Ernest, 99
Meet the Press: Grenada coverage, 147; Vessey's appearance on, 150–51
Merick, Wendell S. (journalist), 151
Meyer, Edward C. (Army chief of staff), 154
militaries: ignored in sociology, 10–13, 11, 17; intrinsically political, 13–15, 17, 22, 215; military autonomy, 3–5, 13; military discipline, 8; military power, 7. *See also* Army
militarism, 54–55, 58
militarization, 54–55, 58, 60
Military Assistance Advisory Group, Vietnam (MAAG-V), 77, 80
Military Assistance Command, Vietnam (MACV): Army's control over public affairs, 89; democratic oversight, 122; information practices, 84–85; MAAG-V redesigned as, 80; Op. Lam Son, 111; on press communications, 108; press embargo, 110–13; resilience to critique, 94; rosy picture of Vietnam War, 94; Vietnamization strategy, 100–101
Military Assistance Command Office of Information (MACOI), 87–89, 93
Miller, Karen, 17
Milwaukee Journal: Gulf War coverage, 175–77
Min, Brian, 222n34
Minor, Dale, 30
Mohr, Charley (journalist), 97
Moore, Arthur, 29

Nagasaki, atomic bomb on, 59
Nation, The: Gulf War coverage, 181–82
National News Council, 151
national press pools. *See* press pools
National Security Act (1947), 61, 70
National Security Act (1949), 59
NATO, 210–11
Navy, 70–71
NBC: Vietnam War coverage, 79–80, 83

NBC News: Gulf War coverage, 187
NBC Radio, 41
Newsday, 179; Gulf War coverage, 191–94, 198
news media. *See* press
Newsweek: Grenada coverage, 149; Marshall's relationship with, 41; Vietnam War coverage, 81, 109, 112–13
New York Herald Tribune: Korean War coverage, 64; Marshall's relationship with, 41
New York Times: Falklands War coverage, 143; Grenada coverage, 148, 149; Gulf War coverage, 174, 179; Korean War coverage, 64; Marshall's relationship with, 36, 41; Vietnam War coverage, 79, 81, 83, 84, 85, 93, 97, 116, 148; World War II coverage, 44
Ngo Dinh Diem, 81–83, 86
Nguyen Van Thieu, 111
Nightline (ABC): Gulf War coverage, 178–79
Nixon, Richard, 105, 106, 112, 113–14, 124
Nolting, Frederick, 81
Noriega, Manuel, 164–65
North, Don (journalist), 97–98, 107–8, 117
Notestein, 56–57. *See also* Sidle-Notestein report
NPR, 175–77
nuclear power, 58–61, 70–73, 74, 113
Nunn, Sam, 194

OCI, 112
OCPA, 133–34, 135–36, 155–56
October War, 125–26, 158
Office of Censorship, 33, 34, 57, 64. *See also* censorship
Office of Public Information, 67
Office of Strategic Services, 33
Office of the Chief of Information (OCI), 112
Office of the Chief of Information and Education, 67, 69
Office of the Chief of Public Affairs (OCPA), 133–34, 135–36, 155–56
Office of the Director of Information, 55
Office of War Information (OWI), 33, 34, 57
OHIO (Over the Hill in October), 39, 41

Oliver, Kendrick, 30
Operation Desert Shield: author's overview, 173–74; intensity of media interest in, 176–77, 178; non-pool reporters, 176–77; non-pool reports, 177; PAO escorts for journalists, 178–79, 180, 183, 190, 191; press pools, 174–77, 178; restrictions on press, 178–80
Operation Desert Storm: author's overview, 173; "big five" weapons systems, 124–25; "death by briefing" and sidelining reporters, 185, 187, 188; live-to-air content, 187, 188; number of journalists covering, 187, 249n79; PAO escorts for journalists, 185, 186, 190, 191; positive relationships with press, 185–86; reporting delays, 186, 188, 192; working outside pool system, 186–87, 193
Operation Duck Hook, 113
Operation Earnest Will, 162, 163, 171, 173
Operation Just Cause, 164–70
Operation Lam Son, 111
Operation Rolling Thunder, 90
Operation Urgent Fury, 144
orogeny of state, 9–10
Ottosen, Rune, 251n28
OWI (Office of War Information), 33, 34, 57

Page Report (1945), 55, 66
Palmer, Bruce, 100
Panama, 164–70, 205, 209
PAO (public affairs officers). *See under* public affairs
PAO escorts: buffering commanders, 185; as censorship, 180; criticism of, 199; hindering journalists, 187; Op. Desert Shield, 178–79, 180, 183, 190, 191; Op. Desert Storm, 185, 186, 190, 191; part of embedding process, 186; Pentagon rules for, 190, 191; requirement for journalists, 183, 185; shaping news stories, 178–79, 188. *See also* embedding journalists
Pappas, Ike (journalist), 180
Parks, Floyd L., 56, 66
Parsons, Talcott, 221n29
Parsons, W. S., 70
Patton, George, 49

Paul, Christopher, 146, 147
Pax Americana, 12, 60
Paz, Robert, 164
Pentagon: Army utopianism, 65; Civil Affairs Branch, 102; Grenada invasion, 146–47, 149; Office of the Chief of Information, 112; SGAC and media access for Gulf War, 190–94. *See also* Department of Defense (DOD)
Pershing, John J., 35
Persian Gulf War. *See* Gulf War
Peterzell, Jay (journalist), 175–77, 180, 193, 247n60
photography: civilianizing photographers, 91; combat photography, 91–92, 178–79; of dead service members, 182; Falklands War, 143–44; propaganda and, 40–41, 48, 143–44
Plato, Kenneth S., 161
Posen, Barry, 127
Posse Comitatus Act, 16
Powell, Colin, 164
press: as critical resource, 195–96, 207, 209, 213–14; expansion of and changes to, 132, 153, 187; as obstacle, 35. *See also* censorship; journalists; media management; press relations; public affairs; television; *individual conflicts*; *individual outlets*
press pools: advantages for Army, 162–63; author's overview, 160–61; combat press pools, 177, 183, 184–87, 193; competition between journalists, 184, 199, 248n69; as compromising reporting, 177; deliberate mismanagement, 194; disliked by journalists, 161–62, 177, 180, 188, 193, 197, 198–99; early experiments with, 162; embedding journalists with units, 181; limitations on, 202, 210; normalization by DOD, 162–63; Op. Desert Shield, 173, 174–77, 178; Op. Desert Storm, 173; Op. Earnest Will, 162, 163; Op. Just Cause, 164, 165–67, 168–69; organization and size of, 246n42, 248n68; public debate over, 180; reporters working outside of, 186–87, 193; SCAG debate over, 190, 193–94; Sidle's advice on, 181, 183;

INDEX   263

support for, by journalists, 247n60; viewed in instrumentalist terms, 169
press relations: alignment of interests, 29; civilian involvement, 87, 90; Civil War, 29; Crimean War, 28; DOD policy revised, 99, 134–35; embedding journalists, 181, 185–86, 195–96, 205; Grenada, 146–50; journalists' access and support, 28–29; Korean War, 63–64; MacArthur and, 50, 63–64; military's unforced errors, 94; omitted from Army doctrinal development, 132–33; personal relationships with journalists, 66, 67, 81–82; post–World War II, 74; press as critical resource, 213–14; Press Relations Branch, MACOI, 87–88; restrictions on journalists, 176, 181–83; Westmoreland, 94; World War I, 29; World War II, 21, 28, 29–30, 31. *See also* Gulf War; Marshall, George C.; public affairs; Sidle Panel Report; Vietnam War
Press Relations Bureau, 33
press work, defined. *See also* legislative liaising; Marshall, George C.
Price, Bryon, 34
prisoners of war, 40
Program for the Pacification and Long-Term Development of South Vietnam, A, 101
Projection '62 (NBC), 79–80
propaganda: "black," 33; criticism of, 69; domestic, outlawed, 57; journalists executing military's, 29, 31–32, 213; under Marshall, 38, *39*, 40–41, *43*, 44–45, 47, 51; photography and, 40–41, 48, 143–44; Smith-Mundt Act, 15, 16, 57, 68; spin, 179–80; USIS and Vietnam War, 90; "white," 30–31, 33. *See also* censorship
public affairs: Abrams's change to doctrine of, 102–3; *Active Defense*, 128–31, 132, 141, 142, 158; *AirLand Battle*, 131–32, 141, 142, 146; in *AirLand Battle*, 131–32; ambivalence toward, 144; AR 360-1, "The Army Public Affairs Program," 65; *An Army Public Relations Plan*, 67–68, 69; bad faith engagement with press, 185; centrality of PAOs, 156–57, 158–59;

character of war and, 151–53; charismatic to bureaucratic authority, 209; command (troop) information, 17; community relations, 16; conveying Army's role to public, 172–73; defined, 231n32; divisions of, 31–32; downgrading of, 132–33, 137, 203; *Field Manual 3-61: Public Affairs Operations*, 207, 210, 214; *Field Manual 46-1: Public Affairs Operations*, 202, 207–8, 210; Gallant Eagle airborne exercises, 162, 175; Hoffman Report, 169, *170*; importance of, 55–57, 66–69; inevitability of, 51, 203, 207; integration in leadership training, 134, 135–36; Joint United States Public Affairs Office, 90; JP 3-61, *Doctrine for Public Affairs in Operations*, 202, 207–8; MACV, 89, 108, 110–13; MACV's rosy picture of Vietnam War, 94; Meyer's concerns over, 154; Office of the Chief of Public Affairs, 133–34, 135–36; openness and honesty, 134–35; Op. Just Cause, 165–70; Op. Lam Son gaffe, 111; principles for dealing with press, 178; propaganda mixed with, 90; Ricks's "thinking forward" notion, 203, 207; secrecy interfering with, 114, 147, 150, 166, 169, 174; spin part of policy, 179–80; troops' role in, 68, 88; Worldwide Public Affairs Conference (1987), 157. *See also* Bureau of Public Relations (BPR); Gulf War; Joint Information Bureau (JIB); PAO escorts; press pools; public information; public relations; security review of news stories; Sidle Panel Report
public information: AR 360-5, *Public Information*, 65; decentralized, 33; defined, 17, 31, 212, 231n32; information czar for Vietnam War, 87, 90
Public Information Division of OCI, 112
public oversight. *See* civilian oversight; democratic oversight
public relations: AR 600-700, *Public Relations*, 64–65; defined, 231n32; post–World War II, 74; shaping audiences, 68. *See also* Bureau of Public Relations (BPR); public affairs

Public Relations Division, 55–56
Pulwers, Jack, 18–19, 133, 134
Pyle, Richard (journalist), 163, 179

Readers' Digest, 36
Reagan, Ronald, 164
Record, Jeffrey (journalist), 171–72, 173
Rehbein, Kathleen, 14–15
reporters. *See* journalists
Reserve Officer Training Corps (ROTC), 56–57
Reuters: Gulf War coverage, 175–77; Korean War coverage, 62–63; Vietnam War coverage, 84
Rheault, Robert, 112–13
Richardson, Robert C., 33–34
Ricks, Charles W., 202, 203
Ridenhour, Ronald, 103–4
Ridgway, Matthew B. (Army chief of staff), 65–67
Robinson, James (journalist), 79–80, 83
Rochelle, Carl (journalist), 176–77, 187, 193
Rogers, Bernard W. (Army chief of staff), 121
Ross, Mike (journalist), 175–77
Ross, Thomas, 135
Rossom, William B., 112
Rostow, Walter W., 73, 79
ROTC, 56–57
Rueschemeyer, Dietrich, 4
Russell, William Howard (journalist), 28–29, 213, 226n6

Sadat, Anwar, 125–26
Salant, Richard S., 151
SASC, 190, 194–96
Saturday Evening Post, 36
Saudi Arabia, 174, 176
Sawyer, Forrest (journalist), 179
Scales, Robert H., 205–6
Schanberg, Sydney (journalist), 191–94
Schuler, Douglas, 14–15
Schwarzkopf, H. Norman, Jr., 175, 194–95, 196
Sconyers, Ron, 165–67, 209
Scroggs, Stephen, 16
secrecy: Cheney's use of, 165, 174; Grenada invasion, 147; interfering with public affairs, 114, 147, 150, 166, 169, 174. *See also* security-review for news stories

security review of news stories: as censorship, 188; delaying stories, 186, 188, 192; DOD, 197–98, 202; during Gulf War, 195, 199; JIB, 190, 191–92, 197–98; live footage, 188; reasons for, 246n39; work-arounds for, 186–87. *See also* secrecy
Selective Service Act, 47, 61
Selective Training and Service Act, 39
Senate Armed Services Committee (SASC), 190, 194–96
Senate Governmental Affairs Committee (SGAC), 181–82, 190–94
September 11, 2001, 215
Sharkey, Jacqueline, 146, 148
Sharp, Grant, 99
Sheehan, Neil (journalist), 82, 83, 84, 93
Sherman, Michael, 179
Sherrod, Robert (journalist), 41, 42, 49
Sidle, Winant: advice on press pools, 181, 183; archival records, 19; on censorship for Vietnam War, 93–94; SCAG Gulf War investigation, 191–94; Sidle-Notestein report, 56–57, 66–67
Sidle-Notestein report, 56–57, 66–67
Sidle Panel Report: author's overview, 22, 150–53, 214; centrality of media management, 153; Grenada invasion, 157; interpretation and simplification by DOD, 160, 161, 165, 168; operations planning as public-affairs planning, 161; recommendations, 151–52, 161, 165, *168*, 169, 209–10. *See also* press pools
Singlaub, John K., 135
Skocpol, Theda, 4, 217n1
Sloyan, Patrick (journalist), 179–80, 198
Smith, Hedrick, 148
Smith-Mundt Act (1948), 15, 16, 57, 68
Solomon, Robert B., 133–34
sovereignty, 10
Spicer, André, 3
Spiller, Roger, 206
spin, 179–80. *See also* press relations; propaganda; public affairs
SS *Bridgeton*, 163
Starry, Donn A., 129, 130–31, 132–33, 137. *See also Field Manual 100-5: Operations (AirLand Battle)* (Starry)
Stars and Stripes, 100
state, the, 2, 3–4, 5–10, 13

INDEX 265

State Department: maximum candor policy, 88, 89, 95; Vietnam information policies, 80; Vietnam War leadership and, 80, 85
Steuck, Jay C., 198
Stevenson, Charles A., 134
Stewart, Richard, 147
Stimson, Henry L., 33
Stiner, Carl W., 164
Sullivan, Gordon R. (Army chief of staff), 205–6
Sullivan, Michael, 155
Sullivan, Robert A., 133–34, 135–36
Sully, François (journalist), 81, 82–83
Summers, Harry G., Jr., 191–94, 196
Surles, Alexander, 34, 44–45, 48
Sylvester, Arthur, 87
Syria, 125–26, 158
Syvertsen, George (journalist), 107

Tait, Thomas H., 205–6
Tait Report, 205–6
Taylor, Bob, 175
Taylor, Maxwell (Army chief of staff): as Army utopian, 71; conventional warfare championed, 121; public affairs and, 67, 90; Vietnam War and, 73, 79, 87, 99
television: Gulf War coverage, 176; security review of live footage, 188; Vietnam War coverage, 79–80, 90
Tet paradox, 21–22, 78, 98, 106, 122
Thompson, Hugh C., 99–100
Thurman, Maxwell "Mad Max" R., 164
Tilly, Charles, 4, 220n25
Time: Gulf War coverage, 175–77; Marshall's relationship with, 41, 50
Training and Doctrine Command (TRADOC), 123, 126, 128
troop (command) information, 17, 31
Troop Information Branch, MACOI, 87–88
troop morale, 39–40, 41, 67, 88
Trumbull, Robert (journalist), 79
Turley, William, 83–84, 89, 93
Turner, Nick (journalist), 84

UMT, 54–55, 57, 61
United Press International (UPI): Gallant Eagle coverage, 162; Gulf War coverage, 175–77; Korean War coverage, 62–63, 64; Vietnam War coverage, 83, 84
United States Information Agency (USIA), 57, 69
United States Information Service (USIS), 87, 90
Universal Military Training (UMT), 54–55, 57, 61
USA Today, 191–94
USS *Maddox*, 89

Vagts, Alfred, 54
Vessey, John A., 146, 147
Vessey, John W., Jr., 150–51
Vietnam 10 Years Later: What Have We Learned?, 153
Vietnam War: Abrams's press relations, 102–3, 106, 108; active marketing of Army during, 88; antiwar protests, 105–6; Army utopianism and, 73, 78, 94, 125; attrition strategy, 100, 101; author's overview, 21–22, 77–78, 214; Battle of Ap Bac, 83–85, 95; bombing campaigns, 89, 90, 105, 106–7, 108; casualty reporting, 99; censorship in, 93–94; competition between journalists, 99, 107–8, 117; contingency of media-military relationship, 109–10; control over MACV's public affairs, 89; control over supply of information, 81, 83–85; conventional force, 121–23; credibility gap with American public, 113; credibility gap with press, 80–82, 84–85, 94, 98, 111, 116; daily information briefings to press, 88; decreasing in newsworthiness, 111–12; democratic oversight, 118–19, 121–23; DOD reassessing press relations, 99; expectations of a compliant press, 78; fall of Saigon, 116–18; First Team, Army, 108–9; Gulf of Tonkin incident, 88–89; information policies, 78–80, 81, 84–85, 87, 89–90, 92, 95, 99; journalists' autonomy, 84–85; Kennedy downplaying involvement in, 78–80, 86; lessons from, 95, 118–19, 121–23, 132, 141, 153; MAAG-V, 77, 80; Marines at Da Nang, 90; maximum candor policy, 88, 89, 95; media-management paradigm,

Vietnam War (*continued*)
79, 80, 86; militarizing the mission, 86–87, 88–94; mission creep, 78–79; My Lai, 99–100, 103–5; news embargo, 110–13; Op. Duck Hook, 113; operational versus political success, 98, 106; Op. Rolling Thunder, 90; perspective difference between military and press, 93, 111; press censorship debated, 93–94; press relations, 80–82, 83–85, 88, 95, 108–10; press restrictions, 89–90; propaganda, 90; *PROVN*, 101; restrictions on press, 83, 92, 93–94, 99, 108, 109, 110–13; Saigon press corps, 82–86, 87, 93, 95; shift from State to DOD leadership, 80, 85; as shooting war, 79–80; Taylor and Rostow's proposal for, 73; on television, 79–80, 90; Tet Offensive, 96–98; Vietnamization strategy, 100–101, 113, 114, 121; withdrawal discussions, 112. *See also* Military Assistance Command, Vietnam (MACV)
violence, state's monopoly on, 5–6, 7–10, 13. *See also* Army; militaries
Voss, Frederick, 30
Vuono, Carl E. (Army chief of staff), 156–57, 171–73, 174, 177–78

Walker, Lynne (journalist), 187
war, ignored in sociology, 10–13, *11*, 17
Ward, Orlando, 48
Washington, George, 2–3
Washington Post: editorial on Army's future, 171–72, 173; Grenada coverage, 146; Marshall's media consumption, 36; Op. Just Cause coverage, 168
Weber, Max, 2, 5–9
Webster, Don (journalist), 107
Weigley, Russell F., 74
Weinberger, Casper, 146

Weiner, Sharon K., 215
Weintraub, Bernard (journalist), 149
Westmoreland, William C. (Army chief of staff): attrition strategy, 100, 101; Big Army conventional warfare, 121; as chief of staff, 100, 121; leading Vietnam War, 87; My Lai, 103–5; press relations, 88, 94, 98, 99; Tet Offensive, 96–98
Weyand, Frederick C. (Army chief of staff), 100, 114–15, 121
Wheeler, Earle (Army chief of staff), 85–86, 99, 121
Whitney, Craig (journalist), 237n35
Wickham, John A., Jr. (Army chief of staff), 154–55
Williams, Pete: debate on *Crossfire*, 180; media management, 191–94, 197; press pools and, 174, 246n38; replaced under Clinton administration, 202–3; spinning news stories, 179–80
Wimmer, Andreas, 222n34
Wines, Michael (journalist), 174
Woerner, Frederick F., 164
Wolf, Marvin J., 91–92, 109
World War I, 29, 34, 55, 213
World War II: golden age of press relations, 21, 28, 29–30, 31; information management expanding, 32–33; journalists exporting military propaganda, 31–32; lessons from, 50–51; North African campaign, 44, 45–46; press censorship, 30, 33; propaganda, 33
Wyatt, Clarence, 30

Ydstie, John (journalist), 175–77
Yom Kippur War, 125–26, 158

Zald, Mayer, 15
Zorthian, Barry, 87–88, 90, 151, 191–94

GPSR Authorized Representative: Easy Access System Europe, Mustamäe tee
50, 10621 Tallinn, Estonia, gpsr.requests@easproject.com

www.ingramcontent.com/pod-product-compliance
Lightning Source LLC
Chambersburg PA
CBHW031237290426
44109CB00012B/337